WHAT I BELIEVE

Jacques Ellul

TRANSLATED BY
Geoffrey W. Bromiley

William B. Eerdmans Publishing Company
Grand Rapids, Michigan

Marshall Morgan and Scott
London

Copyright © 1989 by William B. Eerdmans Publishing Company
255 Jefferson Avenue SE, Grand Rapids, Michigan 49503

First British Edition 1989 by
Marshall Morgan and Scott Publications Ltd
Part of the Marshall Pickering Holdings group
Middlesex House, 34-42 Cleveland Street, London W1P 5FB UK

Printed in the United States of America

Translated from the French *Ce que je crois*
©Éditions Grasset & Fasquelle, 1987

Library of Congress Cataloging-in-Publication Data

Ellul, Jacques.
   [Ce que je crois. English]
   What I believe / Jacques Ellul; translated by Geoffrey W. Bromiley.
      p.   cm.
   Translation of: Ce que je crois.
   ISBN 0-8028-3658-5
    1. Ellul, Jacques. 2. Faith. 3. Christianity—20th century.
  4. Civilization, Modern—20th century. 5. Christian life—Reformed
authors. I. Title.
BX4827.E5A3 1989
230—dc19   89-1623
                                           CIP

Marshall Morgan and Scott ISBN 0-551-01940-9

CONTENTS

Translator's Preface   **vii**

Introduction   **1**

PART I VARIOUS BELIEFS   **11**

1. Life Has Meaning   **13**

2. Chance, Necessity, Accident   **19**

3. The Word   **23**

4. Dialectic   **29**

5. Harmony   **47**

6. Evil and the Thirst for Good   **57**

7. Lifelong Love   **66**

PART II THE HUMAN ADVENTURE   **87**

8. Chances of History   **89**

9. The Prehistoric Period and the
   Natural Environment   **104**

10. The Historical Period and the
    Social Environment   **115**

11. The Posthistorical Period and the
    Technological Environment   **133**

PART III   END WITHOUT END   **141**

Introduction   **143**
12. The Seventh Day   **152**
13. God for Me   **167**
14. Universal Salvation   **188**
15. Judgment   **210**
16. Recapitulation   **214**

TRANSLATOR'S PREFACE

Jacques Ellul's reputation rests in the main on his vigorous opposition to beliefs, convictions, slogans, illusions, and developments, both ancient and modern. As he himself confesses, he would have found it easier to give an account of what he does not believe than of what he does. In fact, even in this book entitled *What I Believe* many of the things that he does not believe naturally and necessarily emerge. Nevertheless, readers of Ellul, friends and critics alike, will surely welcome this succinct but characteristically powerful statement of the basic convictions that lie behind his life and writings and activities.

There is, of course, little or nothing here that might not be found in a wider reading of his enormous output of books and articles. We see, for example, the same personal involvement, the same commitment to dialectic, the same emphasis on freedom, the same concept of the secret divine presence, the same strenuous (if not wholly convincing) defense of universalism, and the same vision of a final ingathering of everything good into God's holy city. The style and methodology will also be familiar, the dangerous combination of hyperbole and paradox, yet through it all the incontestable erudition, the penetrating insight, and the passionate fervor that make Ellul worth reading even though (or perhaps because) he provokes the most urgent questioning or the most vigorous dissent. As Ellul himself modestly admits, he is stating here only what he believes, convinced of its final compatibility with God's revelation in Christ according to the Scriptures. He recognizes that he might be wrong, and therefore he does not insist upon it as doctrine or seek a committed following for it. Yet it is no mere academic construction, for it obviously constitutes for Ellul the meaning and motivation of all that he writes and speaks and does.

Geoffrey W. Bromiley
Pasadena, Advent 1987

INTRODUCTION

It would finally be much easier for me to say what I do not believe than what I do believe. This initial statement might be attributed to a negativism with which I am wrongly charged because I have repeatedly said that the first duty of free people is to say no, or because I have often taken up the Hegelian concept of the positive nature of the negative. But it is a mistake to infer pessimism or negativity from this perspective, for no one is at root more optimistic than I am. My ultimate vision is always positive. Hasty reading allows of rash judgments.

For me the difference between what I do not believe and what I do believe has a very different origin. What I do not believe is very clear and precise. What I do believe is complex, diffuse — I might almost say unconscious — and theoretical. It involves myself, whereas what I do not believe can be at a distance. I can regard it as exterior and therefore relatively well-defined. It can be the object of a taxonomy. What I believe finds me totally implicated personally. I can speak about it only as I do about myself. I do not believe in an object but in a network of relations which I cannot really expound because exposition demands a didactic procedure, the dividing up of realities that belong to one another. I cannot deal with everything at once. Persons of great talent might with a touch of genius offer readers the whole complex of what they believe without snapping the bonds and relations, authoring a great poetic text and also giving readers the sense of a vibrant complex and the illuminating clarity of a reality suddenly grasped. But I am not such a person. As an industrious scholar I need to unravel the complexities, to follow a lucid and rational path, to take up objects that I can examine one after the other. I thus deprive things of their nature, I make patterned planks of living things, I break up the relations between them. I can evoke the complex but not reconstitute it for others. I put something definite and bounded for something infinite.

Nothing, then, is more discouraging for me than to try to say what I believe, for in so doing I give rise to all kinds of misconceptions. Yet I do not know how else to proceed. To say what I do not believe is simple. I do not believe in progress, or religion, or politics, or science as the final answer. I do not believe that in society as it now is we can resolve in the coming century either economic problems or the problems of the Third World. What complicates things is that what I do not believe is closely linked to what I do believe. The two cannot be dissociated in practice. Yet they are not direct opposites: I would not say that if I do not believe in progress it is because I believe in nonprogress. The relation is more intimate and less logical. The two things depend on the taking of positions to a higher, more definite, and more decisive hierarchical degree or degree of abstraction. I have to go back to essential data in order to see what will become what I believe and what I do not believe, the one along with the other. I cannot say what I believe without implicitly tracing a path in a flood of possibilities, choosing one and rejecting others that are not necessarily contradictory but simply different. I cannot say quietly that I do not believe in this without at the same time referring to an implication of what I do believe. Thus we have to grasp the two together. Yet the one can be clearly defined, whereas the other remains even for me an object of constant deliberation and inquiry. In what becomes didactically separate there is a need to retie the bonds, to bring the themes together again, to play the subtle game of multiple relations. For here as in each of us everything is connected with everything else—nothing is isolated, without reference or referent. Yet only the reader can do what is required, and to do so is not just a game or a matter of curiosity, but the only path to understanding.

I also need to say something about the subject of belief itself. Two words call for notice, *faith* and *belief*.[1] We have an annoying tendency to confuse the two. Belief is an everyday matter and sets the foundation for all that constitutes our existence. Everything depends on it; all human relations rest on it. Unless I have good reasons to the contrary, I believe spontaneously what people tell me: I have confidence in them a priori. If this were not so, human relations would be impossible, as in the kind of speech that only causes confusion or derision. I also believe scientific truths. I believe that $E = mc^2$ because I have been told it. The whole educational system is based on belief. Students believe what their teachers or their books say; they learn on a basis of belief. We also believe spontaneously the witness of our senses, even when they are disturbed. We believe similarly in certain words, such as the good, or freedom, or justice, which we do not define plainly or consistently but to which we cling firmly no matter what their content. A society could not function if it did not rest on beliefs hidden in the deep recesses of each of its members and producing coherent sentiments and actions. A society without collective beliefs (which are, of course, individual in the eyes of each member) would soon fall into lawlessness and enter a process of dissolution. Beliefs are definitely the raison d'être of society.

Faith is very different—it is addressed to God. But beliefs may also be religious. There has always been an assimilation of belief to religion, and there still is. Religious beliefs are part of the whole. Often (in a debatable way) *religio* is connected with *religare*, "to tie." Religion binds people together and binds them as a group to their god. It is precisely this binding character that causes the problem, for it plunges us into a sociological analysis of religion. It is finally for the sake of fellowship with one another that people refer to a more lofty being or god that will serve as a group guarantee and symbol. The objects of this religion may be very different, whether one or more gods projected in heaven, or the Universal. Other dimensions than the human can be apotheosized. Reason can be deified, or science.

1. I have dealt with this theme, but rather differently, in *Living Faith: Belief and Doubt in a Perilous World*, trans. Peter Heinegg (San Francisco: Harper & Row, 1983).

Hitlerism made its own religion, as did Marxism-Leninism up to the 1970s. The country can be regarded as divine. Progress has become a key term in modern religion. Each cult has its own rites and myths and heretics and believers and raison d'être and believing potential. But the object of religion is not necessarily God.

Faith in God—in a God who does not incarnate some natural force or who is not the abstract and hypostatized projection of one of our own desires or aspirations or values (Feuerbach), faith in a God who is different from all that we can conceive or imagine—cannot be assimilated to belief. For this God cannot be assimilated to one of the representations that we might easily multiply. If God is God, he is inevitably different from all that polytheists call god. Each of those gods can be described and defined; each has its own function and sphere of action. But the God of faith is inaccessible and inassimilable. He is so fundamentally other (if he were not, if he could be measured against one of our values or beliefs, he would not be God) that we can neither define nor contemplate him. The God of faith is totally inaccessible. The affirmation of Feuerbach, that God is an absolutized value, was simplistic and puerile. For one thing, we have no idea of what the absolute or the infinite is. We cannot say anything about it or assimilate it. To talk about an absolutized value might be to talk about God, but it is not possible for human beings to absolutize anything.

In regard to the innumerable attacks made upon God, we may simply say that those who make them do not know what they are talking about. Often with just cause they are attacking the image of God that in a given time and place people have made. But this is their own image of God, made for convenience —it is not God. A commonly repeated formula that is now accepted as self-evident is that we have made God in our own image. But to say this is not to know what one is saying; it is childish prattle. For if God is God, then all that we can say about him is just our own approximation or perception, as when a child takes a pail of seawater, stirs it until it foams, and then says he is carrying the ocean and its waves. On our own we know nothing about God. Only when he chooses to reveal a tiny part of his being do we achieve a tiny knowledge and recognition. In this revelation God has to put himself on our level of apprehension, on our cultural and intellectual level, if what he wants to communicate is to be accessible. Thus there are variations, not because God is variable, but because those whom he addresses are. He uses the most appropriate means to establish communication with us — the word. When he addresses himself to a person, it is always a very personal interrelation.

The question arises, of course, why God chooses to give this partial revelation. Why does he not keep an absolute distance? Why does he not remain solitary, at work or at rest, and let us solve our own problems on earth? The first answer is that no answer is possible. God is unconditioned. If he were conditioned by anything else, he would not be God. There is thus no "because" in his case. No prior reason can be given for his decisions and acts. He decides to reveal himself in a way that we can bear simply because he decides to reveal himself. But when I look at what I am told about revelation in Judaism and Christianity, I can give another answer which is not contradictory but complementary. As Creator, God does not want to leave his creatures without relation or reference, like a newborn infant cast out on the highway. In love God cannot remain alone; love has to address itself to someone outside the self. God is not solipsistic. He directs his love to creation, to his creatures, and tells them what they need to know about him if they are to survive and flourish.

We can see now the difference between faith in this God and all beliefs. A belief that enables society to maintain itself is necessarily collective. Apt at seizing on the fulness of its object, it is an uplifting force that carries us above ourselves (even though it may do much mischief when it pretends to be absolute and exclusive). Faith is at every point the opposite. First of all it is a personal relation. It does not grasp the fulness of him to whom it is directed. It is not useful to society; on the contrary, it is a disturbing force, causing breaks in social ties. Above all, it can arise only because it is God who comes down to us. This is the key point. Belief always tries to mount up to what it regards as God. Faith receives him who comes down from his transcendence to set himself on the level of the child that he wishes to rejoin. No two things could be more different.

Yet history shows that faith can turn into belief, though belief cannot become faith. Faith undergoes this metamorphosis when it claims to have full knowledge of the God to whom it is directed; when it brings with it the establishment of institutions to conserve and transmit it; when it tries to explain itself in radical formulas that serve to determine what is true; when it pretends to embrace the whole of society (and at that moment undoubtedly becomes the cement of this society); when it takes fixed form in definitive and unchangeable affirmations; when it thinks it can force people to recognize the truth of its God. Whenever any of these things takes place, there is no more faith but belief and institutional religion. But in this book, though the title refers ambiguously to believing and I am forced to speak about believing, I am also trying to say what faith means for me.

I have not finished with belief, for if one aspect of belief is belief in what I call absolute values, there is also a very different sense. Belief means esteeming, thinking, valuing. I believe what I regard as accurate, what I accept in appraisals, though these might be irrational and subjective. I believe that someone is my friend. I believe that it might be useful to me to read a certain book. I believe that an event will take place. I believe that such and such an act or decision will have such and such consequences. This believing all takes place in a confluence of things internal and things external, of things sensory and things intellectual, of things imaginary and things experimental.

This believing can vary a great deal, but finally it stays the same. The mystery of identity! What proves to me that I am myself? All my bodily cells change every seven years. I become quite different, and yet I have an invincible conviction that I am the same person I was some years ago. I have seen my body deteriorate, yet I am always myself. Similarly, those who have had organ transplants or significant prostheses are convinced they are still the same persons. Beyond the different parts of the body there is a sort of totality that changes and yet remains the same. Elements in the system might be stilled but the system maintains its identity and processes. Another and even deeper meaning of belief, then, is that without any proof or guarantee I believe intensely that I am myself, and that there is nothing more false or futile than for me to say that I am a different person. If all that this means is that I never know myself completely, that there is a good deal of shadow in all of us, and that perhaps a different person resides there, that is a truism. But if it means that I am someone else and not myself, that is a falsehood along the lines of all the attempts of European intellectuals to destroy being, to unravel personality, to dilute and weaken things. To this I oppose staunchly my belief that I am who I am and not just a label that corresponds to nothing living. I realize that what I have held to be true for some years is no certainty, yet also that my belief is enriched by experiences and encounters and chances and quests which have not given me certainty but which have made me different and still the same.

Yet another point is that not wanting to believe, or refusing to do so, has always been for me an important aspect of belief. One may look at this aspect in two ways. An event takes place, clearly interweaving and combining many factors, which I find horrible, unacceptable, and very painful. I see the results of the acts and decisions of politicians. I see the spread of foolish and disastrous opinions which engulf the masses under the guidance of the mass media. For me there is here a tragic certainty; the developments of the situation seem to be ineluctable. But while I may be unable to change things, I refuse to believe them. I know they will be fatal, and I will not believe it. I do not say that they will not happen, but my feeble protest lies in the refusal to believe. I remember that in 1939, one month before the declaration of war, I was walking along a road outside Bordeaux, and the more I thought about the situation the more I saw that war was inevitable. But in a revolt of my whole being I would not believe what I knew to be certain. All my life I have in fact been torn in this way between what are clearly the evil results of something and my refusal to believe, a fragile obstacle which in my distress I try to put in the way of things irresistible. The only thing I can do in such circumstances is to utter warnings, telling others what is likely to happen so that they will be on guard and refuse to believe that things will turn out well. Today, alas! I am haunted by the terrible certainty of a nuclear war, but I do not want to believe it. When I announce what is going to happen, what is the logical result of actual decisions, people cannot believe it because they all support the actual event that carries implications beyond their conception. It was thus with Cuba, Vietnam, and Cambodia. It is thus with belief in the technological society, with unemployment, and with the fatal evolution of a leftist government in France.

Regarding this leftist government, I wrote an article on the election of Mr. Mitterand which caused much offense because I said that nothing important had happened. It was clear to me that except for some spectacular but futile gestures such as nationalization the Socialists would be forced to enter the same path of technological progress as any other government, that they might alter the rules of the political game with mandates and political careerism but that they could not alter the structures of society or the economic domination of multinational corporations, and that like all other regimes they would have to take such measures as circumstances demanded. All this seemed certain to me. But I like the Socialists, I like the ideals of justice and freedom, and I could wish that they would bring about a true Socialist revolution, as I have often said. Thus I did not want to believe that things would happen as I saw they would. I was charged with attacking the Socialists when I really wanted to show them that the task was harder than they thought. It was all in vain.

There is another and rather different aspect to my refusal to believe. I see existing objects, whether political or economic; I see the tendencies and irreducible elements in them. I see them as I might see a rock. Yet I refuse to give them my adherence, I refuse to believe in their excellence or value, I refuse to add my belief to their existence. I see the modern state, or bureaucracy, or money, or technique[2]—they are what they are. I just will not believe in them. They are self-sufficient, although in fact they constantly solicit my adherence and even my veneration. I let them be, but do not believe in their value or good-

2. For Ellul *technique* means *"the totality of methods rationally arrived at and having absolute efficiency* (for a given stage of development) in *every* field of human activity" (*The Technological Society*, trans. John Wilkinson [New York: Knopf, 1964], p. xxv). See also Jacques Ellul, *Perspectives on Our Age*, trans. Joachim Neugroschel, ed. William H. Vanderburg (New York: Seabury, 1981), pp. 32-33.—TRANS.

ness or truth or utility or gratuitousness. Let them be content with their existence. I myself am not, though I know very well that I cannot free myself of them. What we see here is that human belief adds to such objects an incomparable value. It at once makes them much more than things; they acquire a human look. Marx often compared capitalism to the legendary vampire. I think one might extend the comparison to all social, political, and economic objects. They are only things, but they suddenly become active, prominent, and incontestable. They have effects when people begin to believe in them. They do not feed on blood like the vampire but on belief that verges on confidence and even affection. I for my part rule out belief of this kind.

These, then, are my clarifications of the simple word *belief*. Each time it is a matter of what *I* believe. This is not psychoanalysis. There is in fact no spontaneity or immediacy about belief, contrary to a common sentiment. To find out what we believe and do not believe we have to examine ourselves and reflect on ourselves. We are also challenged, for the question arises whether it is legitimate for me to believe this or that. To talk about belief is to inquire at the same time into its validity or truth. It is to enter into a critical study that is not without danger. There is no place for the facile skepticism that says it believes in nothing precisely because it is blind to what it does believe in. We have to be serious because our whole being is at stake here. When I ask what I believe in, I am "searching my conscience," as they used to put it. I am passing judgment on what I believe as this is brought to light. As one advances, a double movement takes place which causes one constantly to come across another belief that is often hidden but which also provides the pause needed to move on to its criticism. "As one advances"—we either have to advance here or be silent. I cannot say easily what I value or think just now, what I regard as true. I have to do something more difficult, which will undoubtedly involve some political evaluations, if I am to try to bring the roots of my beliefs to light.

PART I

VARIOUS BELIEFS

Chapter 1

LIFE HAS MEANING

I believe that life has meaning. We are not on earth by chance; we do not come from nowhere to go to nowhere. This is a statement; it cannot be proved. Meaning implies both orientation and significance. Not every event or act or word has meaning, but everything is set in that orientation and signification. Orientation covers a series of chances that push the race from the Paleolithic Age to the Neolithic Age and then to the Bronze Age and the age of information. I am careful not to talk about a philosophy of history or of agreement between this chance adventure and a goal to be attained. I do not follow Teilhard de Chardin when he talks about qualitative leaps to higher periods and a convergence in every case.

But I reject absurdity. Here again I am making an arbitrary statement. Absurdity does reign, of course; I find it everywhere. I am convinced that human conduct is often absurd, and many events seem to be irrational. But they seem to be so because we cannot put them in the total context. It is absurd for the parents of an abnormal child, mongoloid or mentally deficient, to want to bring up this child instead of turning it over to a specialized institution. But when we consider the miracle of love that this situation might represent, the mutation that it might cause in those around the child, the human and psychological development that it might carry with it for all concerned, the absurd act becomes a model of humanity. I have seen this.

I have also known a man who, when his wife became a grave hemiplegic and lost her voice, sold his business and devoted all his time to daily care for her in her sickness. This care claimed his whole life from the time he was fifty. He came from a humble background but he worked out a genuine philosophy of life. He could say to me: "Life is good and wonderful. We all have a mission on earth. But we have to realize above all that life is always good." An absurd act? A meaning of life? He moved on steadily to personal enrichment and fulfillment instead of seeking petty comfort and happiness. He was no believer and knew of no end beyond death. But this did not prevent him from giving meaning to every moment in life. To find meaning we have to look at an event in the complexity of human interrelations and in the long term. What seems to make no sense to me now, what I am thus disposed to ignore, can show itself tomorrow to be full of positive implications and can give direction to a series of events that seem to be inert.

But we need to make some distinctions to avoid ambiguity. The statement that life has meaning might be taken in two ways. First, it might mean that life has meaning intrinsically. In this case, no matter what our attitude, all that happens has meaning. Meaning qualifies life itself. Our task in this case is to find the meaning.[1] This is the point of the well-known dictum: History has meaning. For the successors of Marx the meaning of history was unveiled by the discovery of the class struggle. We need only apply this criterion to each situation, they said, and we find its meaning (in the twofold sense of the term — significance and direction). And whether we discover it or not, his-

---

1. When he received the Nobel prize for literature in 1985, Claude Simon began his speech by saying that he had nothing to say. He did not need to say this because his novels demonstrate it. There is no truth anywhere. But more seriously, he added that in all his life and after all his many experiences he had never found any sense anywhere unless it was (as Barthes, he believed, said after Shakespeare) that the world simply has the significance of existing. But not to mean anything is not to denote anything but oneself, not to be the sign of anything, not to have any direction or value (but then why, for example, did Simon himself escape from prison camp during World War II?), not to be able to conceive of any truth. If one holds to the strict sense of these words, there is no meaning, there is no point in living except as a mere pot that is there because it is there. And if there is no point in living, why go on? I think that to say there is no meaning brings us up against a final choice: either to go mad or to commit suicide. Unless talking like that is just a way of talking, a literary device. I believe that this was the case with Simon, for if nothing makes sense, then his books make no sense either, and in that case why write them?

tory goes its way and has its own meaning like a watch that ticks away whether we look at it or not.

But, second, Marx also said that we make our own history. This is not a simple matter. In one case all we have to do is to consider what act or decision will enter into the meaning of history. In another case we make independent decisions that can complicate the course of history and apparently put it off track, or we might say that our specific calling is to give sense to what takes place, that nothing has meaning on its own, but that we can find the meaning, that doing so is the dignity of human beings, who establish history and morality. On this view events are the fruit of chance or the play of multiple neutral factors, and we rise up and say: "This is what all this means, and this is what I am going to do now in consequence."

I believe that in the long run both interpretations are correct. Life has an orientation, a final end toward which everything moves. I realize, however, that I can say this only because I am a Christian. I know that the human adventure moves on to fulfillment, not in glory, but in a rupture followed by a recreation which is the consummation of this whole history. If I step outside this faith, the human adventure has no orientation of its own. It is not true that history as such has meaning. It is not true that the movement from the Paleolithic Age to the Neolithic Age and then to feudal society and industrial society was logical and coherent. Human history is in fact a tale told by an idiot. The Bible says as much when it depicts history as the headlong gallop, without direction, route, or reason, of the four horses of the Apocalypse: the horse of political and military power, the horse of economic power, the horse of death with the cortege of its causes, and the horse of the word, the Word of God. In a furious ride they cover the whole earth, and it is the combination of their tracks that we call history. History as such has neither goal nor meaning. Only in retrospect can I lean upon it and give it meaning. The situation is such that prior events lead to this point and therefore they have this orientation and value. But a posteriori explanation does not help to throw light on tomorrow. I do not know what to do in order to keep within the meaning of history. There are too many factors and parameters. I make a chance throw, convinced that I am

doing what ought to be done. If I cannot find a logical and rational sequence, I still attribute meaning symbolically and myth-
ically. To do so is not silly. It gives us a very rich and profoundly
true bouquet of meanings. Myth is the symbolical explication
of the meaning that we rightly attribute to what we see eter-
nally, globally, and personally. Yet the human adventure, real-
istically viewed, makes no global sense. I can give it meaning
for the sake of honor or coherence, and to fight futility, the absurdity that is no proper climate for humanity. I cannot stand
being meaningless.

At the level of personal life, I am convinced that every
event, adventure, and encounter has its own meaning. Nothing
in human relationships lacks meaning: neither a chance meeting nor an illness that attacks us. Everything makes sense because everything concerns these strange beings that we call
human and that are significant in themselves. Each word and
glance has meaning (in the twofold sense of the term). Some
things orient me to life and some to death. Some have for me
a signification that I must integrate into my life if I deserve to
be called human. If there is no meaning collectively in global
history, our human calling is to attribute meaning to it. (We may
make mistakes but that is not important; we survive them.) But
in personal and interpersonal life every event has meaning.
Those who think human life is absurd have only two replies,
either suicide or the transformation of the absurd into the
proper meaning of existence (as definitively in Camus). Each
of us must ask about the meaning of what happens to us or of
what we have tried to do. This is the proper work, not of the
intellect, but of the conscience. For finding the meaning of life
is not a mathematical problem that one can solve by reasoning.
It is a problem of life and responsibility.

The meaning—discovered, discerned, or merely glimpsed
—needs to be integrated into what, again, the living are called
upon to live. The meaning of yesterday's event is for me today's
decision and helps me to see the new meaning in what is now
before me. Even apparently insignificant things in life may be
vital, and that means we must be on the alert, on guard against
routine and repetition so that we can discern in what seems to
be futile or fleeting something dazzling and determinative if

only we have eyes to see it, if only we are ready for it, if only we are attentive to it and not diverted by distractions.

We live today in a strange and unsettling world in which we are caught as in the clamps of a vice. On the one side we are claimed by jobs that are repetitive and impersonal (whose model is the assembly line), or so swift and pressing that we can hardly see what is going on or achieve the distance needed if we are to appreciate the significance and orientation (the utility) of what we are doing. It seems as if the production and utilization of all our vital forces are organized in such a way as to prevent us from putting the question of meaning. This is indeed a dangerous question, for if we find out that what we have to do makes no sense, we will object. But this organization itself means that protests, for example, by workers, leave on one side the things that really matter in life. They make superficial demands and miss reality (denying its existence) because they never have the chance of putting the question of meaning to what they are doing. I refer to laborers, but I might just as well speak of all those who are engaged in the collective order of modern work.

The other side of the vice, which often comes into play through excess of information, might be defined as the refusal to put the question of meaning. If our life in modern society and what we see of the world in the media is so horrible and distressing and frantic and dangerous, I not only refuse to be invaded by its horrors but also refuse to believe that it can have any meaning. I refuse to seek any meaning. But I also refuse to live in absurdity. Hence my only option is to turn aside and find distraction. I escape from horror in play. This is an ancient attitude illustrated in Boccaccio's *Decameron*. During the Black Death, some young men and women fleeing the scourge took refuge in a well-barricaded and well-provisioned castle, and while people were stuffed in open carts outside they gave themselves up to pleasures and games, telling the famous stories imagined by Boccaccio. The work of horror and death makes no sense. I do not want to tire myself out trying to discover what it might mean for me to attribute signification to it. In face of the absurd and the horrible, it seems best to resort to play, evasion, absence.

But what once a few privileged people could do, all of us can now do. So that no one should put the disturbing question of meaning, a maternal society provides us today with scores of games designed to claim our interest and attention. We also acquire the habit of so watching television that the horrible news broadcast by it finally becomes part of the game. The way the news is presented also helps us to avoid the traumatism of meaning and questioning. After seeing a famine in Sahel or the ruins of Beirut (in a mere three minutes) we pass at once and in the same way to the oddities of modern fashion or to soothing sports. No one must enter the labyrinth of meaning, where one risks indeed an encounter with the Minotaur, until everything is explained and determination is possible. I think, however, that people are not yet totally enslaved or robbed of all disquiet. Not yet! If ever they are, then in the abundance and the play and the risk we shall witness the worst regression of humanity since the Neolithic Age.

By way of final clarification, although I have tried to show the difference between collective life and individual life in the matter of meaning, it is life alone that can have meaning. There is no meaning in the infinitely big or the infinitely little, nor in the banal matter of our daily environment. Neither the orbits of the planets nor corpuscular movements correspond to any history (only people, not matter, have and make history), and therefore they have no meaning. They have no signification or orientation, for their changes and evolutions are directed to no end. There is nothing ultimate about them from which we might deduce such an end. This is why it seems so futile and unimportant to try to find links between the stars and us (astrology) or to try to find in the chances of the material world mysterious meanings or indications of the way we should live or decide. All these things are neutral and blind. But I am well acquainted with those who, coming up against some absurd and unexpected event, a simple play of circumstances, begin at that moment to examine their life and choices, so that if they do not find the meaning of this chance event in itself, they do at least come across some truths about the meaning of their own lives.

Chapter 2

CHANCE, NECESSITY, ACCIDENT

Concerning matter, I accept the play of chance and necessity demonstrated by Jacques Monod.[1] In the initial situation nothing is established in advance for matter. There is no unilinear causality or finality to determine a course leading to a prescribed end. Millions of combinations of millions of possible factors are possible, and these are random combinations. Most of them fail and come to nothing. One, at times, succeeds. But when it does, it imposes itself by force, takes its place in the universe, and obeys at once not the joyful intoxication of freedom but the law of necessity dictated to it by its own components and its place in the universe. From the moment that the play of chance has thrown up from millions of possible combinations one that is unique, lasting, stable, and coherent, it obeys laws that enable it to persist but that also prevent it from becoming anything else. This is the necessity that we can know scientifically.

What stops me from accepting Monod's system in its totality is in the first place the ambivalence of what he calls chance. At the outset he puts us in a world of chance but never tells us what he is talking about. Philosophers, mathematicians, and physicians offer us many definitions of chance. The term is not clear or univocal. I have the impression that in the course of his exposition Monod plays with different possible meanings. A second and more serious objection relates to the fact that Monod

---

1. See Jacques Monod, *Chance and Necessity: An Essay on the Natural Philosophy of Modern Biology*, trans. Austryn Wainhouse (New York: Knopf, 1971).— TRANS.

wants to make of his presentation a kind of metaphysics or universal system. Everything everywhere is reduced to the play of chance and necessity. He thus becomes no less dogmatic than those whom he criticizes constantly, for example, those who see a final goal. In particular, he rejects the specificity of living things.

As for myself, with many modern scientists I accept the uniqueness of living things. They cannot be reduced to the mechanistic play of cells and molecules. Even if one could explain or even reproduce the innumerable interrelations and interconnections of neurons, one would not achieve thought. I like Mumford's comparison of the brain and thought to the disk and music. One can reproduce the disk but that is not the music. The music existed before the disk. The play of neurons does not produce thought in any systematic or original fashion; it simply makes it possible. An additional, heterogeneous factor causes the extraordinary combination that produces thought. To reject teleology is fine, but it is obvious that the eye, for example, is truly inexplicable. Why should the different and atypical cells that compose the eye, present in an embryo, finally come together in a coherent way and form this organ? What leads them to associate so as to bring about this result? How are we to explain the attraction of one cell to another that produces the organized totality that will be this organ? I refer to the eye precisely because it is made up of cells that are not identical or repetitive. No answer can be given if we simply look at the intrinsic features of each cell. I believe, then, that there is something specific about living things that corresponds neither to chance nor to necessity.

Nevertheless, unceasingly in the composition and reproduction of this universe there are series of accidents. In what seems to be a very fixed and closed game, an accident is possible, that is, the production of something other than what might have been expected (and again one might see chance here). Hence there is no clear evolutionism. Not only are there apparently inexplicable leaps in evolution; there are also qualitative changes. The implication is that no single system can explain the reality of the world and that which constitutes it. There is no formula of reality. Yet this is what we have been trying to achieve by the increasingly complex models that are now presented, by the bringing into play of feedback (positive and negative), by the importance attached to crystals and vapor, by allowance for an ever greater complexity. The more we advance, the more the complexity grows. As order comes out of disorder, so information grows out of reports. Chance and necessity are not by a long way adequate to explain things. Order growing out of disorder is a fine image, but the process is as inexplicable as the mathematical transition from zero to one. Yet the problem there is only intellectual, whereas here it is real and even existential. We learn the measure of it from the enormous work of E. Morin.[2] In other words, with living reality we are placed before a complex system that is set even further beyond our grasp by the possibility of new phenomena appearing. Attempts have been made to make these new things logical and accessible, but far too often at the expense of rationalization, schematization, and reductionism.

In our own day, there are new things of a different kind. Up to now one could talk of new things produced by the interaction of natural elements themselves, and in some cases only as the prelude to a goal. It seems to me that the supernovae are symbolical in this regard. Astronomers see them appear suddenly. They are particularly bright and dazzling stars, but we now know that the excess of light is simply a last sign of termination and death. Now, however, we find different new things on earth, artificial things humanly produced. Human beings are introducing new substances, chemical products that did not previously exist, and new materials made of these products. They are introducing new bacilli and new and unexpected disturbances of nature. They are not just imitating nature (talking machines and active robots) or making things like it. They are also upsetting nature by interventions no less traumatic than earthquakes or typhoons. And there is a difference, for whereas the latter are accidental and sporadic, our human interventions are permanent and regular. We are killing off lakes and rivers. We are destroying forests either by massive deforestation (the Ama-

2. See E. Morin, *La méthode:* Vol. I: *La nature de la nature* (Paris: Seuil, 1977); Vol. II: *La vie de la vie* (Paris: Seuil, 1980).

zon basin is a victim here) or by acid rain. We are depleting the level of oxygen and raising that of CO_2, which lies in the atmosphere and will lead, scientists think, to either a warming or a cooling of the planet. We are similarly increasing the level of radioactivity, and although this seems to be negligible in comparison with natural radioactivity, it accumulates indefinitely and is never lost. We keep producing materials that cannot be broken down, though we are already swamped by them. These are not the angry arguments of an ecologist. They are facts recognized by scientists, with long-term results that we cannot calculate, producing a new, irreducible factor through human activity, and altering the whole ecosystem.

The situation becomes even more difficult if we adopt the perspective of certain physicists such as d'Espagnat who espouse the principle of nonseparability, that is, that no phenomenon in the universe can be validly separated, scientifically, from any other, that all things belong together, and that everything produced at one point has repercussions upon everything else. This is simply a generalization of what has been known for a long time from observations in microphysics, namely, that even the presence of the observer modifies the phenomenon observed. In a different sphere, that of systems, the same has been given emphasis by the demonstration that in a closed system any modification of one of the components can transform the whole system and all the other components. The old certainties regarding fixed data, limited causality, and the separability of factors (whether in history, physics, or any other discipline) have all been called into question in what one might truly call a crisis, not of science, but of the ideology of science and its univocity. We live in a universe of both solidarity and contingency, susceptible to what is new and unexpected.

Chapter 3

THE WORD

As human beings, we have to take this contingency and unity into account. We can do so only by the word. I move here into one of the commonplaces of our day. We are above all speaking beings. I will not trace the great attention that has been paid for the last thirty years to analyzing word, language, and discourse. From a much earlier date and without the scientific apparatus, I myself have been gripped by the unique and irreplaceable character of the word, but for very different reasons: because God created the word, because he has revealed himself uniquely by his Word, because the incarnate Word is the Word of the eternal God, because the God in whom I believe is Word. Hence every human word is for me decisive and irreplaceable. I have noted elsewhere the radical antithesis between speaking and seeing.[1] I will be brief about this so as not to be redundant. We have to understand that both are indispensable. They belong to different orders which we must not confuse — they are complementary.

The word is of the order of truth; it is located in the sphere of truth. It can also at the same time be falsehood if it does not speak this truth. For me, this possibility results precisely from the fact that the human word is a response to the Word of God. In this response it can lie. It is never dictated by God's Word. It has its own autonomy as we ourselves do, and thus it can say things different from what it hears in God's Word. Let us not

---

1. See Jacques Ellul, *The Humiliation of the Word*, trans. Joyce Main Hanks (Grand Rapids: Eerdmans, 1985).

engage in ridicule in this regard: I do not mean that one ought to reserve the word only for chanting canticles or delivering sermons. I mean that every word ought to carry the meaning that God has given to life (even though it may never refer to God). It ought to carry joy, hope, forgiveness, love, reconciliation, light, and peace in the order of truth. It contributes to the elucidation of the meaning of life.

Seeing is of the order of reality and is indispensable if we are to grasp the world. It sets us in the world and incites us to act in it. It does not lead to truth,[2] and it does not give meaning. The word is what can give meaning to what we see. Seeing enables me to apprehend at a stroke all that reality presents to us and that the word is ill-equipped to describe. But the word (I am thinking of poetry), with reference to the real, can bring out what is hidden in it. The two things cannot be separated. Truth must incarnate itself in reality; reality is empty without truth. If truth is the unfolding of meaning, this is the meaning of what we see to be real and not of an illusion or dream or phantom. This is how it is with us.

We have different temptations today, especially that of action. We are immersed in a world of action, and the word seems to be incredibly futile. We have all expressed or accepted the slogan: Actions speak louder than words. Action is the decisive test, especially in politics. Politicians are despised if they simply make speeches and do not act. But I would say that their words may be classified as lies. Action does not prove the validity of the word, nor is it more important. If we properly consider what action signifies, we never find more than three answers. First, it may be an affirmation of power, an expression of the will to dominate. This is a daily experience. People act in order to succeed in their undertakings, to crush rivals, to assert their nature, to triumph over obstacles, to be hailed as great or illustrious. No matter whether the opponents be individuals, nations, or natural forces, action always denotes power. Dominating action takes many forms: money, science, war (armed or padded by liberalism), technology, politics, publicity, and many other means invented

2. On religious visions and depictions see Jacques Ellul, *Humiliation of the Word,* especially pp. 71-106, 237-54.

by people from the very beginning to overcome active or passive rivals.

I am not judging, for if human beings had not acted to conquer they would not have survived. But we must make no mistake. Action is simply an expression of a will to dominate which in itself is illimitable, and those who win seldom have the wisdom to impose limits on themselves. It is the word that will indicate the limits in the name of truth, but the word is weak, and this is precisely why it is the servant of truth. All that we can do is keep on repeating that this victorious action makes no sense and that it will perish faster than it triumphed. What has been the good of all the wars of this terrible 20th century? War, as action at its peak, is always futile. What did 1918 achieve? Nothing but wind and storm. What did 1945 achieve? An extension of the gulag and a lot of mediocre talk. What do wars of liberation achieve? Even worse dictatorships and misery beyond anything previously known. But why continue with this balance sheet of action? Elsewhere I have attempted similar analyses of technique or revolution, and I have always concluded: Vanity of vanity, all is vanity and a pursuit of wind (see Eccl. 1:14).[3]

The second and third answers relate to individuals, whose passion for action may have two sources. The first is pleasure. By action people hope to achieve enjoyment, to feel that they are alive and young and vigorous at an elemental level. Games, sport, sex, creative work, the intense pleasure of speed — a hundred other forms of action, but all fleeting and momentary. Action here and now is a transitory thing that can have only two results. Either we go back and reflect on what we have done, and it is all dust and ashes; or else we keep on doing it, day after day heaping up sensuous pleasures, ecstasies, and delights. In the former case we have an Epicurean restraint that demands great discipline and can be achieved only by the word. In the latter case we are in a headlong flight like Don Juan, *Mille e tre*, with a round of conquests, each testifying that it is already over, and that there must be a search for new pastures with in-

3. For example, on technique see Jacques Ellul, *The Technological Society*, trans. John Wilkinson (New York: Knopf, 1964); on revolution see Jacques Ellul, *Autopsy of Revolution*, trans. Patricia Wolf (New York: Knopf, 1971). On the theme in Ecclesiastes, see Jacques Ellul, *La raison d'être: Méditation sur l'Ecclésiaste* (Paris: Seuil, 1987). (English translation forthcoming from Eerdmans.) — TRANS.

creasing dissatisfaction. Action uses up action, and it uses us up even more swiftly until the point is reached where there is only the sad recollection of what was once action but has now become impossible.

The second point is that action serves as a substitute for truth. It is the great intoxicant of society and individuals. We ask for no reason; we plunge into action as into a party. Since action validates itself, we do not ask about its why or wherefore. What we have here is the frenzy of movement. We must not shut ourselves up in ourselves or in our rooms; we must be on the move to something new in an illusion of renewal. We must get out of ourselves in order to live only for entertainment, or we must forget ourselves in highly qualitative actions, for example, in our work or in deeds of charity, in the service of a cause or our country, in the distraction of a hundred possible actions that are always open to us and that are constantly renewed by an inventive technology that offers support for all actions and that authorizes the greatest possible dispersion of our being in its enterprises and fascinations. My acts allow me to escape the haunting question: Who am I? Action suffices. Above all, when I have gone to the edge of the world, when I have explored the most paradisal of islands, I must not come back to myself and make the ridiculous discovery that I am the same person as I was when I set out. Action evades the word; indeed, that is one of its main functions.

The word is irreplaceable. After many hesitations and contradictions we have come back to the certainty that the word specifies humanity. This was once believed; then people shrugged their shoulders. On the one hand, discourse was reduced, thanks to a rigorous systematics. Structural linguistics enabled us to elucidate the mysterious elements in the word. Refined analyses brought to light the inconsistency of belief in the unique character of the word. The new novel offered a form of speech which came from nowhere and was going nowhere, which had no content, no author or reader, no purpose, nothing to say, simply being set there as an object. On the other hand, great discoveries were made about animal language. We are not the only beings that can talk. Linguistics has also taught us that animals have their own language and can communicate with one another. At the same time the meaning of the term *language* was greatly extended. We now hear about film language, television language, etc.

Yet the wheel always turns, and more swiftly today than ever. Recent studies have tended to recover the unique character of spoken human language. The fixed and stereotyped nature of the language of bees and ants is especially contrasted with the fluidity and novelty and openness of human language. It is the strength of language to be always adaptive, though this is also its unavoidable weakness, for it allows of uncertainties and ambiguities and internal contradictions. The plasticity of human language that specifies us also places us in an indefinite world of interpretation. This is precisely the situation that makes human beings inventive and innovative. Our word is not just a simple game of communication. The celebrated schema "sender—information—receiver" is false as regards the word. So is the oversimple dichotomy of signifier and signified. Two primary dimensions are now perceived. First, human language takes on its value from what is not said and from the margins. By itself, of course, what is not said says nothing. But it begins to be full of meaning when it relates to a word that *is* said. The omitted, hidden, avoided word that is hinted at is what enriches dialogue and makes it human. The margins play the same role: to have a margin one must have a text. And in these margins are all the glosses and additions and interpretations that discourse leaves out.

There is more. We now know that language takes on meaning for the interlocutor only because there exists a metalanguage. This concept is taken in different ways. I will confine myself to one. If what is said is to make sense, it must kindle a collection of images, feelings, recollections, aspirations, judgments, etc. in the interlocutor. The word always refers to something beyond it. A phrase apart from the speaker and hearer has no meaning. What gives it value is the secret intention of the speaker and the individuality of the hearer. In other words, language is never neutral. We cannot analyze it objectively. It depends on the makeup of those in dialogue, and it is inseparable from these persons. We can engage in as many analyses as we like; the essential point escapes us. The whole person speaks and the whole person receives. Even to try to put ourselves on a purely conceptual plane does not help. Information systems created by systems experts might serve as an example. In order to work, the system has to be fed by human experts (without this human input, no such system is possible). This input conveys part of the experts' knowledge, and one can easily see that this knowledge, being objectifiable, can be transmitted to a machine as it is. A more subtle point is to see how the experts proceed. What are their methods, their savoir faire? Being human, they have had to be in their line of work for a long time to find the most effective method. Theoretical apprehension is not enough. They have to have practical experience that they can analyze and reduce to a minimal vocabulary in a domain of action and knowledge that is easy to circumscribe.

But we come up against a limit here. For example, expertise on works of art, especially paintings, cannot be programmed by a systems expert. "In effect, though there are well-qualified experts in the field, paintings offer a description of the world that can be reproduced only with all the power and wealth of natural language."[4] This is why there can never be communication between computers and human beings. Computers can understand human phrases relating to acts and limited objectifiable concepts. They can give information and obey orders. But this plainly has nothing whatever to do with the word or speech. The real danger and serious risk that we run with the proliferation of computers and robots is that being forced into relation with machines will slowly reduce our word to the nonhuman, external, objective aspect, and this in turn will make of the word something that is of use only for action. Once this comes about, we will lose our human distinctiveness. Without what is not said, without what is beyond itself, the word will simply be a utilitarian cipher. Face to face with speaking robots, will we still know how to speak in human fashion? This is one of the dangers of using computers in schools. One may see already the incredible poverty of the vocabulary of the young, their thirst for the inaudible word of rock music, the replacement of meaning by rhythm, the lack of aptitude for any thought that is not mathematical. The domination of the computer will complete this work of mental destruction.

4. J.-G. Ganascia, "La conception des systèmes-experts," *La Recherche* (October 1985).

Chapter 4

DIALECTIC*

We have not yet reached that stage. And here I am, expounding the importance that I attribute to the word at the very time when I am setting us in the nexus of chance, accident, and totality. I believe that, voluntarily or not, we are led to think and express ourselves dialectically. I must also try to bring out again the truth in the word *dialectic*, which is so botched and overworked and despised today.

It might seem presumptuous for a nonphilosopher to embark on a discussion of dialectic. But dialectic is so much a part of my way of thinking and being that I am talking about myself and my studies rather than about an academic mode of exposition or a philosophy outside myself.

During the last few years I have been looking at comments, criticisms, and reservations concerning my work, and I have profited by them, as will be apparent in my future writings, if God wills. In saying this, I am not saying that I will correct my mistakes. I have no thought of reviewing my faults and listing them as a theologian once did.[1] That demands a great dose of humility but is not of great practical use. Furthermore, there is another way of proceeding. In a dialogue, listeners reconsider their own positions in the light of what they hear. They thus reach a new stage. There is no need for self-criticism, for going back over

---

* An earlier, nearly identical version of this chapter was published as "On Dialectic" (trans. Geoffrey W. Bromiley), in *Jacques Ellul: Interpretive Essays*, ed. Clifford G. Christians and Jay M. Van Hook (Urbana: University of Illinois Press, 1981), pp. 291-308. — TRANS.
1. St. Augustine in his *Retractions*.

what has been said and modifying what has been found to be wrong in it. There is also no need for self-defense, for trying to show that the other speaker is mistaken. Both these attitudes are sterile. We need to cross a new threshold, taking two contrary positions into account and thus making progress possible.

This brings us to dialectic. Dialectic allows me to explain some of my "contradictions." Since my two intellectual origins are with Marx and Barth, dialectic is central for me, and it might be useful if I explain this theme more precisely.

I. General Sketch of Modern Dialectic

I am not attempting here to advance a general theory of dialectic. Dialectic comes from the Greek *dialogein,* "to talk with," as in "dialogue." But the *dia* also carries the sense of distance or contradiction. Dialectic can be the art of dialogue, of developing thought by question and answer, but it is also much more. The main problem in grasping what it is comes from the fact that it is used and defined in scores of different ways. There is the dialectic of Heraclitus, of Zeno, of Plato, of Aristotle, of Kant, and also that of Hegel and Marx, who have given the term its modern significance.

Let us begin at the simplest level. We are used to logical reasoning in terms of cause and effect, to the sequence of algebraic equations, to the linear expression of thought, and to the principle of noncontradiction (black cannot be white). We are also used to a binary system of alternatives (0 and 1, good and evil). We can accept intermediary nuances, but we always find the one ruled out by the other. True, the principle of causality has been seriously questioned by some sciences, so that today scientists prefer to speak of groups of referents or concomitants or more or less determinative factors. But this does not greatly change the process of thought. The principle has also been challenged by Marshall McLuhan, who relates it to writing and printing. But the comprehensive mythical thinking that has developed with new media and electronic transmission does not seem to me to be very convincing. I myself stand in a different world.

The simplest comparison with which to begin is as follows. Put a positive charge with a negative charge and you have a powerful flash. But the new phenomenon does not exclude either pole. Are we sure, then, that positive and negative factors exclude one another and that it is impossible in thought to uphold a no and a yes at the same time? The two ways of posing the question illustrate the fact that there are two sides to dialectic. There is a dialectic of ideas, but perhaps there is also one of facts, of reality.

In the first place, is dialectic merely a play of ideas functioning according to the familiar classical schema of thesis, antithesis, synthesis? Already in Plato we find a larger view than that: "The dialectician is the one who sees the totality" (*Republic* VII). Dialectic, then, is not just a way of reasoning by question and answer. It is an intellectual way of grasping reality, which embraces the positive and the negative, white and black. Descartes has an equally interesting remark to the effect that dialectic teaches us how to handle all things, just as logic gives a demonstration of all things ("Conversation with Burman," in the *Discourse on Method*). In other words, dialectic is not demonstrative reasoning or a system for the formal deployment of thought. It claims always to be dealing with reality, to be a means of taking account of reality. But reality includes positive and negative things. It includes contradictory things that do not exclude one another but coexist. Hence a system of vigorous thought ought to take account of both the yes and the no without ruling out either, without choosing between them, since every choice excludes one part of reality.

Hegel did not make dialectic a means of apprehending reality but a means of expressing truth by the dialectic of ideas. From another angle, how can we perceive the totality without also perceiving that it is in the process of changing? This is why reference is often made to the dialectic of Heraclitus, the philosopher of flux *(panta rhei)*. Reality includes not only contradictory elements but also a permanent process of change. If we relate two elements, it is easy to see that the negative element acts on the positive and that this action brings about a modification. In other words, contradictory factors do not relate to one another in a way that is inert or static. They are in interaction. The simple formula: thesis, antithesis, synthesis, implies already the transformation of the first two factors into a third that neither suppresses one or the other of them, nor confuses them, nor adds to them. One might also think of a living organism in which forces are constantly at work. Some of them tend to keep the organism alive while others tend to break it down or destroy it. At each moment there is a synthesis of the two groups of forces which produces the state of the organism at that time.

The concept of time or history comes into the dialectical relation here, and it is a decisive factor. Dialectic has often been viewed as a type of reasoning or as the coexistence of contradictory elements. The important point, however, is that the contradictory factors cannot exist without eliminating one another unless they are correlative in a temporal movement that leads to a new situation. On the one side, it is coexistence that in real history rules out any idea of an inert and immutable absolute, and hence that rules out metaphysical thinking. On the other side, the manner of knowing must also be in evolution if it is to keep up with the contradictions and evolution of reality, for even when I begin to think, reality is in a process of change. Thus there is no fixed state that I can impose on the object. The flux of time comes into knowledge itself. This is why, for example, in Marx, there is reference to the dialectic of history.

For Marx history proceeds dialectically, that is, by confrontation, by the contradiction of historical factors that mutually negate one another yet do not exclude one another, producing after a certain period of contradiction and conflict a new historical situation. Thus we can conceive of history only in terms of conflict. Each actual situation is made up of tensions. In every social and political context we have to discern the contradictory forces and interpret their present relations in such a way as to foresee their possible evolution. In a sense one might appeal to the celebrated interpretation of Toynbee that each civilization evolves thanks to the challenges it meets, surviving only as each time it finds an answer to the challenge hurled against it. This is true, and there is something here that corresponds to a dialectical view of history, although Toynbee's own thinking was not strictly dialectical.

If we want to understand the historical process successfully, we obviously must not make any mistake regarding the contradictory factors. In every society there are hundreds of contradictory forces. Most of them are irrelevant—they have no dialectical value—but some constitute the dialectical process. One of these is the familiar contradiction that Marx perceived between the forces of production (technological and economic) and the social relationships of production (which organize society).

To make it clear how dialectic has been an influence for me, I must now explain two points. In a well-known formula Hegel talked about the positivity of negativity. Negativity is essential, for if the positive remains alone, it is unchanged, stable, and inert. A positive element, for example, an unchallenged society, a force without counterforce, a person engaged in no dialogue, an unstimulated professor, a church without heretics, a sole party with no rivals, is enclosed within the permanent repetition of its own image. It will be satisfied with what it has done thus far and will see no reason to change. Facts and circumstances and events that might be contrary to it will be for it no more than tiresome inconveniences.

A contrary fact, be it noted, is not enough in itself to bring about change in us. Often we obliterate it or disguise it. We interpret it in such a way that we can fit it without harm into an understanding that has an answer for everything. This is how we finish up with the sclerosis, the paralysis, the redundant monologue of self-satisfaction and auto-production. We find this in a totalitarian society (I say "society" and not necessarily "power"). But to say this suggests also that there is never any true innovation. There might be apparent innovations, formal changes, but these will not produce any real mutation. The result is increasing strain between the actual situation and the organization or individual. The only thing that can bring about change or evolution is contradiction, challenge, the appearance of the negative, negativity. This factor carries with it a transformation of the situation.

In the human condition it is not enough that the contradiction be one of facts or events. There has to be an express contradiction made by a contradicting subject. This is how negativity induces and provokes innovation and the consequent history of the group or individual. One thus sees clearly that negativity has a positive aspect. Where there is transition from one state to another, we owe it to negativity. I am intentionally not referring here to progress. I am not certain that transition or innovation necessarily signifies progress. In this respect I differ totally from Hegel and Marx. For them the new state has to be an advance on the previous one; the synthesis (though Marx does not use the term) of the positive and negative factors implies that the new state is better. I am not at all sure about that, and in Hegel and Marx this conclusion rests purely on a belief in progress or an ideology of progress. What I am sure about is that life presupposes innovation, that humanity is a history that includes negativity, and that to remain in a given state is to deny both life and history, that is, to deny human distinctiveness, to try to arrest history and in this way (perhaps) to enter the kingdom of God.

For me, negativity has a positive value even though I am not sure that the product of the dialectical march of history will necessarily be superior to the preceding state. There are always favorable and unfavorable elements. The new state or synthesis — or, if one will, equilibrium — gives rise unavoidably to a ‚new negativity which will reproduce the contradiction and ineluctable movement. But why should this be better than a fixed order and repetitive organization? I will not enter into a debate about entropy, about the total disorder that constitutes ultimate stability. I will simply underline the fact that human life makes no sense if there is no possibility of change of some kind, if we ourselves have no role to play, if there is no history begun but not yet consummated. It is in this respect that negativity comes to the fore. In one of my books I thus adopted the well-known formula of Guéhenno that our first task as human beings is to say no.

To give greater precision to general considerations, we must think about the question of crisis. When we talk about thesis, antithesis, and synthesis, we cannot stop imagining the tranquil intellectual work of philosophers in the study. Yet we know that a chemical synthesis releases a great deal of energy and might bring about the dissolution of the structure of the bodies brought into synthesis. We must not have any illusions about intellectual synthesis. When we engage in minute demonstrations and study the process of intellectual analysis, synthesis escapes us. When synthesis is achieved by a poet in a creative act, or by a philosopher who suddenly arrives at a new understanding by intuition, it is inexplicable. Creative synthesis is achieved only by explosions and acts of destruction. This applies to the whole dialectical movement.

No temporal or historical transition is peaceful. None moves self-evidently from a prior state (positive-negative) to a final state. To reach the second state there has to be a crisis, a time of intense trouble, of fire and explosion, in which the first elements are dissolved and destroyed. In the historical and social field we call this crisis *revolution*, in the spiritual field we call it *conversion*. If the dialectic is dealing with reality, we see that neither conversion nor revolution is ever once and for all. Both constantly have to begin again. Thus crisis in society or the church or human experience is always a sign of confrontation with a negativity that must be transcended to create a radically new state. What we find here is undoubtedly the theme of challenge. Does this living organism have adequate resources to meet the crisis and to achieve a new equilibrium, or will it fall into neurosis, disorder, and incoherence? The latter is always a possibility. Dialectic is not a machine which automatically produces results. It implies incontestable human responsibility and hence a freedom of choice and decision.

II. Biblical Dialectic

A tradition among philosophers would have it that dialectic began with the Greeks. Some propose Heraclitus at the end of the 6th century B.C. In his theory of becoming, conflict is the origin of all things, contrariety leading to concord. Others, following Aristotle, believe that Zeno of Elea invented dialectic in the 5th century B.C. Even if he used the word, however, he did not seem to go beyond the idea of argumentation and the technique of discussion. Others would derive dialectic from Plato. I for my part believe that long before these intellectual formulations dialectic had arisen from as early as the 8th century in Hebrew thought, and that the Old Testament as a whole expresses a dialectic.

I am not saying that the Hebrews had an express theory of dialectic, or that they used the word, but that in the Old Testament we come up against an original process of thought which bears the marks of what would later be called dialectic (in the ontological sense and not merely in that of the technique of discussion). I am completely opposed to the idea that if a word is not present the thing itself cannot be there. On the contrary, I believe that the reality comes first here and that the term comes later only in an effort to understand a reality of which there has already been experience. In other words, the Hebrews formulated divine revelation dialectically without examining what they were doing intellectually and without expounding the noetic aspect. I will offer five examples of the dialectical process in the Bible, simply giving brief remarks and referring to well-known questions.

First, we have the global affirmation that God enters history and accompanies the human race in its history. This fact is no less astonishing than the incarnation of Jesus Christ. We are told that the one God and Creator comes to be with his people; that a people bears his glory, chosen to do so because it is the least of all peoples; that this God, who is so different from the gods of Egypt and Greece which either symbolize nature or have a kind of intrinsic temporality, enters into relation with a people as the partner in a dialogue in such a way that all that one can know of this God is by way of his people; and that all that his people experiences is defined, though not foreordained, by this God. This is dialectic precisely because the God in question is the contradictory pole of all that is lived out by the people indissolubly bound to him.

The process represented by such terms as *commandment, disobedience, judgment,* and *reconciliation* is precisely a process of total dialectic. It is not a chance process. It is not that of a little story (as among the Greek gods) that might have been different. We find the same schema repeated at each stage in the people's history. Each time there is a synthesis of the preceding factors (including disobedience) by way of a crisis. The historical process does not allow the God who is thus revealed to be a metaphysical God whom one may construct and know by a metaphysical process. To define God as omniscient, omnipotent, impassible, imperturbable, eternal, etc., is not to have understood the biblical revelation. These things might all be said of any kind of God. The God of biblical revelation, however, enters time and history, bears with the suffering and sin of the race, tolerates its initiatives, and limits his own power. He repents, he revokes his judgments, etc. We cannot have the one side of God without the other. Is this a contradiction? Precisely. It is logically insoluble. Yet it creates the biblical dialectic which means that our relation to God is not a mere repetition, a fixed thing, a ritual, an exact submission, but a permanent invention, a new creation on both sides, a history of love, an adventure whose outcome we cannot know in advance. It is all an incredible revelation of the freedom of God.[2] The one thing does not exclude the other. The whole expresses the dialectical development of the relation in revelation. One cannot understand this revelation unless one thinks dialectically instead of thinking in terms of either-or as one is tempted to do: Either God is omnipotent and we are slaves, or we are free and God does not exist. Nor is this just a matter of philosophical formulation. At issue is a new understanding of revelation such as there has never been elsewhere, and that implies that if we are to attempt an intellectual account of it we have to proceed dialectically.

A second aspect of this basic biblical dialectic, and one that brings to light many others, is that which Moltmann has shown, for example, in his *Theology of Hope*,[3] namely, that throughout the Old Testament the process of development leads from promise to fulfillment, and that the fulfillment contains new promise leading to new fulfillment. We must not simplify this movement, as many Christians do, by merely saying that all the Old Testament promises have been fulfilled at one point in Jesus Christ. This is no doubt true, but in saying it we must not leap over the route that leads to Jesus Christ and that equally begins with him. For we, too, live by a promise (the *parousia* of God and the kingdom). But this is not a theoretical and global

2. I tried to show this in my commentary on Kings, *The Politics of God and the Politics of Man*, trans. Geoffrey W. Bromiley (Grand Rapids: Eerdmans, 1972).

3. Jürgen Moltmann, *Theology of Hope*, trans. James W. Leitch (New York: Harper & Row, 1975).

promise. On the contrary, it multiplies in the course of the church's life and our own in the form of partial promises and fulfillments which always for us, as for the Jews, contain new promises and indicate a new way ahead. This is how it is in the relations of grace, sin, and repentance. Is grace given before repentance? Does repentance have priority over the fact that salvation is free? To this insoluble biblical question Luther replies with his famous formula that we are always at the same time sinners and righteous and penitent. (We must not forget the third word.) "At the same time" means each moment afresh.

One might quote innumerable biblical passages that express this contradiction. Let us simply adduce Psalm 130, where we find the astonishing affirmation: "There is forgiveness with thee, that thou mayest be feared" (v. 4). Forgiveness ought to bring with it love or gratitude. Fear ought to be kindled by justice or wrath. But no, the biblical text puts fear in relation to love and pardon. God is feared because he is the one who forgives. He manifests his final greatness, not by refusing to pardon, but by being the only one who can do so. The dialectic of forgiveness and fear is essential.

Thus the whole deployment of the existence of the people of God (the church) and individual Christians is dialectic in the constant renewal of promise and fulfillment (or, in other words, of the already and the not yet). The kingdom of heaven is among you, in the midst of you, or in you, but it will also come at the end of the age. The God of Abraham is fully revealed but not yet revealed except in Jesus Christ. Jesus Christ is already the Lord of the world, but not yet, for he will be so at his *parousia*. To all this we must not add words aiming at a logical reconciliation. We must say neither that Jesus Christ is virtually or secretly Lord of the world, nor that his lordship will be revealed in the last days. To take this course is to relax the tension. It is to accept a hypothetical explanation instead of living with the contradiction of what is fully accomplished yet obviously not yet accomplished. The Christian life is lived in this contradiction.

If it is true—and we have shown that dialecticians believe so—that historical life develops and evolves only by way of dialectical contradiction, the same applies to the Christian life. If everything is accomplished and we are content with that, then we have no useful or worthwhile life to live. All is in vain. If nothing is accomplished, then no life is possible. Yet we must not mix up the two things. Our job is not to accomplish what is not yet accomplished (a regression to moralism). An actual fulness of accomplishments goes hand in hand with an actual experience of total nonaccomplishment. This is the indissoluble relation that makes the Christian life possible and gives it meaning in its movement from crisis to crisis (as the historical life of the church shows).

The third aspect of biblical revelation that I like to recall is that of the relation between the whole and the remnant. On the one side developments obviously lead to an apparent reduction of the election, from the race to a people, from the people of Israel to a remnant, from the remnant to an individual (Jesus). Yet on the other hand the proclamation is in each case more universal until we come to the recapitulation of all history, all nature, and all human works in the last days. The more the elect remnant is reduced historically, the more real is universal election. Thus the remnant represents the whole. At the same time, although this is not the same thing, the process is dialectical in the sense that each break or fracture results in the reintegration of the excluded whole with the manifested remnant. The election of the chosen people implies the reintegration of the human race, that of the remnant the reintegration of all Israel, that of Jesus the reintegration of the remnant. From the standpoint of the Bible, then, the development of judgment is never a mechanism to separate the good from the bad (as though the latter were merely rejected, eliminated, or excluded). It is an election of the bad achieved by that of the good. Jesus is not just the mediator between God and us. He signifies the salvation of all Israel and therefore of the human race and therefore of all creation. Clearly this is not a fixed schema that one can reduce to a formula; it presupposes historical development and constant tension between opposing factors.

Having given these three examples, I want to point out the mistake in a whole theological movement influenced by a certain type of Greek philosophy. I have in mind the view that what is one is good, that every break or fracture or division is bad, and that we are thus to seek metaphysical unity (e.g., mystical fusion in a great totality). This obsession with the one, which has led some to rejection of the Trinity, others to theism, and yet others to pantheism, results in a complete misunderstanding of revelation and its replacement by an explicative system (e.g., the pyramid of the one in Gnosticism).[4] The temptation to follow this path recurs constantly, structuralism being a recent example.

The first three examples I have given come mainly from the Old Testament. I will now give two specifically from the New Testament. We undoubtedly find there the dialectic of the already and the not yet (in the kingdom, as already shown). On another level we also find an essential dialectic in the thinking of Paul. Thus at the center of his thinking we find the statement that we are saved by grace through faith (Eph. 2:8). This is clear and simple. We are familiar with the important developments of this statement. But then the same Paul tells us to work out our salvation with fear and trembling (Phil. 2:12). This is an evident contradiction. If we are saved by grace, there is no need to work out our salvation, and vice versa. There is then a further contradiction in Philippians, for in 2:13 Paul tells us that it is God who works in us to will and to do of his good pleasure. Now we must not try to reduce the contradiction by establishing some sort of continuity. On the contrary, the contradiction itself constitutes life in Christ. As God works in us to will and to do, we have to accept our responsibility as if [5] we were without God and everything depended on us. For God is at one and the same time both unknown God and love. Thus there can be no place for a pietism that tries to discover in every situation here and now the response and will of God. If we work out our own salvation with fear and trembling and do the impossible, then in the last resort we can only give glory to God, who has

4. In *Political Theology and the Life of the Church,* trans. John Bowden (Philadelphia: Westminster, 1978), André Dumas has clearly shown the inadequacy of monism and dualism. Dualism separates us from God. It is a structure of distance, whereas the Bible is a history of covenant. Covenant, of course, takes place only between beings that are distinct and separated but still united.

5. I have often insisted on the "as if" in the life of Jesus. Jesus was no clown, but the divine splendor was concealed beneath a humble appearance, and he was ready to suffer and die as if he were not God.

already saved us. But to think that this attitude means we need not work is to misunderstand the incarnation, to despise salvation, and not really to believe in salvation by grace.

The dialectical process in the individual Christian life consists of unceasingly rediscovering what is meant by salvation by grace and by the glory of God which shows us grace, but only by way of the crisis which arises when in the very grace that is shown us we are summoned to advance, accepting the judgment on all that we have done thus far. This judgment pushes us toward the new situation of receiving, the receiving of salvation by grace, and this alone can make us live without looking for a guarantee of salvation. Thus all Christian ethics, all conduct in the Christian life, can be thought of only on the basis of the dialectical relation between the two opposing factors of salvation by grace and works.

I will now give as a final example history and the *parousia*. Linear and logical thinking tends to say that history is a cocreation with God, that it moves naturally toward the kingdom of God, that there is continuity between the two, that history is a kind of beginning of progressive evolution toward the kingdom. Some millennialists espouse a similar ideology, believing that we are establishing the kingdom of God on earth by social reforms, and then when we have finished the Messiah will return. Roman Catholic theology says something similar, as when Péguy calls carnal cities the image and commencement and body and sketch of the house of God. Similar views are held by those who champion a theology of liberation or revolution. From another angle the same linear and logical thinking would say that everything is destroyed at the judgment, that the kingdom of God is something absolutely new, a gracious gift of God, that there will simply be new heavens and a new earth where righteousness will reign, that all old things will be done away, and that history and politics and so on have no meaning, value, or interest.

In my judgment, both views are biblically incorrect precisely because the Bible depicts a dialectical process. On the one side history moves toward judgment and disaster, so that no continuity is possible. But on the other side and at the same time history is extraordinarily important. What shows it to be so, we might say, is the decision of God to write himself on the pages of history. The note in Luke 2:1-2 regarding the decree of Caesar Augustus and Quirinius the governor of Syria is enough to remind us that history is not without importance for God.

What does all this mean? First, there is always one history, not two (secular and sacred). In this one history we have the conjunction and opposition of independent human work and God's "relational" work. Every actual event in history expresses this twofold force. It is a product of human activity. There is no progress in it but a multiplication of the results and capacities or potentialities of the race. I am tempted to say that history will not end until every possibility of combination between human initiative and divine initiative is exhausted, or rather, until all human initiatives are exhausted (for God's are eternal). I might take as an illustration the musical theme and variations on it. Like a piece of music, history will end when no further variation is possible. I believe that this takes account of the relation between human invention and the basic theme of covenant or promise. But all this moves, not toward the kingdom of God, but toward the crisis triggered by the absolute contradiction between vain human effort and God's exclusive novelty. The crisis or judgment, however, does not mean the annulment or insignificance of history. As in the dialectical crisis, no factor is suppressed. The two are integrated in a synthesis. All human history, then, will enter the new Jerusalem.[6] The creation of the final city is the obvious consummation, not the result, of all that we attempt in history. Nothing in history (collective or individual) is lost, but everything is qualitatively transformed. There is a natural body and there is a spiritual body, but incontestably if there is no natural body there will be no spiritual body. Hence we can understand the revelation of the kingdom only dialectically.

These brief examples are perhaps enough to show that in my view only dialectical thinking can do justice to the scriptural revelation, since this revelation itself is fundamentally and intrinsically dialectical.

6. Cf. Jacques Ellul, *The Meaning of the City,* trans. Dennis Pardee (Grand Rapids: Eerdmans, 1970); and also Part III below.

III. Dialectic in My Books

To discuss my own work may seem pretentious, and yet my books constitute a totality conceived as such. To the extent that I have arrived at the conviction that it is impossible to study modern society in its unity without a spiritual reference, and also that it is impossible to engage in theological study without reference to the world in which we live, I have found myself faced from the outset with the need to find the link between the two, and this link can be nothing other than the dialectical process.

I have found it impossible to join Christianity and the world into a single whole. From my very first writings I have shown that there is no such thing as a Christian politics that a Christian party can espouse, nor is there a Christian economics, nor, epistemologically, a Christian history or science, etc. In the first place, there could only be a kind of ideological cloak, and in the second place, there would be a deformation of methods and results. Naturally an ethics written by Christians can be a Christian ethics, but only Christians can accept it. Similarly, Christians can study history or biology, realizing (like all scholars) what their presuppositions are and how they will affect their conclusions. Again, Christians may be members of a union or a political party and play their own part in it, but they will not pretend to be Christian politicians (something I have found by experience to be impossible and untenable).[7]

From another angle, it seems no less certain to me that we cannot think in a Christian way in isolation from the concrete reality of society. Christians cannot live by eternal principles without reference to the real world. It is idealistic and fanciful either to think that Christianity can permeate or modify the structures of society (and here I come up against the function of ideology according to Marx), or, conversely, to think that Christianity ought to be adapted and modified according to the necessities, exigencies, and orientations of the world. This has always happened even to the point, politically, of French Chris-

7. I have written to this effect as early as 1937 and repeated it in 1944 in *Foi et Vie* and *Cahiers des Associations professionelles protestantes*.

tianity being monarchist under Louis XIV, revolutionary in 1792, Napoleonic in 1800, republican in 1875, and in process of becoming socialist in 1950. The theologies of liberation and revolution seem to me to be simple attempts to adapt Christianity to circumstances. At the same time, it seems to me to be impossible to proclaim that the world is lost and, conversely, that the church is without significance.

Thus I have found myself forced to affirm both the independence of analysis of contemporary society and the specificity of theology, to affirm both the coherence and importance of the world in which we live and the incomparable truth of revelation in Christ—two factors that are alien and yet indissolubly linked. Thus the relation between the two factors can be only a dialectical and critical one. Noetically we can only affirm two contradictions, pressing contradiction to the limit. Actively, we can only introduce the dimension of mutual criticism, the world criticizing the church and science criticizing theology, the church (as we should not forget) criticizing the world and theology criticizing science. Since the synthesis, the negation of the negation, or the appearance in some form of a new state can be only a product of history, there can be no question of presenting this synthesis in some arbitrary intellectual fashion in a study which will simply correspond to an appearance of response. I have thus been led to work in two spheres, the one historical and sociological, the other theological. This does not represent a dispersing of interest nor does it express a twofold curiosity. It is the fruit of what is essentially rigorous reflection. Each part of my work is of equal importance and each is as free as possible from contamination by the other. As a sociologist, I have to be realistic and scientific, using exact methods, though in this regard I have fought methodological battles and had to contest certain methods. As a theologian, I have to be equally intransigent, presenting an interpretation of revelation which is as strict as possible, and making no concession to the spirit of the age.

If the final result is a dialectic, however, the whole is not made up of unrelated parts: there has to be correlation. The negative exists only in relation to the positive, and the positive only in relation to the negative. The two have reciprocal roles as in musical counterpoint. Hence it is perfectly possible to think in terms of correspondence between apparently unrelated works. There is counterpoint, for example, between *The Political Illusion* and *The Politics of God and the Politics of Man,* just as *The Ethics of Freedom* is the exact counterpoint of the two books on technique (*The Technological Society* and *The Technological System*).[8] I have worked out at one and the same time a way of acquiring knowledge and a way of passing through the crisis. The crisis may be seen in our society, in the political and economic sphere and also in the sphere of Christianity and the church. But it cannot lead to a positive result or escape incoherence and nonsense unless there is a clear recognition of the two factors present in it. This is what I have tried to contribute. In truth my attempt may seem to have failed. People do not use my studies in correlation with one another so as to get to the heart of the crisis with an awareness based on Christian understanding. They continue to react at the level of reflex rather than reflection, adopting Christian positions upon which they have not reflected.

Having said that, I ought to note in conclusion that dialectic does not simply operate between the two parts of my work but also functions as a twofold element: on the one part as that which permits understanding of some of my positions, and on the other as my very profound conviction regarding the actual situation.

To illustrate the first element, I might say that it is a dialectical attitude that leads us to consider that we are impotent in relation to structures and necessities but that we ought to attempt what can be attempted. The same attitude causes us to affirm constantly that as an expression of determinism and as an exclusion of freedom, society must be unceasingly attacked and yet that all our efforts will tend to maintain this society, so that we must not give way to destructive anger but simply try to keep society open. It also leads us to say that our human enterprises are highly relative and represent no supreme value,

8. Jacques Ellul, *The Political Illusion,* trans. Konrad Kellen (New York: Knopf, 1967); *The Politics of God and the Politics of Man,* trans. Geoffrey W. Bromiley (Grand Rapids: Eerdmans, 1972); *The Ethics of Freedom,* trans. Geoffrey W. Bromiley (Grand Rapids: Eerdmans, 1976); *The Technological Society,* trans. John Wilkinson (New York: Knopf, 1964); *The Technological System,* trans. Joachim Neugroschel (New York: Continuum, 1980).

but that nevertheless they ought to be taken in hand with absolute seriousness as if they had supreme value. It leads us to say, too, that human values and the morality produced by human groups are not real values, not natural or absolute morality, not the will of God, and yet that we ought to defend and uphold and practice them (whatever they are) because the groups in question (and hence the human race) cannot live without them. Thus we have not to establish rivalry between such values or morality and Christian truth, which is supposed to deliver us from the errors inherent in other beliefs, nor between such values or morality and an exclusively good Christian morality, which is supposed to take the place of every other morality. If there is dialectical contradiction here, that is healthy. If there is a judgmental attitude that wants to eliminate all else, that is unacceptable.

The second element is my basic conviction regarding the actual situation. I will sum up my conclusions briefly. If, as I think I have shown, the technical system is a totalitarian one that embraces all other activities, that has its own logic, and that progressively assimilates all other cultures, there is no longer any dialectical factor in relation to it. It tends to become a totality or unity. But if we believe that the dialectical process is indispensable to life and history, it is absolutely necessary that this factor exist. If the technical system is totalitarian, then this factor must exist outside it. But only what is transcendent can be exterior to it. For me, in the concrete situation in which technique has put us, the transcendent is an essential condition of the continuation of life, the unfolding of history, and the mere existence of human beings as such. But this transcendent cannot be one that is self-sufficient and unknown. It has to be one that is revealed to us if we are to be motivated and to launch ourselves into a dialectical movement in spite of the autonomy and universality of technique. In saying that, I am not engaging in any kind of apologetics. I am simply pointing out what is the unavoidable result of the double movement of my research, sociological on the one side and theological on the other.[9]

9. We shall develop this point in Part III below.

Chapter 5

HARMONY

Bachelard has talked about this better than I can do, but I cannot avoid it, for harmony is a reality that I maintain. Again, we must try to understand one another. I do not believe in the existence of a natural or cosmic harmony, which would be the expression of the free play of chemical and physical laws. The cosmos whose harmony for a long time commanded admiration is, as we now know, an immense battlefield. I do not believe in an economic harmony such as liberalism imagines. I do not believe in a harmony of evolution that ensures the survival of the fittest. This survival is at the cost of the weak, and that is not harmony but massacre. Those who come off best are not better, and simply to talk of some coming off best rules out harmony. I do not believe in a spontaneous harmony between people, or in a society that is good from the start. Wherever we go, no matter how far back, war reigns. Heraclitus was right. Hence I have no hope that one day there will be established a paradise of anarchy, or the paradise of Marx.

It is not the authority or domination of a minority that obstructs harmony. The cause lies deeper. Undoubtedly the world as God created it was harmonious. The human race had its place there without violence, and the animals lived at peace with one another. All was very good, the Creator said. But the world rested on the harmonious relation between the Creator and his image or partner in an exchange of love. When this correspondence was broken, disorder came, diversity became exclusiveness, and plurality became competition. Human beings were no longer in harmony with nature, which brings forth thorns, or

with animals, which go in dread of them. They created fear and
live henceforth themselves in fear. There is no harmony in the
world. There is no harmony in nature. Left to itself, nature is
the tragic scene of complementary life and death—life thrives
on death. But because death *is* death, we cannot speak of harmony. What triumphs from a human standpoint is death. This
earth is our only possession. It is called a garden. But is it a garden? We think of the constant disasters that afflict us, tornadoes,
earthquakes, volcanoes, floods, fires, the terrible disorder, the
incredible waste, a thousand octopus eggs that hatch in order
that finally only one will live to adult age, a thousand butter-
flies that almost all fall prey to birds, a profusion that simply
moves on to destruction. Death supports other life, but is this
vast slaughterhouse a place of harmony? We have to look elsewhere and not just rely on positive observation.

God created a garden called Eden in order to put Adam
and Eve there. In the midst of creation, in the midst of the stars
and the cosmos, he created Eden, a garden, whose very name
denotes pleasure and delights. The earth was our garden, our
delight, conceived to give us pleasure. Everything in it was good,
beautiful, harmonious, and pure—all there for our pleasure. But
then discord came. This earth, our unique home, was meant for
correspondence and joy. If these are no longer present, they
must be restored. For this fragile and shattered earth is our only
place, our only home. We must rise up with all our force against
the absurd ambition of the human race to colonize the galaxy,
to place colonies on other planets, and to set up space stations
in the universe. Fiction is already anticipating human colonies
set up on other planets in flight from an earth made uninhabit-
able. I say no. I say no because it is a matter of colonizing. Do
we still not realize what this word means? Do we still not realize it even after the colonizing of North Africa by Islam and of
the rest of Africa by Europe? After the colonizing of the Indians by the American melting pot? After the colonizing of South
America by the Spaniards and the Portuguese? Do we still not
realize that all colonizing brings twofold disaster, both to those
who colonize and to those who are colonized? Do all these experiences count for nothing even though there is not a single
example of successful colonizing? We still want to colonize

space, but what do we begin to set up there? In reality, and above all, it will be phenomenal war gadgetry. This is the point of space vehicles and communication satellites — they are all devoted to war. Let us return to the earth and try to make it humane, livable, and harmonious. This is our real business. The earth is our only place. Let us rediscover joy in the earth. Instead of hating it because of disasters and destroying it by the senseless exploitation of agribusiness, mining, and hydrocarbons, instead of squandering its riches that were slowly accumulated over millions of years and that we scatter in a few decades, let us regard this home, this garden, this place that was made for us, on its own terms. Let us contemplate the wealth of the countryside, the grandeur of the mountains, the majesty of the oceans, the mystery of the forests. This earth was made for us. We have here all that we need to make us happy, as people have been for centuries.

But this earth, having been ravaged, is no longer just a garden. It is also a place of tragedies and disasters. Our task is to restore it to itself. In placing us on it, God gave us only this command—to till it and keep it. This is all that we have to do. We have to till it well and not to waste it, or make it ugly or unnatural. We have to keep it, even against itself at times, in such a way as to restore its lost harmony, and also against ourselves in such a way as to find in it the limit and measure of our arrogance. No doubt we human beings are the measure of all things. Yet the earth, our garden, is also the measure of all things, of actions that are reasonable and legitimate. We must cherish it, making it the object of our favor and thus making it more amenable, more in conformity with the spirit of its creation. Harmony is the issue.

But once again our perspective is radically mistaken. For the last five hundred years our genius has been for conquest, exploitation, and aggrandizement, when harmony was our real vocation. We have begun to destroy for our own ends. We have accumulated possessions and in the process destroyed and lost everything. We are breaking up the garden, and if we continue to devour it as we are doing, the earth will soon be no more than a pile of lifeless bones. The last traces of Eden are on the point of disappearing. Is this an ecological discourse? I am afraid that it will be instead an elegy on the death of the earth, which was no part of our human calling. As we vaguely sense, we were called to create a harmony or balance or just equipoise of forces and means, an equitable distribution of earth's bounty. But this concern has been snuffed out by power. I might say the same about society, finding there the same battle between harmony and power.

A harmonious society would be a utopia, dearly bought. What would we not give to evoke this harmony, to arrive at the conviction that we are living in the best of all possible worlds, or to close our eyes to the reality of nature in order to trust in a system of laws in which nothing is lost? But we now know that this is no longer true. There are constant losses and unceasing conflicts. And yet harmony, like liberty and justice, though it does not exist and we cannot define it, is something to which we aspire with passion and despair. Again and again, in spite of the challenges of reality, we dream of it and are obsessed by it. Because we desire it in this way, I would say that it does exist. I reject the skeptical and simplistic analysis which offers a rational explanation of the way in which we have invented the thirst for harmony and justice, these being unstable dreams which exist only in the psychological mechanisms of the human constitution, and which therefore do not exist at all. But rational explanations are not definitive. An opening always exists through which this particular dream slips, and not another. What is created is harmony and not something else. We may not know what we are talking about, but we do know from what we suffer, and we thus know from time to time that it is possible to live where harmony is at last a living reality. And when it is there, we can know it. We want it to last, but it is fleeting. If it were to last, it would mean the sudden stoppage of that which makes up life, the appearance of a machine that repeats itself indefinitely and that would no longer be harmonious. Or it would mean the great silence of absence and nothingness. No one can define or delimit harmony. We can talk about it only in parable and metaphor. Yet we know something about it by experience.

Already a first misunderstanding arises in this regard. We have the impression that harmony survives as a kind of miracle independent of our will. The setting sun produces a sky which is as dazzling and changing as an opal. Harmony is achieved for a few minutes. It seems like chance. This chance concerns me, for I have to see it. I have to be there to grasp the harmony and live with it. If there were no one to do this, it would still take place, but I could not call it harmony. It would be no more than a combination of light without significance. There is harmony only when human beings are involved. Face to face with a given situation, which has no significance of its own, we human beings can catch the thrill of harmony. Thus I would say that it is never there on its own. It does not exist apart from us, objectively, with no one to recognize it. There is harmony for *this* person when there is nothing for those who are not there. Harmony is not an indisputable, objective datum.

This is why, I repeat, we cannot talk about a harmony of the laws of nature. We cannot talk about economic harmony, the free play of the laws of the marketplace. Harmony is to be found when certain events come together, but above all it is to be made, created, invented, and produced. Harmony is our affair. This is why it is so important to destroy the idea of an independent, established harmony that goes with the package of the universe. This idea undermines human responsibility. I believe that our vocation on earth is to establish a harmony that includes all that we call justice, liberty, joy, peace, and truth. Our vocation is to set up harmony between people, between earthly things, between the elements that compose our universe. This is why all arrogance, all desire for domination, and all attempts to exploit other things or beings run contrary to our vocation. Yet this is the way things go. Everything tends spontaneously toward disorder, and we have to try to introduce a harmonious order.

I have in mind the passage in Genesis in which God says that it is not good for man to be alone (Gen. 2:18ff.). God brings all the animals to him so that he may find a helpmeet, but also *name* them. We must not forget the importance of the name in this Semitic world. The name establishes the spiritual quality of that to which it is given and fixes its place in the world's order. Thus when man gave names to an innumerable host of animals, he did more than something useful or utilitarian. He established harmony between himself and the animal kingdom.

But this parable brings out another aspect of harmony. Adam acted by means of the word. There is nothing more fleeting or fragile or transitory than the word. Once spoken, it is gone. It is not without effect, but it is no longer there. Hence harmony set up by the word is not a fixed thing like a butterfly pinned in a collector's case. It is a creation that comes and lives and then tends to vanish as the effect of the word decreases progressively. Harmony, being set up by the word, is also fleeting. This is what I wanted to show when I spoke about the sunset. A few moments, and then darkness falls. Perhaps there will be another striking sunset tomorrow. But harmony does not last; it is not a fixture. It is created. It lives for an instant. Afterward, there is only a happy and illuminating memory (a happy memory perhaps being more true than happiness on earth). Or else we may find only dust and ashes as we dream of the great happiness that we have lost. I have in mind the uplifting moment in a revolt when a group of people is gripped by the certainty that at last a truly new world has come in which justice and universal brotherhood are possible, and along with victory there unfolds the rainbow of all the hopes so long built up. This joy lasts only a short time and then the opposite of harmony returns quickly. It cannot last, for harmony has always to be a new creation, a renewing, a fresh beginning. The opposite of harmony is fixation or installation, the transformation of the illuminating glory into an acquisition that we never want changed. Fragility is undoubtedly a part of harmony, for if we could be sure of finding it at any moment as long as the world lasts, it would say nothing to us. In cold fixation it would cease to be "for us." As the poet says, it is the law of nature to live on unceasingly, scorning like a goddess pilgrim man who ought to be its king, but it is for us to love what we will never see a second time.

I am saying in effect that when stability is achieved there is no more harmony. It is pointless to argue that a work of art exists forever on its own with its harmony. To be sure, the Pietà is always the Pietà. But there has to be someone to see it if it is to be more than a block of marble and if harmony is to be born. The stability of things or groups or relations or labors works against life in harmony. What it brings is the ongoing institution. The magnificent exaltation of the moment of revolt produces a society of blood and bitterness in which the revolution may undoubtedly be successful but people lose themselves in the institution and society loses itself in the repression of everything that will not accept the new conformity.

This hostile installation of harmony may take two forms. There is that which kills instantly. I have in mind the opposite of a glorious revolt, that is, a planned revolution, calculated like clockwork, in which people are mere pawns and strategy is dominant. Inhuman and barbarous, this revolution has terrorism as its inevitable child. It thus sets us in a permanent renewal of horror and a triumph of inhumanity. Terrorism is the exact opposite of harmony. But the inversion of human creation is more insidious and subterranean when it involves a simple recommencement of what was once harmony, or when measures are taken to ensure its permanence. Harmony is created when human beings bring a certain order into society by setting up a morality that all feel to be vital and joyous, or by establishing a law that is absolutely essential if life in community is to be possible. Each of these is a creation of the word and is so fragile that the morality easily changes into conformism and insignificant commonplace, and the law into absurd and burdensome constraint. As the world changes, the moment passes when there is exact correspondence between the morality or law and the social situation, the common aspiration, the shared values. Then the morality is established and the law becomes mortal. We have to live the moment of harmony intensely, but we cannot seize it. It is a state of grace. But we cannot trade on this grace and think that it countenances all our mistakes.

I realize that what I have just said does not help my readers to see what is definitive about harmony. There is no such thing as a hard and fast definition. Harmony is not a matter of the intellect but of life. It is the moment of birth. It is the feeling of fulfillment that we find in certain human relations, or in certain places of special beauty (banal though it may be, I recall my emotion on viewing the Parthenon), or in the past of which we are heirs. It is the fulfillment of the joy of first love, or of the absolute consolation that one might receive in the midst of great grief, or of still being alive in a heavy bombardment. We experience such fulfillment in sparkling bursts when suddenly, without being aware of it, we have the vital certainty that there is nothing to add, that nothing can possibly be added to this moment of life, but that the least that might be taken from it would destroy at once the miracle of what we experience as an absolute accomplishment. Once again, it is because I am there that harmony is there. It is an exact correspondence of subject and object. It is an exact correspondence between three parts of us that we irresistibly tend to sever: being, having, and doing.

I believe that here we come to a central aspect of harmony. Philosophers since Gabriel Marcel have certainly had good cause to show that having alone (which obsesses the people of our time) makes no sense, and that we must give preeminence to being. Yet being can do nothing without having. Having is undoubtedly secondary, yet asceticism, by cutting out all having, is a terrible danger that brings with it sclerosis and aridity. Having does not enhance being (notwithstanding the stupid ideology of our technicians), but there is no expanded being without some having: the golden mean. Thus we read: "Give me neither poverty nor riches; feed me with the food that is needful for me, lest I be full, and deny thee, and say, 'Who is the Lord?' or lest I be poor, and steal, and profane the name of my God" (Prov. 30:8-9). Being that is totally without having cannot know harmony.

Similarly, being has to express itself in doing. The ideal would be for doing fully to express being and being alone. This is a radical challenge to our technological society, in which doing is completely dominant, expelling being and circling in upon itself. But when dominant being finds nourishment in having and keeps control of it, and when active being expresses itself in a doing that does not go beyond it, then there is harmony no matter what the circumstances are or the spheres in which it applies. There will be, for example, the harmony of the couple when the one is everything for the other, when there is no excess or lack on either side, when possessions are equally shared, and harmony re-creates itself each moment, whether passionately or patiently. This harmony is not the fleeting instant of sentimental exaltation.

One might also refer to the harmony of art, to the exact correspondence between the being of the painter or musician and that of the spectator or listener. An artist has the gift of an invaluable having that is suddenly grasped by someone else who finds nourishment and lifeblood in it. The artist with his act gives something to the world, and the spectator performs a corresponding act, for we must not delude ourselves: if there is truly to be harmony in art, the spectator must also act, taking hold of the proffered gift in order to make of it a new and living work. This is why what we are offered as modern art in both painting and music has nothing to do with art so far as I can see, for it does not carry with it any possible harmony. It is wholly based on the refusal of harmony, on disharmony, on fracture, on disorder, on incoherence, in which there is neither being nor having, and at most only a mad doing whose products slip through our fingers like dry sand. I think of the difference between the admirable harmony of classical dance or ballet, of which every element or pose is symbolical and ties into a perfection without collisions, and the abominable dancing with which we are incessantly presented today, in which the human body engages in acrobatics, the face is devoid of expression, a mask of nothingness, and the poses recall those of robots. People today no longer know what harmony is. But the consequences are serious, for what this means is that we can no longer achieve balance, and there are no longer all kinds of possible openings for us.

Harmony in its fulness responds to two human desires, the desire to discover and the desire to create, both in the world and in dealings with others and the self, an equilibrium, a moment of equilibrium, when contrary forces will coincide exactly, and many possibilities will open up. In other words, it seems to me that harmony is the opposite of fatality, of rude causality, of the closing of possibilities (which is why old age is the great enemy of harmony). With harmony many possibilities present themselves among which we can choose. In politics, for example, constraint often rules. Things become necessary because the economic, electoral, and sociological possibilities are such that they rigorously dictate decisions. But then there are fleeting moments of harmony when, as Hugo would say, destiny hesitates. That is to say, situations are fluid. There have been breaks in the framework. Action has not yet begun. There are mass movements that have not been fabricated. Parties are in flux. Alliances have broken up or are not yet made. Economic data are not yet in. There are moments when human decisions can really shape what will soon happen. These are what I would call the harmonious moments in politics in contrast to what people usually have in mind, that is, the vision of a perfect society in which there is no play and everything is regulated. That is destiny, not harmony.

Chapter 6

EVIL AND THE
THIRST FOR GOOD

Evil does not come on its own. It is not the product of a combination of uncertain and irresponsible events. Human beings bring it. They are fundamentally evil. This statement might seem to contradict what I have just said. Not at all! Our vocation is to establish harmony in the world. If harmony does not rule, that is our doing. The obstacle is that we are evil. But we must be more precise. I am not making a moral judgment here. I am not talking about moral or metaphysical evil. I am not talking theology. I do not want to say that we are sinful. The idea of sin is not what I have in view when I say that we are evil. To talk in that way would be a serious theological error, for sin has been taken away by the sacrifice of Jesus Christ. We have not become good, but before God all the sin of the world has been carried by Jesus Christ, and consequently, although we are still wicked, we are no longer sinners eschatologically before God. Reconciliation has been effected. It is true that we are always sinners *(semper peccator et iustus)*, but this does not carry with it the concrete consequences of sin. When we do evil, we rediscover the lived out reality of sin. We rejoin it. Sin is no longer the cause of our wickedness. Hence I do not take up an ethical or a theological position when I declare that human beings are evil. The statement is to be taken in the simplest and most unobtrusive and elemental sense. We do evil. We all do evil. We do it to neighbors, spouses, prisoners, enemies, and the natural environment. To say that we human beings are fundamentally evil is simply to say that in almost all our actions we do evil to what is around us.

I do not want to make a hard and fast generalization. I am talking today in the world we know. It may be there is some exemplary Indian tribe in which such monstrosities as war and adultery and similar follies do not hold sway. There might have been some privileged epoch in world history that knew no hatred or exploitation or egoism. I know of none and have records of none. In all the civilizations of which we have accounts I find wars and massacres and religious sacrifices and slavery and deceit and duplicity and oppression.

But there is no need to consult the witness of history. We have only to look around us today. Is there a single country where evil does not reign? Not only does evil exist everywhere; it also affects everything. It affects policies and economic actions. It affects propaganda and information (which, unfortunately, increasingly serves the ends of propaganda). We live in a warring world. In Western lands everything is geared to preparation for the next war. To pretend that this does not reveal human wickedness seems to be cowardice to me. For if I prepare for war with ever more powerful weapons, it is because I am convinced that the other is wicked, and this very conviction brings to light my own wickedness, for I judge the other only by myself and my own feelings. If I think that the other is wicked, it is because I judge that I am wicked myself. There are wars in preparation and there are also wars through intermediaries. The latter are those in peripheral countries related to the two blocs and stirred up by them, for example, Iraq and Iran, Ethiopia and Somalia, Afghanistan, Libya, Nicaragua, Colombia, and Angola. There is also the worst of all wars, the holy war. This is the worst because it is insatiable. It allows of no peace. No treaty can be arranged. The holy war is absolute war, waged without declaration of war, by every means, by people made mad by fanaticism, aiming only to destroy the non-Islamic adversary. Newly proclaimed in our world, the holy war brings to light the horror of unbounded wickedness. Evil reigns everywhere. The drama in Cambodia offered a new version of Hitler's genocide. Can we really say that the adherents of Pol Pot were not fundamentally bad? We recall also the many lands that have concentration camps or labor camps or retraining camps, from Vietnam to Cuba, from China to the dictatorships of South America.

And what are we to say about torture? We know that this, too, is used more or less universally. On the eve of the German attack in 1940 there were innumerable discussions and analyses of the astounding and almost incredible fact of torture. How could we have come back to this evil? But far from being effaced by the victory over Hitler, the Nazi model has spread across the globe. Now, the political system plays a role in torture, yet those who do the torturing are not just simple cogs in a machine. They are also people engaging in this act and taking pleasure in it. They are giving free rein to their will for absolute domination, to controlled ferocity. They are themselves fundamentally wicked.

Why recite facts that we all know? I do so because all nations without exception engage in these things. We all engage in them. Every so often, of course, we take part in a collective process of psychoanalytical purification. We collectively select a scapegoat upon which to place all the world's wickedness. Forty years ago it was Israel, now it is South Africa. By the massive and crushing propaganda of all the media, people have to be convinced that this is where all evil resides, so that we ourselves can have a good conscience and clean hands. For we are not involved in apartheid. South Africa wipes out the fact of the refugee camps of Cambodia, the boat people, the terrorism of the Shiite militia. The unique guilt of South Africa purifies it all. For years now we have been playing this scapegoat game. It has a profound source, as Girard has recalled, but the possibility of universalizing it is the exclusive work of television, the radio, and the press. These attach the label and thereby justify whole nations and each and every individual.

Individuals unceasingly do evil to others. We must not forget the individual act: aggression, interpersonal violence, drugs, automobiles that claim far more victims than terrorists. (I am told that the driver means no harm. What a mistake! The desire to pass, to go faster, to make more noise, the liberation of instincts of power, scorn for the pedestrian or the quiet driver, all these are an expression of evil.) This is a well-worn refrain, too well-worn, yet it needs to be repeated. For people are afraid to say that this act, too, is an expression of human wickedness in keeping with the lawlessness of our society. The brave attempts to free people (even children) from all taboos and prohibitions and principles—liberty, cherished liberty!—have led finally only to a lawless society, without rule or law, in which people are plainly shown up for what they are with neither fear nor limit, that is, evil.

We are experiencing the democratization of evil. This statement will shock people. Naturally, I do not mean at all that democracy is evil. Quite the contrary! Nor do I mean by evil moral evil. I simply mean the evil that we do when we cut loose, or the evil that we do to our neighbors when we overwhelm them with the noise of our amplifiers. Evil has many dimensions. But there is value in using the same word for this very concrete and material evil and for moral evil, for in effect the material evil that we do to others very often proceeds from the moral evil that is in us. The general idea is very simple. An increasing number of people among us is acquiring instruments that can hurt our neighbors or unknown people who, whether we like it or not, are close to us. This is the democratization of evil. Means that were once reserved for the powerful, for the rich, for aristocrats, and which constituted their privilege, are now within the reach of all of us. These means were always means of power by which the rich and mighty could ensure their domination and do wrong to the rest. It is very important to realize that these privileged means are now within the reach of all of us. This seems quite natural to us, for it is a democratization of comfort, of well-being, of a higher standard of living. From this optimistic standpoint it is good. But it is also a democratization of the evil that one can do to oneself and others. Previously only the rich had horses and carriages and could sometimes cause accidents to pedestrians and, as seventeenth- and eighteenth-century reports tell us, do minor damage, splashing mud, scattering stalls, and breaking windows. But such things were not numerous, and they were disliked mostly because they were disdainful rather than harmful acts. Today most people have automobiles. And it has often been noted what a change comes over gentle and polite people when they begin driving powerful vehicles. Relations between drivers are always relations of vanity, scorn, competition, and anger expressed in insults and finally leading to fatal accidents. I could multiply examples of the same order in almost every sphere.

The democratization of evil involves two things. First, the more people reach a higher standard of living, the more they have means to provoke disagreements with others. Second, the use of more potent and efficient means of action demands people who are not only competent but who also have control of themselves, who have respect for others and take into account the effects of what they undertake. In other words, what we need are more moral people. To be sure, people in our society are no worse than those in past centuries. But they are also no better, and they now have more powerful agents at their disposal. At a very simple level, those who hated their neighbors might once have attacked them with a stick, but they would have done so far less effectively than if they had a submachine gun. But everybody today in many different areas has the equivalent of a submachine gun. Think solely of noise. Extreme noise, as we all know, is dangerous from many angles. In the 18th century, however, the means of making noise were very limited. But today we can all swamp our neighbors with noise. People in the West seem to need an affirmation of their power in this way. In default of other means of satisfaction, they need to overwhelm their neighbors with noise.

We might refer as well to other areas of life. Pollution and accidents are the result of power placed in the hands of almost all citizens and their irresponsible or aggressive handling of it. The other day I saw an outboard vessel weaving between boats in a highly dangerous manner. A wave had diverted it slightly, and it struck a boat, damaging the hull, but it did not stop. We have to think of such possibilities which arise when drugs are readily available. Years ago they could be had only by the wealthy, by artists, and by half-mad intellectuals. Now they have been democratized and they recruit their victims among the people. This is the democratization of evil. We might also mention the ease with which explosives are obtained. A century ago attacks with explosives were difficult and dangerous. Nihilists were heroes who were ready to die with their bombs or dynamite. In fact we now find plastic and other explosives everywhere, and attacks, the taking of hostages, and the seizing of airplanes occur all the time.

The great writers of the 18th century who demanded democracy (Rousseau among them) all maintained that virtue must accompany it. This is very true. To grant people freedom presupposes that they will act reasonably, having regard for others and for the community as a whole, and not abusing their liberty. Institutions have never been adequate to make democracy work, to make people good, to prevent people from doing evil. But if this is true of political democracy, it is a hundred times more true of the democratization of technological means, their proliferation, and their placing within the reach of all. If violence is mounting in countries today, it is not because people are more violent. I believe they are less so. It is because they have much simpler and easier means of being violent. A weak impulse toward violence will produce very violent effects when the means of violence are multiplied.

If we want to make society livable, people will have to improve themselves. Moral progress is necessary. Political organization, economic change, or psychology will not do it. The actual situation shows us that contrary to what Marxism imagined, moral progress does not result from raising standards of living or bettering economic conditions or increasing the means placed at the disposal of all. On the contrary, these things simply trigger a frenzy of evil. The urgent need is not to establish a moral order, which cannot be done externally even by superior authority, but to find the way of self-mastery, of respect for others, of a moderate use of the powers at our disposal. This is the way of wisdom and morality. Such words are not greatly valued by our age—so much the worse for us! We have to consider that not taking this path will lead ineluctably to the impossibility of living in concert, a situation far worse than an economic crisis or war.

In rebuttal, one might appeal to many acts of kindness, generosity, and solidarity: medical help, Mother Teresa, the many unknown people who care for their neighbors, those who perform devoted acts at their own peril to save what can be saved in a fire or earthquake. I am aware of all this. But there is no comparison. Contrary to a familiar doctrine, there is no balance between good and evil. Evil is a massive, global fact embracing the crowd, the mob, the nation, and all who do harm to others. Exceptional individuals show what good might be. There are, of course, individual assassins, but what strikes me is the collective nature of wickedness. In the mob people bluntly bring to light the ill that they want to do to others and that they refrain from doing when they are alone out of fear or shame. Yet do we not see generous impulses in crowds as well? Not at all. Is not antiracism a sane and positive reaction? No. It is inverse racism. The deep conviction is that the bad people are the whites. To stress incessantly the racism of the whites, and to point to all the crimes that Europe has committed through the world, may well be good, but it leads to a global condemnation of everything white. We see this in Rhodesia. When Rhodesia came under black rule, whites who had always been well disposed to blacks were massacred along with the rest.

The human wickedness that tends spontaneously to respect nothing coincides with the collective imbecility of the race. The same people who can be refined and intelligent and cultivated become imbeciles when they are caught up in mass movements: Heidegger and Nazism, Sartre and Stalinist communism,[1] and how many others. I watch hundreds of people

1. I have again and again asked myself how Sartre, whose quality as a writer I do not deny, nor perhaps his worth as a philosopher, could have had the influence he has had. When an intellectual cannot understand a monstrous phenomenon like Stalinism, how can people have confidence in him? For it was not merely with the Twenty-First Congress that Stalinism appeared in its true colors. The Moscow trials of 1935 (which were decisively important for me), the massacre of anarchists by communists during the Spanish Civil War (Franco had no better allies than the communists), the pact between Germany and the Soviets, and the partition of Poland by the USSR, were not these enough to show clearly what Stalinism was? Sartre, however, showed neither knowledge nor understanding. He could not draw the obvious conclusions. He had to be either ignorant or a fool. His efforts to justify and reanimate Marxism expose his limitations. For him, Stalin never existed. He stayed with the thinking of Marx. He wanted to give it a purer sense, abstracting away from history. There is an illuminating sentence in Chapter 1 of Book II of *Critique of Dialectical Reason* (trans. Alan Sheridan-Smith, ed. Jonathan Rée [London: NLB, 1976]) to the effect that the dialectical intelligibility of history can develop only in and by action, i.e., in the living and practical discussion of one involved thinker with other equally involved thinkers. Not being places of this kind of action, concentration camps did not exist. We also recall the spiteful and angry attacks of Sartre on Kravchenko and on the first who had the audacity in 1959 to talk about Soviet concentration camps, D. Rousset and P. Barton.

plunge into absurd and wicked causes. There was no reasoning with the crowds that shouted for the liberation of Vietnam and Cambodia. We now see the fruit of those liberations. Today the same ardor is shown in attacks on South Africa. An un-fathomable imbecility renders people incapable of any judg-ment, appreciation, or nuance, of any reflection, comparison, or prevision. The media undoubtedly bear much of the blame for this imbecility by consolidating opinion. Imbecility is the other side of the coin of wickedness. Such we are, and again this judg-ment is neither pessimism nor the product of a religious con-viction of sin: it is a striking fact for any who wish to look care-fully at what is taking place.

But I love people as they are. I love them in this evil, this perversion, this cruelty. I love individuals. For twenty years I have worked to prevent delinquency and social maladjustment. I have worked on behalf of blacks, drug addicts, etc. I love them because in all the evil that they do they are essentially unhappy and not just malefactors. I do not say that they can be excused. The evil they do is still evil. I do not advocate irresponsibility. That would be to dishonor them. No, they are responsible. But they are also unhappy, and I consider this first rather than their wickedness or their imbecility. There are no degrees. All are guilty. But all are also unhappy, even the executioners of Auschwitz and Pol Pot. As the poet puts it, it is no exaggera-tion when people say that they are naked and that they tremble, that they are unhappy, that they are under the stroke of death and cold, when they say that they shiver and tremble, that they are wanderers with no refuge, that they are under the stroke of man and God. I have devoted my whole life to making people more aware, more free, more capable of judging themselves, of getting out of the crowd, of choosing, and at the same time of avoiding wickedness and imbecility. My books have never had any other goal. Of all the people that I have met, no matter what they are, I can say that I have tried to love them. I have lived my whole life in terms of the great theological affirmation: "God so loved the world [the place of absolute evil] that he gave his only Son, that whoever believes in him should be saved and have eternal life" (John 3:16).

Human beings are the most surprising beings imaginable,

for the very people who are so evil have a fundamental thirst for good. They do evil but they aspire after good. They want a world of justice and liberty. They are moved by the sight of the misery of starving people. Even when they do ill to others, they always try to justify themselves. For a long time I thought that such attempted justification merely redoubled the evil. I said that I would accept what people did so long as they did not look for excuses to show that they had good reason to do it. Undoubtedly there is truth in this view. I still believe that excuses add hypocrisy to the evil. At the same time, however, the attempt at self-justification is an expression of the thirst for good. We cannot be content to do an evil that is simply an evil and is recognized as such. We have to give ourselves a certificate of good conduct. In other words we can never be purely and simply cynical. When we come before the just Judge, we cannot look him in the face and simply say: "All right, I did it, and that is all there is to it." We always act as Adam did when first he fled and then he blamed someone else (his wife), or as Cain did. We have to convince ourselves that we have done good even when we have done evil. We are pursuing such goods as liberty, happiness, equality, progress, country, truth, or love. Millions of our neighbors are killed in the pursuit of such goods. Convinced that there is good in what we have done, we have no remorse precisely because of this thirst for good. We kill to save. Think of the unheard-of action of the church when it burned heretics and witches, not to punish them, but to save their souls. Such an act was called an *auto-da-fé,* an act of faith. I am not accusing anyone of hypocrisy. I believe that this thirst for good is one of the deepest of human tendencies even though we can only do evil, and if we could only be aware of what we are doing we would agree at once with the statement of Paul: "Wretched man that I am! I do not do the good I want, and I do the evil that I hate" (see Rom. 7:15, 25). The essential difference is that Paul, thanks to the light of the Holy Spirit, clearly perceives and takes note of his situation, whereas those outside the Christian faith glory in doing evil, convinced that it is for a greater good.

Chapter 7

LIFELONG LOVE

Since Western civilization achieved awareness of itself, no theme has been more scrutinized in literature, and later in music, than love. Everything has been said and written about it. Our own age is particularly explosive on the subject. People discuss every aspect of it: homosexual and heterosexual love, plural love, free love, transitory love, extrovert love, trial love, love without limits. Everybody is concerned about it: the psychoanalyst of course, the scientist, especially the geneticist, the doctor, the psychologist, the moralist, the bishop, and the philosopher. All have their own remedies and conceptions and proposed orientations. I might adopt once again a formula I have used many times without ever being refuted: "In a society which talks excessively about a human factor, the point is that this factor does not exist. People talk excessively about freedom when it is suppressed." This formula has always proved to be true. I would thus apply it here as well. So many novels and essays and studies and experiments and propositions are made precisely in order to hide the basic absence of love. Love does not exist in our society. It is no more than a word. Someone might object: "What does it matter what an old man says about love; he no longer knows anything about it and cannot do so; he is unaware of the beautiful blossoming of it all around him. He is simply looking at the past." Nevertheless, I think I have something to say on the matter, the fruit of long experience, something that is not often put forward today. But I must begin by challenging certain actual orientations under the heading of the disintegration of love.

In April 1985 an international conference on bioethics discussed the various problems raised by genetic manipulations. What can we do, and where is it all leading? Obviously when we intervene in the process of birth, whether it is a matter of cloning, in vitro fertilization, artificial insemination, chromosome mutation, or surrogate motherhood, a new age has come and the customary morals are shoved aside. Two positions regularly confront one another. The first is that of freedom (the freedom of abortion, of the pill, or of having a child artificially), a view held by progressivists and feminists. The other position is that of a pseudo-Christian traditional morality, which seems to be retrogressive and reactionary.

Here I want to present another point of view. What we very generally call love is the fruit of prolonged human evolution. Like all animals, human beings at the very first coupled together as male and female, and we do not know whether this coupling then took a permanent form. But the earliest records available to us show that by that time it was not a matter of a few minutes or of chance. There was a more complete union between a man and a woman (or several women). The sexual act was linked to a totality of life and of responsibilities. In relation to the woman the man had certain functions, as had the woman in relation to the man. This was not fleeting, temporary, or contingent coupling. The sexual union was a lasting one. In every country and tribe it had become a marriage with various taboos and with a prohibiting of adultery or incest. The world of sex was integrated into a larger reality and regulated as one of the most important factors in life. Man and woman had a totally reciprocal life which included the sexual act, though this was neither primary nor exalted. The sexual act normally resulted in the birth of children. Ideas relating to the union developed; it came to be magnified; it found expression; it became religious. Thus the stage of love arrived, the express commitment of one person to another, a choice, and even by way of prohibitions and taboos a sublimation. Love consisted of this emotional, voluntary, reciprocal, and vital totality. And the love of the two led to love of a third, the product of the union, when it came. If romantics have fallen into idealistic excesses regarding incorporeal love, those who deny the existence of total love fail to recognize the profound reality of human beings for at least five thousand years. The corporeal and physiological aspects are indissolubly related to the spiritual aspects, to the total relation.

But what we see today is the complete disintegration of this totality. Already easy abortion breaks it open, though in a secondary way.[1] But what we are now seeing is the breaking apart of the constituents of total love. Sexuality has been detached from the whole. To give people the right to procreate freely without any personal relation either to the donor or the recipient of sperm is to detach human love from one of its basic functions. What becomes of total love if the husband gives his sperm to some other woman, or the wife is pregnant by the sperm of another man? Or if there is in vitro fertilization? It has been well said (by a scientist!) that when a woman bears the seed of a man who is not her husband there takes place real biological adultery. And when in the discussions of the conference mentioned above someone asked what is meant after all by a couple, he was referring to the breaking up of that total complex of love. Procreation is no longer the fruit of a shared delight, a reciprocal joy, a tenderness, and a venture. It is a purely mechanical and technical act. Similarly, abortion as a merely practical and often invalid procedure has become no more than a technical operation without good reason or sense of responsibility for the life that is broken off.

The division of what was once love into a number of technical procedures, the separation of the physiological from the psychological, the emotional, and the relational, seems to be fundamentally very serious. This is not for me a moral or religious matter. It is a matter of the negation of all that is human. Do we not have to consider the totality of being human? Or do we have to see the human merely as a collection of separate pieces, a machine with many cogs that one can take apart and then put together again in a different way? This is the issue in all the present-day genetic operations. They imply a denial of human beings as persons, their treatment as automatons or

1. I am not opposed to abortion as long as there are serious and well-considered reasons.

robots the parts of which can be taken away or added on or replaced. But if human beings are simply collections of detached pieces, if there is no such thing as a couple, if love is unreal, then we should have the courage to make the final inferences. Why should we respect this human machine? Why should we not manipulate it even more than is proposed here? If abortion is now given on demand, and if, as ministers say, artificial insemination can be arranged with no therapeutic necessity and simply for personal convenience, why all the grandiloquent talk about human rights? Whose rights? The rights of this machine that one can manipulate and of which one part has already been detached, namely, love? And why ban experiments with toxic products (such as take place in the USA)? But in this case are we not validating the medical experiments of the Nazis? Are not these in order if human beings are no more than machines? This is the real question in all its dimensions that genetic advances raise. And why talk about freedom in this connection? Whose freedom? Once again, that of beings that have been partly taken apart and are negated as persons.

The final objection to my viewpoint is obvious: You are reactionary, you cannot stop progress, we now know how to clone and graft, there is no more room for discussion, the moral or humanistic criticisms are those of the rearguard that has already been left behind. This is a fine argument. What it amounts to is that we have no choice or decision to make, but have to accept what technological progress makes possible and necessary. Is this a triumph of freedom? In reality it is a triumph of bondage, of the very opposite of freedom. As slaves of progress we have to watch one of the main reasons for living, namely, love, being debased and destroyed before our very eyes. This is the question. And this is why we should pay heed to Monsignor Lustiger when he asks whether we have adequately reflected on these matters.

All this is just a preamble. But I want to say how sad I am when I see before me the thoughtlessness of many love affairs, and how compassionate I feel when I note experiences that show such a fundamental ignorance of love. When I witness the end of a marriage because one of the spouses is gripped by a passion for someone else, I am as sad as at the death of a child.

I am sad, too, when I see what is now the traditional confusion between the sexual act and love. People are constantly talking about "making love." But we do not "make" love. It is love perhaps that makes us by edifying us. No one has ever been able to "make" love. At best we live it. But this is another matter. For many people, however, love is no more than making love. No matter with whom! And the partner is no longer flesh of my flesh or bone of my bone or more myself than I am. The partner is simply a partner in a game or in momentary pleasure. This is what love has become. Am I a romantic? If so, then people five thousand years before Jesus Christ were romantics. I am sad when people enter into preliminary experiences to find out if they are sexually compatible, for this shows that marriage is not a matter of love but of putting the pieces together well, of constructing a good machine. I am sad when I see a union in which there is no mutual commitment but only an agreement to live together. For this means that it will last only so long as it lasts.

But why am I sad and not scandalized? Why do I not judge and instruct? I am sad because I realize that those who are living in this way do not know what love is. They are missing a whole number of possibilities. Throughout their lives they have no knowledge of the finest of human creations. They are missing the truth, the only possible meaning of life, in the name of theories and passions. From the very outset they are failing to find the vital path of life.

I am sad, then, as before a life that has failed. Love is not fleeting or experimental. It is not a child of Bohemia. It is a permanent thing and not a butterfly flight dependent on those who feel it. It is made to last because it is *life*. Life comes from it, and not life alone, but the only possible relation to the other. We cannot live without this basic relation that presupposes myself in the other and the other in myself. Love cannot exist without this existential presence. But we need to find it again and not view the other merely as an accidental instrument of my pleasure or as an absolute stranger who has nothing in common with me apart from habits and experiences. Love is not just a matter of the I-Thou that one can have in a social relationship. Here is not just some other but the other that is also myself, unique and not indeterminate. I am in this other as this other is in me. The complete otherness comes to completion in an identity which excludes mere selfhood. This is the most basic experience that we can have in life. And in it alone the statement becomes true that love is stronger than death (Cant. 8:6).

But the word *love* is full of ambiguities. We must give it its true sharpness. At issue is simply the love of one human being for another. To use the term to qualify feelings relating to abstractions like country or humanity seems to me to be ridiculous. Love involves freedom. It is not an emotional upsurge relating to something imaginary that simply demands sacrifice. I have just referred to freedom. There is a close relation between love and freedom. Yet it is a tragic confusion to speak of free love. Free love has nothing whatever to do with real freedom except as a caricature of it. In free love I take a person and then leave that person. Nothing keeps us together. Nothing binds us. There is no love here except in the sense of making love or sleeping together. Sleeping together entails no life commitment and in it there is no need to talk about freedom. There was certainly a time when free love could have an air of truth in the battle against the tight and socially unassailable bond of marriage, and of marriage without love. Those who protested against a lasting tie where there was no longer any love had some reason on their side. But even at the commencement of such marriages could one really speak about love? And if there was love at the commencement, in what name was it then challenged? In the name of a sudden new passion? But was not this a romantic illusion?

In any case, in our own age the question no longer arises. Obviously in free love each is "free" in relation to the other, for the other counts only to the extent that he or she offers pleasure. Am I free then? In reality I am merely following my impulses, the determinations of my glandular system, in the name of freedom. If we are to be serious, let us talk about love and freedom, but not about free love. To say love and freedom is easy. There is no love without freedom nor freedom without love.[2] We can-

---

2. See Jacques Ellul, *The Ethics of Freedom,* trans. Geoffrey W. Bromiley (Grand Rapids: Eerdmans, 1976).

not love under constraint. We can love only in the depths of personal freedom. We have to be free to demonstrate love. We have to be free either to initiate it or to respond to the love of another. No constraint, whether moral, social, or contingent, can give rise to love or reciprocate it. There is no imperative here. Love arises only on the path of freedom as two freedoms meet.

But reciprocally, there is no freedom without love. This is less easily acknowledged. We wrongly think that liberty means destroying some despotic power or acting as we will without compulsion. This is by no means negligible but it is often illusory and always inadequate. Freedom that does not involve meaning and end is valueless. Freedom for the mere sake of freedom is worth little. It is the mere freedom to go anywhere or to do anything, no matter where or what. The "no matter" that characterizes our society is simply absurd. But freedom is not absurd. It involves meaning. To be itself it has to be oriented. Its human orientation is the inaugurating, upbuilding, and maintaining of love. If freedom loses this orientation it inevitably becomes either folly or the oppression of others, who are now mere instruments of satisfaction (as in the case of de Sade, who is simply a pale replica of our mad dictators; cf. Bokassa). Freedom manifests itself in love. It is not good for man to be alone (Gen. 2:18). A threefold cord is not quickly broken (Eccl. 4:12). Freedom is respect for others in love. It is self-giving. It is expansion in the joy of love. Without love there is no freedom. Perhaps this is what the revolutionaries of 1790 clumsily perceived when they added fraternity to freedom.

We thus have the image of a love that gives. Who of those who have had a little spiritual or moral experience, or experience of a true human relationship, do not know that it is in giving that we receive ourselves, that we become greater in giving, that we find true freedom in giving? Love that gives, that gives itself, expresses freedom. But love can also have another and frightening side. The love that captures and dominates seems to me to express itself in two main ways. The first is the absorbing of the other in love. As often described in novels, there is the familiar love of a mother enslaving and emasculating her son. An invasive love of this kind eliminates the being and freedom of the other in a pretense of love. This love insinuates itself like a cancer. We find it, not merely in mothers, but also in some couples (cf. the *Sapho* of Daudet). The other does not even need to love. The love of the one amply suffices for both. The one feeds on the substance of the other. The second expression is the erotic one in which the object of love is no more than an object that is used for the private and unshared enjoyment of the one who controls it. I have referred already to de Sade. Eros is dominant here again, but by reducing the other to an object, by negating, utilizing, excluding, and finally slaying the other. When I talk about love here, I mean the love that gives and does not take. This love that gives is made to last, for it is life. It is made to last for life, and has no reason to cease to be prior to death. But if it necessarily lasts thus for the whole of life, it changes, taking new forms and acquiring new and different powers. Instead of growing weaker, it builds up little by little by means of experiences shared, differences overcome, and breaks repaired. It uses different materials to build itself up, and in fact it does build itself up instead of destroying itself. What I want to recount here is the story of lifelong love.[3]

> *"I am sure of my love because I do not want you to die and know that you will"* (G. Thibon).

The first step is undoubtedly that of passion. This is the explosive discovery of the other for whom I was waiting, who corresponds to all my desires and hopes. There is no reason for this irresistible feeling for the one who can fulfill all my deepest wishes. The other becomes my universe. I see everything in and through the eyes of this other. But there is no need for me to write about this enchantment. All the books and novels that deal with love have presented it. This is love as passion, as exaltation. It is the love that gives us a sense of transcendence, as the novels have described it. Whether it is the emergence

3. Naturally I have unbounded contempt for writers like Léautaud and Jouhandeau, who offer a false picture of love on every page and thus secure the admiration of ninnies who misconstrue as nonconformism the worst conformism, that of weakness in self-satisfaction.

of first love in the adolescent, or the marvel of a love that will change a life mired in a marriage without love and that involves adultery, or the exalted tension of the mature adult finding new youth in a love that seems to be incomparable (and which is so because it will be the last), in each case it is the passionate love to which people refer us as if it alone represented the totality of love. And in a sense I can readily understand this, for this is love that uplifts and gives promise of joy. It is love at its most visible and thrilling, love that easily turns to obsession and invades the sphere of conscience. This is the element in love that is easily confused with sexuality, for it is true and good that in it human beings should find fulfillment in sexual union. Sexuality is not separate from love. The one we love, we also love sexually. Two beings become one flesh. That is very good. For some time new aspects of the other will disclose themselves as my eyes learn to see better. At the same time sexuality will diversify by experimentation and refinement so as not to fall into repetition.

But a first warning signal is flashed here. For as sexuality becomes more subtle, there is a danger of being carried away with it and of going where it goes. A desire then arises to change the sexuality by changing the partner. From that moment sexuality achieves domination over love. Passion is no longer exclusive. It is directed to others. And this again is what most novels show us. Sexuality is no doubt a fulfillment of love, but to confuse the two is to destroy love. Here is the first great temptation of a couple, and our generation has made the astonishing discovery that one can exchange partners or engage in round-robin sex in order to satisfy diversity of taste but without breaking up the couple. Such things, however, have nothing whatever to do with love. Soon a break comes and this will shatter at least one of the two. I have known couples who were at first agreed that both should retain their freedom, but after a time, when one of them made excessive use of this freedom, it hurt the other profoundly. The one who is thus hurt is naturally the weaker partner, that is, the one who really loves. Here again Western novels in abundance tell us how breakup, divorce, and shipwreck follow adultery. But all couples do not have this experience. For after love as passion, after sexual illumination, after a summit, there is a descent (an apparent descent) toward something else.[4]

If we are not to search indefinitely for a renewal of amorous prowess, then we must look together for another way of love that I would call common responsibility. There are children, there is a job, there are tasks to share. Complementarity is not in sexuality alone but in the totality of life. Literary works that venture into this field are very critical. They describe the reign of habit which begins to take the place of adventure and freedom, the reign of slippers and boredom. I do not agree at all. If we refrain from assimilating love to sex, then at this point we find love again, and I would say a much deeper love because it has already integrated other parts of life. We do not enter into banality but into an encounter with life, an encounter which in all its fulness and difficulty we cannot go through if we are alone. With the common task, bad days may well begin. There is a new battle for life. It is a common battle against weariness and boredom. It is a battle to give new meaning to the union. This is a less brilliant matter, but one that is very serious and profound. This love is not flamboyant but it brings with it the test of truth. The question is the radical one whether what one has said thus far is true. In the exaltation of an amorous haze there can be no question of truth. It is all passion and illusion. The acceptance of joint responsibility is the test of the veracity of the love declared. The one was ready to die with and for the other. But it may be revealed that this one was not ready to live with the other, to undergo the test of everyday habit, the test of life, which is no picnic. After passionate love must come responsible love (which is certainly not boring or prosy but more subtle and refined).

A parenthesis is in order. In traditional sexual relations the woman was responsible for not becoming pregnant. Hers was the risk of pleasure and the burden of responsibility. She had to be responsible for what she did. The man had no such

4. R. Barthes described it as a descent in *A Lover's Discourse: Fragments,* trans. Richard Howard (New York: Hill and Wang, 1979) when he called the fact of love an episode with a beginning (the lightning stroke) and an end (suicide, abandonment, disaffection, convent, or travel), and no possible reconstitution of the initial experience.

responsibility unless he was willing to accept it. He could act irresponsibly, rejecting both woman and child. To do this was despicable. But for him responsibility was a matter of choice. Now, thanks to the pill, the woman has the same choice. This is hailed as freedom for the woman. She can accept responsibility or refuse it. She can be responsible for a child by choice. But most often, like the man, she prefers irresponsibility, and this is strange in a society that is constantly asking for responsible people, that sets a high value on responsibility, while still heaping up means to permit human beings to flee it, for example, the pill. We reach a higher stage of love, however, when it integrates responsibility into life. Nevertheless, each stage of the creation and development of love carries a danger with it. I have talked about the common task. Perhaps it will become so demanding and consuming, or so engaging and vital, that love will be transferred from the other to it. Each will talk in a monologue about his or her own work and problems and career, or about the education of the children (I say each, but in most cases the mother raises the children; the father's interest is only accidental). What ought to be a common responsibility for the richness of love becomes a personal matter. Love tends to diminish. In the thinking of both there is recollection of the first stage, of the passion which is renewed from time to time by means of parties, vacations, and anniversaries. Yet love made up of memories is not a vital love. It slips back, and life resides only in the past. If, however, the couple overcomes this temptation, if the work of the one is also of interest and concern to the other, if there is co-responsibility, then the couple lives out a richer love whose history is by no means at an end.

Far from being a time of habit, this second stage of love ought to be one of awareness of all that separates me from the loved one. Not just sex or character but different interests and activities, and perhaps a polarization of life. The one may be working while the other takes care of the children. We have to learn to love in such a way that the other is truly other for me: not a sphinx, nor a praying mantis, nor an object, nor a lamb for the slaughter, nor a spider lying in wait, nor a fly in my web, but the other loved as bone of my bone and flesh of my flesh, yet the one to whom I can talk most honestly and intimately, who brings me something that I am not, and with whom I have a true exchange because love makes it possible and authentic. Growth comes with the dispersing of the falsities and illusions that passionate love sometimes brings.

A new stage of love comes that I would call the stage of recognition, the moment when the one truly comes to know the other. This is perhaps surprising, for it is finally clear that in the illumination of love there is knowledge and recognition of the other. To believe that love is blind and that lovers cannot see each other as they are was always a gross error. I believe on the contrary that it is love alone that sees truly, and that when a lover says: My wife is like this, then even if his judgment runs contrary to that of neighbors and friends, it is he who is right. He is not blind to her faults and limitations, but he finds in her (and she in him) what is really there even though others cannot see it. It is the others who are blind. Love can bring to light the truth of a person. To know someone, to know a gift, we have to love. Hatred, scorn, and irony do not know that to which they refer. They know only their own caricature of it. Thus knowledge seems to be there from the very first day of love.

What is meant, then, by this third stage of recognition? It seems to me that a moment comes when one really knows the otherness of the other. After passionate union and the responsibility of common tasks, a kind of distance comes to a couple when each sees the specific otherness of the other. We find this already in Adam's discovery of Eve. She is other in spite of their unity, and he gives her her own different and special name, *Ishshah*. She is truly different from me. She has feelings and thoughts and instincts that are not mine. This recognition is an advance, for continued recognition of otherness means enrichment of the one by the other.

But as at other stages two paths are possible. The discovery of otherness may separate. We are in truth very different, and as there is no longer any passion we go our different ways. Or the recognition may bring a new relation beyond habit and routine. I might use for this relation the overworked word *dialogue*. We can really have dialogue only with those who are truly different from us, and dialogue is basic in love. But this dialogue becomes more profound — it is not just a matter of conversation on common or separate tasks, on everyday household matters. It is a matter of dialogue on the depths of the being of each as perceived by the other, and that they cannot be content to leave isolated in distinction. Dialogue is vital for the couple, for each of the two within it, and for love itself. Nothing is less easy, for this dialogue can bring out differences and even stir up opposition that in a good household people try to hide as much as possible by way of diversions. Some of these differences are essential ones, so that if dialogue is to be possible, it is not enough merely to state them, which may cause rupture by way of incomprehension. A basic rule in life and speech is forgetfulness of self. In dialogue we have to bear in mind that the one is made for the other. Thus I have to efface myself. I have to listen without reacting at once or wanting to impose myself. The important law in dialogue is not to try to be right over against the other, and therefore, even if we are convinced that what we know or think is right, to be silent and to accept all that the other says. To accept being wrong in a dialogue, to do so against our own convictions, is not at all easy. But it is necessary if the dialogue that is to promote the unity of a couple in its otherness is not to become instead a sterile discussion. We have to invert a common formula and say that we love truth, but we love our spouse even more. In this way love will grow as the truths that we surrender at once show themselves to be fertile. When we think some months or years later of the bitter discussions that we have perhaps had together, we see at once how useless and futile they were. But when we recognize otherness in dialogue, a new epoch in the growth of love begins.

We grow older, and love changes again and grows. Two inseparable people who see that they are different, but who cannot separate after overcoming so many trials and differences, can no longer think of the one without the other. This is the period when forgiveness covers over many bickerings and faults. But it is not just habit that keeps the two together. Again, this time of inseparability has its risks and temptations.

The first risk is in fact that of habit. I can no longer separate because the other is so much a part of the customary scene that I would be ill at ease alone, and my habits and fads would all change. Nothing could be worse than this. Love has to be always fresh and vivid. It must not become a ritual of words and gestures.

Another danger is that of the absorbing of the one into the other. This is, of course, a risk at every stage of love. That is why the period of the recognition of otherness is so fundamental. It has often been said that in a couple one partner is stronger, has more personality and authority, and progressively absorbs the other. How many authors have used the comparison of the praying mantis, of the female that devours the male when he has done his work. The difference is that in a human couple it is often the husband who absorbs and annihilates his wife, reducing her to nothing. This is why, I repeat, the period of recognition of otherness is decisive. After it, the two inseparables are safe within the equality of their mutual love. But it may be that in spite of his age, or because of it, the man experiences a new sexual passion. This does not break the inseparability. But it is a severe crisis which can be overcome only by truthful dialogue and by the law that I have already indicated, that is, that of always, a priori, being ready to be in the wrong oneself.

A final deviation in this period of inseparability is that of love as friendship. How often we are told that as couples grow older true love changes into true friendship. The two travel life together like the best of friends. But friendship is one thing and love another. We do not arrive at friendship merely because there can be no more sex. I have had wonderful friends, and I think I know what friendship is, but one aspect is independence. No matter how close friends may be, they remain independent the one of the other. Much of their life is lived outside the strong bond of friendship. The friendship may remain a vital one even though their political opinions, for example, are opposed, but friends also have separate families and jobs, and times apart. They meet again with joy. In being together they find a fulfillment and correspondence that are one of the most complete of life's happinesses. But friendship is not love. Love orients the one totally to the other. Every moment of life is devoted to the other. No interest separates the two. No concerns are not common. Even though this love of inseparables is no longer erotic or passionate, it is not friendship, for it is the product of a long history in which they have progressively conquered and integrated the totality of what makes up a human life.

I thus arrive at what I consider to be the last stage of this venture and development. I call it love as union. Union is not achieved the first day by a lightning stroke, as is evident from the large number of separations and divorces. If these are possible, it is because there is no union between the two. To arrive at this union, it is not enough for a couple to go to bed together or to play together. For a full and complete union there has to be a growth of love. The two have to go through the stages that I have sketched, to overcome the temptations, to accept the common responsibilities, to recognize their otherness even while maintaining unity in dialogue, to become progressively inseparable and not to be strangers living side by side. Love as union accepts the impossibility of separation. This is why it is also so tragic, for it is toward the end of life that this inseparability is accepted, at the very moment when death threatens both the one and the other. The frightening thing, that which causes the greatest anguish, is not my own death but that of my partner. Love as union presupposes intimate acquaintance with the whole life of the other. There is no need to ask, or to ask oneself. We know what the other suffers and fears. We know what gives the other pleasure or satisfaction. We know what causes the other to bloom or to wilt. We know all this because we have lived in the same way at the same time as the other. The union has become such that the two are no longer strangers. After so many years, then, the saying is really true: "This at last is bone of my bones and flesh of my flesh." This does not mean that the man has integrated the woman into himself. She has not become a part of him. I dislike the expression "my better half." For the opposite is just as much true. The wife has integrated her husband. He has become she. And this is perhaps the point of the well-known story that is so often ridiculed, namely, that God took a rib from Adam to make Eve. Eve integrated this part of Adam into herself. In reality the one is the other with no question of supremacy.

Naturally I am not saying that dialogue is no longer necessary. But there is understanding beyond dialogue in true "sympathy" or "consolation." To suffer with the other and to

find a common way out presupposes a kind of divination of the
feelings and thoughts and expectations and desires of the other.
And I have nothing more important to do in life than to respond to these expectations and desires and feelings, and to
enter into these thoughts. As at the first flamboyant moment of
love, the other becomes the most essential thing in life. During
the course of life, the grandiose statement that without the one
there is no one,[5] which is true in early love as passion, seems
to fade somewhat and to be less certain. But now at the end it
is full of truth. I am nothing without her. If she is not there,
there is no one.

In this union there also takes place a singular exchange
which couples who have arrived at this point know very well:
the exchange of needed strength. When the one grows ill or
feeble, the other finds unsuspected resources. Even though
weak and with little power of resistance, this other is suddenly
endowed with unexpected forces, becoming weaker again when
the partner recovers. The relation is such that all that the one
needs, the other gives. And when the one needs to be defended,
the other is ready to defend. This is what counts. It is not good
for man to be alone. "Two are better than one. If they fall, the
one lifts the other up. If someone is stronger than one who is
alone, two can resist" (Eccl. 4:9-12). This is the final stage of a
whole life in love.

The circle is thus closed. With love as passion it was
thought that love as union was already achieved. Such is the
experience of those who discover with astonishment the fusion
of two into one. Everything is in fact already given, by grace I
would say. But this is a fragile union that life will test, and when
the great rushes of affection die it will tend to weaken. If we
have seen that it is both beautiful and true, then we have to
want it and work at it. We have to guard the shining memory
so as to go on to what we do not yet know, though we have
some presentiment of it as the fulfillment of what was there at
the first. We need much time and must go through many aber-
rations and experiences to pass from the first radiance to the

5. Ellul is quoting the famous line of Lamartine: "Un seul être vous
manque et tout est dépeuplé."—TRANS.

sweet and peaceful light of the full moon. The moon is so at-
tractive that many peoples have treated it as divine. When union
is fully achieved, there is built up the complete human being
which is the image of God. Not otherwise: the masculine alone
is never the image of God, nor the feminine — only love as
union. The basic responsibility of both men and women is that
the image of God should be present on earth. But nothing lasts.
And if in love as passion the union is menaced by life, at the
end of the road love as union is menaced by death.

Thus I believe that throughout life, in spite of descents
and setbacks, only one love resists the wasting of time and the
diversity of our desires. How poor and unhappy are those who
have not been able to grasp it or to live it out because they have
not given their whole selves to this venture which is so much
more uplifting than all the foolish passions and accommoda-
tions of sleeping around. Love of a single person is marvelously
exclusive. This is the point of God's statement in the Decalogue:
"I am a jealous God" (Exod. 20:5) — not through weakness or
in the sense of human jealousy, but because of his fulness which
includes all things in itself.

I am not saying that all this has been my own experience.
Readers must not think that I am telling my own story. I am not
setting up myself as an example. When I think about my own
life, I have nothing to be proud of. As love has developed to
fulfillment, I have known all the temptations to which I refer,
and I have not been able to resist them all. I am human like
everyone else, and I have failed some of the tests of love and
not met all the challenges. I simply know what is true even
though I have sometimes lived out what is false.

The long march of love toward love carries with it some
conclusions that are not without value. The first is that lifelong
love has to be for one person. A couple is one and has to remain one even though it consists of two. We cannot carry
through this venture or construct this royal palace with many
partners or with an exchange of partners. If we change in mid-
course, we will not have the time to build the edifice of life.
"What does it matter?" someone will say. It certainly does matter. Love matters. I would simply ask those who think otherwise not to use the word *love*. Let them erase it from their vo-

cabulary and talk about pleasure or enjoyment, or a liking for change, or the need for new beginnings. I know that these things are part of our "nature," but let us then cease this constant talk about love. For all such people know are sterile beginnings that soon wilt. Once we change partners we have to go on doing so. At once Don Juan is right. In the same way love cannot be plural, whether polygamous or polyandrous. I realize that in this area there are social customs and traditions, but we always find them among peoples that do not know what love is. I am less open to the idea that polygamy is natural because we find it among many animals (and after all there are some animal species that give fine examples of fidelity between a couple). We may indeed admit that people act like animals, but again let us not talk about love in this connection. For I cannot love two people at the same time. I cannot divide myself up.[6]

But supposing we have made a mistake the first time. Can we not rectify it? This is the theme of innumerable novels. I cannot judge in the abstract. Yet it must be said that we were not aware of any mistake at the beginning. For union, there had to be that flame, that liking, that passion (I am not talking about forced marriages or those arranged by the family) which impelled the one to the other. Are we sure in these circumstances that we were mistaken? Is it not the meeting with someone else that suddenly makes the union seem to be dull, unsatisfying, peevish, bad-tempered, etc.? It is an illusion that things will go better with someone else, for the first experience will spoil in advance all those that follow. I am not saying that there cannot be a happy second marriage. I am simply saying that each experience renders the next more doubtful and difficult. And it is almost always possible, if we forget ourselves, to change a limping marriage into one that involves joint responsibility and a recognition of otherness.

I talk about marriage, not because I attach importance to the ceremony, but because I value that which distinguishes marriage from concubinage—quite simply, the intervention of

6. I do not like quoting authorities, but I would like to refer to Pascal when he said that the aberration of loving in many places is just as monstrous as injustice (*Discours sur les passions de l'amour*).

the word. Concubinage is a factual state which we can begin and end without difficulty. Marriage is an act of the word, the word given, the word exchanged, the word witnessed by others. For those who attach the value to the word that in it the whole being is pledged, I would argue that publicly saying yes is infinitely more of a responsible commitment than moving in with someone. It is no mere matter of a legal tie or of making divorce difficult. It is a matter of realizing that we are fully committed to our word and that full seriousness is withheld so long as we do not give it. No beginning has yet been made of the construction of love.

The evolution of love that I have tried to sketch gives us a better appreciation of the fine saying that lovers are alone in the world. This is rightly said about the passionate period. Lovers mock at what others might say. They are alone in the face of society, neighbors, and parents. They are self-sufficient. They need neither counsel nor encouragement. Their passion protects them with a mighty wall of fire. They see only one another eye to eye. They know only what interests each other. They are exclusive, and no one can try to help them. Even when they run up against obstacles and problems, no one can do anything for them. Yet the story of a love that begins in this way is really that of a love which progressively opens up to others to their enrichment. It ceases to be exclusive and sets them in relationship. Lovers are no longer alone to the degree that their love becomes adult and strong, like the tree in the Gospel that grows so large that birds can nest in the branches. An inseparable couple, a united couple, is an extraordinary force on behalf of the lonely, the suffering, the deprived, those who need a comprehensive and attentive love and who can draw strength from the venture made by this couple, finding in it support, and confidence, and secret riches. This story of love is the opposite of a narrow restriction, an extreme shutting away, an egoism of two. In a joy that cannot be alone it makes room for the welcoming and understanding of all.

In this regard I might make a final observation. In writing these pages I have been aware that what might be said about a human couple might also be said about the love between us and God. After the revelation of divine truth, the ardent days when God's constant presence penetrates my whole being, there comes the time when it is no longer my own salvation that counts but the task that must done on the basis of revelation. This is the time of responsibility, of work of all kinds. It can also be the time of the temptation to put works first, or to institutionalize, or to give the church primacy in a progressive forgetting of the freedom of the Spirit. If we pass this stage, we reach the time of the recognition of the otherness of the other, of perhaps a vivid realization that God is the Wholly Other, and there is now the danger of remoteness or even discouragement for lack of sustained dialogue. Next comes the time of inseparability when the Wholly Other is no nearer but I cannot think of myself without him. It is not a matter of whether I am a Christian but of what would become of me if he were not there. The last stage, then, is that of union, when I fully accept the fact that my life is in Christ and that I can only die to self because in fact the incarnation of Jesus Christ has achieved all that I could hope for in terms of relationship with God. And this is true even in routine, in the silence of God, in the nongranting of prayers, in exile, for the whole history unfolds from the initial point where God was present even if only once in my life, and I have to live the rest of my life on the basis of this victory, preserving this memory that shapes my whole existence. Similarly, at each stage of human love we have to preserve the precious memory of the first period of ardent passion. It is always present even when hidden. And if this parallel can be true, then, as I have said, the human couple in its love is the only true image of God that we can have among us.

I like the thought of Thibon that old age is the time when we need not be careful or economical. What do we lose if we burn up quickly the time that remains, the bit of dry and worm-eaten wood that is left? Age without promise may be age without prudence. Undoubtedly an indifference is associated with age, as we have all experienced. Yet fundamentally this indifference is a refusal to prepare for death. It is a refusal to know at a time when, it is true, none of us is worried about the experimental knowledge which at other times we regard as wisdom, and which all of us, when old, already have at root. Old people grow harder, lose relationships, and cover themselves with armor.

They do so also against their uselessness. For I contemplate the dissolution of this body that ceases to obey me and that is no longer myself. Great vitality is still attributed to me, but I sense within myself the invasion of death. There is a difference between aging and the choice of the spiritual life, when we are in full possession of our resources and choose not to use them. In old age "it is not we who withdraw from the flesh but the flesh that withdraws from us. Weakness takes the place of renunciation. But is this weakness of the flesh really of benefit to the soul? This is the problem of sickness and of old age."[7] The summons of Ecclesiastes is basic: "Remember also your Creator in the days of your youth" (12:1). I know that people still expect something from me and I fear that with loss of memory I can give only twaddle and empty repetition. The future has no more promises, only threats. But I must live one day at a time as though all things were to be given me. I must not give up, for the hour that approaches is the hour of the truth of my life.

---

7. Some of my reflections here have been inspired by G. Thibon's fine meditation on old age and death, *Le Voile et le Masque* (Paris: Fayard, 1985).

PART II

THE HUMAN
ADVENTURE

Chapter 8

CHANCES OF HISTORY

I must agree that it is intolerably presumptuous to try to present in a few pages, not a description of the human adventure, but some reflections on it that are neither history proper nor philosophy, but simply a framework and hypothesis. All the intellectuals of our day, of course, are asking what history is from their own perspective. I will here give my own answer, the fruit of half a century of studies from a historical standpoint.

A twofold difficulty arises at the outset. (1) As I see it, there is no social, political, or ideological evolution. There is no continuous current from one epoch to another, from one civilized group to another. In a first approach I would say that we can never grasp the current itself. When I taught the history of institutions, I used to show my students that we really advance by successive jumps. Thanks to documents, archives, testimonies, and records, I know something about municipal institutions in southwest France in the mid-14th century, and I can offer a different picture fifty years later. I can see what changes took place, I can bring out the differences, I can set the stage. But how did the transition take place? How does an institution change when it seems so permanent? I have never been able to discover this. Detailed studies enable me to note some factors involved, but never in a complete way. There are always blanks, points of rupture, and even of return. One can establish general "causes" that bring about the overthrow of a whole society, but doing so does not enable us to understand the transition from one institutional state to another. To do this we would have to study every aspect, that of official documents, statutes, and judgments, but also that of the manners, beliefs, and ideologies by which so often, under the facade of a stable institution, a different state comes into being in a way that is much more vital than the documents indicate. The transition is never simple, and it never takes place in the same way. If I grasp its outlines in one case, I can neither generalize nor transfer them to another case. How many times we are the victims of an optical illusion, flattening out time! When I find one institution in the 4th century, and another that seems similar in the 8th or 9th, I am tempted to state with assurance that the second is the offspring of the first. But in spite of the historical memory of peoples and the latent permanence of institutions, I am always wrong to think that one institution or custom can influence another some centuries later when there are no traces of it in the intervening centuries. This is true even for institutions like the Roman Catholic church which are very conservative and careful to preserve their records. There is thus no one current that we can discern, but a great diversity of currents and inflections in the course of time.

Thus it is evident that in the interface of the biosocial and the cultural there is no single determinative factor. The two things are reciprocal and cannot be confused. We all have our own genetic patrimony on which we depend but which also gives us immense possibilities of different combinations. Individuals who are the actors in history are not conditioned by their genes. We can find no individual or collective plan in analysis of this genetic patrimony. No rigorous causality is at work. Individuals are dealt many cards in the game. They have to play these cards, but they can do so in very different ways and obtain very different results.

I would say the same about the cultural environment. The conflict between geneticists and culturalists seems to be a false debate. It is clear that we grow up from birth in a certain milieu, and that there is thus something beyond us that tends to impose itself on us. A modern fad argues that to teach a language to a child is already intellectual terrorism since it limits the child's capacity to learn anything else and cramps its intelligence. This is absurd, for if the child does not learn this language it will learn no language at all. It will be in no relation to others; it will be autistic. Hence we cannot avoid that factor which is beyond us. Yet it no more conditions us totally than does the genetic patrimony. For it is made up of very complex elements — ideas, manners, habits, explications, beliefs, group relations, whether of sex or of generations—and these elements can combine in different ways, so that they are never the same from one generation to another. This is why I am ill at ease with, for example, Bourdieu's *La reproduction* or *Les héritiers*. For I find striking differences between generations (and if we do not see it in ancient epochs, it is again because of the flattening out of time). I cannot understand how these can occur if we apply very strictly the concept of reproduction. Similarly, I think that rigorous determination—the taxonomy of Todd *(La troisième planète)* on forms of the family—represents a mechanical view. Thus if we apply this type of analysis to Rome, I cannot understand how there could be transition from the clan to the agnatic family and then to the cognate family. In other words, neither collectively nor individually can I see any possible determinism. There is no system of the combinations of the genetic or cultural patrimony. There is no single explanation. Instead we find multiple adaptations.

Here again we have to be on guard against oversimplification, against a simplistic pseudo-Darwinism. We must never say that the best adapted survives. For we have to ask: The best adapted for what? There are for us so many factors. There is adaptation to the natural milieu (e.g., climate), to demographic swings (as we now know, rapid increases or decreases bring social, ideological, and other upsets), or to technological change. We have to adapt to so many types of milieu. Nor is it true that the best adapted survive. The best adapted might vanish first. For the best adaptation to a milieu means the greatest sensitivity to any change in the milieu. The best adapted are often the most fragile. Thus multiple adaptations are an essential factor in understanding how the patrimony is utilized, but on the condition of remaining elastic and open to new possibilities. For every development involves a latitude that I find impossible to explain and that allows for innovation or initiation. We have to take into account three phenomena: the determinative factors, that is, the social setting; the possibility that these factors can combine in different ways; and an imponderable element that intervenes to bring something to view. Apart from these phenomena we cannot even apprehend, let alone explain, the historical complexity of life.

(2) The difficulty is increased by the practical impossibility of defining exactly a field of research. The history of institutions used to be called the history of law. The explicit regulations of law were studied, along with changes in them, without reference to the totality of social phenomena. We now realize, however, that law has to be examined in its relation to power, to economic and social structures, to ideologies. To this second stage we now have to add the history of ideas, law being a perfect expression of this or that orientation or conception. Thus we can no longer study wills without referring to the ideas and beliefs of an epoch concerning death. The terms used to define fields of study in the humanities are also subject to wide variation. Social history is an example. Is this the history of society? But this has no meaning —it is at once everything and nothing. We might argue that social history is simply a matter of the structures and evolutions of the family. Some anthropologists take this view. But if students of politics use the term *social history*, they have in mind the complex relations of power and the situation of many powers set in relation to one another. When I myself taught social history, I thought of it as the history of labor and unionism, and of the socioeconomic foundations on which these organizations and practices were built up. We are thus forced to allow for a margin of uncertainty in all these areas.

My most important thesis, then, is that we must eliminate univocal explanations, that is, those which find in one social relation or one phenomenon a guiding thread or a single dominant and determinative factor in human history. I will offer some examples, recalling each time that there is some truth in the contention, but that it is misapplied if the chosen factor is given a privileged position.

Toward the middle of the 19th century historians were enthusiastic over the idea of freedom. They wrote histories in which the guiding thread was the achievement of freedom in the course of human history, and they tried to explain historical phenomena in terms of this concern, this passion for freedom. A little later this idea was replaced by that of the disengagement of the individual from the group. In primitive times the group was supposedly dominant (the class, tribe, people, genus, etc.). Within it people were not individuals but interchangeable, with little awareness of distinctions. But slowly and progressively the twofold fact emerged of the relaxation of integration or group unity and the consciousness of individual will and action. The group ceased to be a unit and gave place to the individual as a unit. People ceased to be group molecules and the group became an aggregate of individuals. These two closely related ideas were in fact essentially dictated by European history. They were Europeocentric. We now see that they cannot be generalized. As recent authors have shown (the school of Durkheim and Gurvitch), we can associate with them the idea of the transition from status to contract. In primitive societies individuals have a status, a definite, assigned place. They have certain rights and duties set by the social body. Their relations to others in the group are fixed, foreseen, normalized, and objectified. Nothing is left to individual initiative. Everything is statutory, and in principle nothing can be changed. But then — and this is the history of humanity — there comes the transition to the stage of contract, which is (or was in 1900) the modern, historical stage. In the constitution of the group, in the organization of economic, legal, and political relations, a situation arose where everything was regulated by voluntary agreements, by contracts. Politically, this is democracy. This hypothesis is very seductive, and one can certainly read history along these lines, but so many other readings are possible that I cannot tie myself to it.

Less familiar but becoming fashionable is the idea that all history is dominated by the man-woman conflict. On this view the first and essential fact is sexual differentiation. How can this not be determinative in the organization of social relations and the structuring of institutions? German writers from the end of the 19th century have thought that at first there was a matriarchate. The group was organized around and in terms of the woman, who exercised authority in it. But man by various ways was able to oust woman from her place and take over her authority. Thus men have organized society, their essential objective being to keep women in a state of subordination, and institutions being set up to keep women in a state of tutelage. But this led to a struggle for independence; women wanted to gain equality, freedom, authority. Feminists scan history for traces of this conflict, accepting the fact that male domination is too obvious to stand in need of proof. Naturally this explanation of history is mostly that of feminists who have retrieved ancient records and testimonies (e.g., those concerning the Amazons). But I will have occasion to show that human history is not so simple, and that the male-female conflict is not its backbone.

I will finally recall the best known of attempts to explain history by a dominant factor. I refer to the Marxist and post-Marxist theory of class conflict, which is simply a form of the dialectic of ruler and ruled. We are all familiar today with what is essential in this vast fresco. In the 19th century Marx argued that there are two antagonistic social groups whose interests are the more incompatible insofar as the subjection of the one makes possible the existence of the other. Their relation is represented by the relation between capital and labor. The former makes possible the purchase of the latter, which then gives the ruling class increasing power in every sphere. The proletariat has no wealth apart from its labor, and it has to sell this, but in so doing it enables those who acquire it to achieve greater wealth and hence to augment the labor force. The proletariat has no way out of its condition, and this exploited group thus becomes a constitutive element of stability in this society. Once the capitalist system is in place, to live in this society one has to belong to one or the other group. Progressively the capitalist class reduces to a proletarian condition all who do not belong to it. This society is organized in stable groups that one might call social classes. (Marx was not the first to use this term, since it appears already in Turgot.) These classes are necessarily antagonistic, since the one can live only on the labor of the other. But the latter cannot tolerate for long being deprived of its substance, and when it sees what is happening, it can only revolt against those who exploit it. Hence this society is totally dominated by the class struggle. Having found this to be a fact in the 19th century, Marx thought that he had found here the key to the history of societies and the meaning of this history. He thus extended his analysis to all history, which in every society he thought to be made up of the battle for liberation waged by the oppressed class against the ruling class. Naturally Marx made the schema more complex so as to be able to find in it an explanation for all social developments, but the one explanatory factor was always the same. In reality, he had to force the facts to fit into his schema, or even at times to ignore them. For long periods of history there was in fact no trace at all of this division of society into antagonistic classes (e.g., in the West from the 5th to the 10th century). No historian (except perhaps in the USSR) really believes any longer in this univocal schema.

From these historical studies over the last half-century we have to conclude that there is no single explanation of history, which shows itself to be extremely complex. Similarly, one cannot establish cause-effect relations. It is better to talk about developmental factors. History knows no direct or simple causality.

But I would go further. I would argue that there is no linear evolution in which each period seems to be an advance on that which precedes and in turn prepares for further advance by that which follows, inheriting the ancient patrimony and augmenting it. This hypothesis coincides with that of a progressive history of the race. I believe that it is totally wrong. History knows both advance and recoil: societies that have reached a high level collapse and are succeeded by "barbaric" societies, so that many centuries are needed to get back to the level of the social body that has vanished. But this is true not only on a global scale or for long periods. I believe it is also true in specific detail. It will be said, for example, that globally women have been moving from bondage to freedom. This is absolutely untrue. In some periods women have been in bondage, shut out, without rights or authority. But in other periods they have known independence, equal rights, sometimes even a superior status. One might refer to the final stage of Greek society, to Hellenism under the Seleucids, or to Rome from the 1st century B.C. to the 4th century A.D. As it was then said, "The senators direct the *res publica,* but the matrons direct the senators." But then everything was lost again. In regions invaded by the Arabs women were reduced to nothing. After the Germanic invasions they lost their rights and status. In the first case their losses were due to the application of Islamic teaching, in the second to the spread of violence throughout society. Yet when feudalism reached its golden age, women were not slaves, and it was not merely by way of compensation that the stories of chivalry gave them an imperial place. Nor was it merely by way of compensation that the cult of women developed as represented by the Virgin Mary. To talk of ideological compensation that masks the true reality is to fail to see the reality. Women could hold fiefs and serve as lords of the manor. As in rural societies, they had their place and participated in decisions. Nevertheless, it is true that their situation and image declined in the 17th century, and especially in the 19th. There is no need to give an account of middle-class women when hundreds of novels have already done so, nor of working-class women, crushed by misery. It was middle-class rule that shut out woman and made her an inferior if expensive object. But we cannot conclude that because the situation of women was bad in the 19th century it was worse in the 17th and worse again in the 13th. Nothing is as simple as that.

The same process of movement forward and back, of advance and recoil, may be seen when we look at political power, and especially at the desire to set up the strong, central, political power that we now call the state, though it is wrong to use that term when we look at Greece, at Egypt, at the Incas, or at the Muscovites. Centralized power that is strong and organized does not have to take the form of the state if we take the state to mean what we find in Western societies for the last three centuries. There is no steady historical development from a society in which power is splintered, decentralized, and divided toward a centralization, concentration, and reinforcement of power to the detriment of local structures. But periods when power becomes centralized and strong, excludes rivals, and takes an authoritarian, violent, ritual, royal, or sacral form, are periods when through an excess of power or concentration no movement is possible (as in the case of Byzantium) or everything is dislocated, so that the empire crumbles. Power then disperses into different hands. This development may be internal or external (e.g., the Aztecs). It may seem to be spontaneous. It may result from collective disaffection (I think of the suicidal surrender of Rome to assassination by the Germanic invasions).

And it is always very hard to know why at a certain place and time the concentration of political power will take place. Why does one type of state arise in Benin or Dahomey and not in neighboring African kingdoms? Hence in the course of history I do not find continuity or accumulation but evolution — not spiral evolution, as people have been accustomed to say for the last thirty years, but jagged evolution, with alternating advance and recoil.

Admittedly, to talk of advance and recoil is already a value judgment. To go back to the phenomenon of political power, I might look at it from the standpoint of the modern state and say that there is advance every time I note a concentration of power, and recoil or decline when I see it scattered. But I would say the exact opposite if I looked at it from the standpoint of decentralization. The point of view adopted depends in fact on a value judgment. If I attach positive value to the state, I uphold it and find centralization of power good or normal. But I might be a supporter of decentralization, of federalism, of self-administration, and in this case my judgment would be the opposite. There is in effect no such thing as progress. There is an ideology, an illusion as Sorel would say, and it is not unimportant that Marx gave himself up fully to this illusion, and that Marxism as a whole lives on the illusion of human progress. As for Teilhard de Chardin, the last to sing the praises of progress, he constructed a theory that is stupefying in its candor. But an indignant reader might say to me: "You cannot deny that we today are every way superior to *homo erectus*. You cannot deny that we know more than he did, that we have infinitely more developed and refined powers, philosophies, techniques, and manners. You cannot deny that we live much better." Granted, yet I am still not convinced. For we have also to consider what we have lost in comparison with this prehistoric savage. Who among us could tolerate the cold of the Ice Age? Who could attack a bear or an auroch with a stone spear? Who could walk hundreds of miles on foot? Who has the same physical strength or detailed knowledge of nature or ability to scent wild animals? In other words, we have lost many personal abilities in comparison with primitive people. (Perhaps not intellectual abilities, but we know nothing about that.) A mutation has taken place. We have made fantastic progress in organization and modes of action, but we have suffered disastrous regress in our senses and physical powers.

It is impossible to measure progress. I might consider the countryside when it was not yet industrialized. I might listen to townsfolk laughing at farmers who come to town on market day and are clumsy and crude. But I might also see how townsfolk out in the country are themselves clumsy and frightened and ignorant. I might think of the scorn of country folk for those who cannot tell one plant from another and do not know the phases of the moon or the time to sow. In the course of history we have gained much and lost much.

As for moral and intellectual quality, I am not sure that people today are any better than the people of Athens in the middle of the 5th century B.C. We have only to look at the horrors of the modern world, the violence, the drugs, the wars, the torture, and it is obvious that humanity has made little advance in these areas. But it is impossible to weigh what is gained against what is lost, or what is lost against what is gained, for we have here values and quantities that cannot be measured against one another. We cannot measure; we have to choose.

If I move to another level, that of rapid change, I might get the same illusion of progress. From one generation to another two situations are possible. The one is that of fixity. Social norms are secure. One generation follows another, repeating the same model. This situation might seem impossible to us, but it functions in very strong traditional societies. More often, however, each generation initiates its own history. It is wrong to think that a generation that follows takes over the legacy of that which precedes and then moves on from there. This relation is conceivable in the scientific and technological spheres, but not in the political, economic, moral, and aesthetic spheres. The generation that comes may adopt some things from the preceding generation, but it may also reject everything and begin its own history (which is often no more than a recommencement). For twenty years I saw how impossible it is to transmit experiences to young people so that they might profit by them. Between 1930 and 1950 we made several experiments, we developed many ideas and theories, and we went through many powerful experiences, in politics, economics, and sociology. I had the vain hope that we could tell young people about our failures so that they would not make the same mistakes or adopt the same approaches. We could say to them: "Do not go this way, we know that it is a dead end. Look what happened to us. That is an example. The same thing will happen to you." But no one listened. The lesson of 1936 was useless in 1968. For my part, I am astounded when I see young people becoming leftist. The Moscow trials, the German-Soviet pact, the Spanish Civil War, the discovery of labor camps, repression in Hungary and Czechoslovakia, the witness of countless intellectuals who enthusiastically joined the Communist Party between 1945 and 1947 and then left the party between 1956 and 1968 —these things count for nothing. In every sphere young people begin again without paying heed to past experience. In settled traditional societies older people had authority because they could transmit to the young the concrete experiences they had had and the lessons they had learned from them. But now the young want to go their own way alone. This is all very well, but they do not realize that they are repeating the same follies as their elders and running into the same obstacles. There is repetition (each time with a new model), but not, as I have said, in the sense of Bourdieu. There is progress in social and personal life, in scientific and technological accumulation. But where is it all leading us?

On the subject of the human adventure, I want to present a reasonably comprehensive hypothesis with the idea of environment as a starting point.[1] By environment I do not simply mean the ecological niche, or, more generally, the place where people live. It seems to me that environment can be characterized by three relations, two of which are apparently contradictory. On the one side, we find in our environment all that we need to live. I say to *live* and not just to survive. We are set in it and we adapt to it, but we also try to adapt it to us. There are in it natural elements, the most rudimentary being air, water, and the plants that feed us and provide for us. Also in relation

---

1. I am not falling into the error discussed above and making this the single factor that lies behind evolution.

to the environment we have occasion to exercise one of the most basic functions of life, that is, symbolism. The environment gives us the chance to create symbols, and here are riches that spur us to development. The environment sets up the conditions of human development and not merely of human subsistence. This is simply one aspect of the environment, and the one that we grant the most readily.

But if we really want to understand the environment in its totality, we have to take into account what I have called the contradictory factor. The environment is what puts us in danger. It is both helpful and hostile. When we die, it is always because of the environment. The danger may be due to the absence of good things: no more water, no more game, etc. But it may also be positive: wild beasts, snakes, etc. We also realize that one of the main dangers may come from other people: war, tribal conflicts, etc. One might be tempted to say that two different environments coexist, the natural on the one hand, the human on the other. But I think that there is a succession rather than a coexistence of environments. When we become a danger to those of another group, a change of environment takes place from the purely natural environment to a different one, the social environment.

The third feature that I discern in the environment is its immediacy. We are set in a direct relation to a given environment. We immediately act upon it (to feed ourselves, to defend ourselves, etc.). It also acts directly on us. We have to adapt to it, to conform to it even as we transform it. The immediate presence of this environment is obviously our constant concern and preoccupation. If the relation to the environment becomes indirect, then it ceases to be our true environment. We are no longer integrated into it. We are at a distance from it and there is no longer any conjoint evolution. When the relation is indirect, we tend to act on the environment as subjects where previously it enforced our adaptation.

As I look at the human adventure from this standpoint, I seem to see three essential stages. The first is the stage when human beings were directly linked to nature around them, to water, trees, plains, and mountains, and when they were part of it. But gradually they formed into groups and found means to act on this natural environment. This is the long period of the ascent to history. Progressively the social group became the true human environment. It was from the group that people now drew all their possibilities of life and also of aggression. Between the original period and the historical period there was the long development of what we call the Neolithic Age. But in the last two centuries the social environment in turn is being replaced by a new one, the technological environment.

Naturally, the transition from one environment to another takes place only over a long period. Furthermore, the original milieu is not completely effaced or annulled or destroyed. It simply becomes a second, indirect environment. When society becomes our environment, it does not exclude nature, but nature becomes less and less determinative, and the dangers come from other people. Similarly, when we pass to the technological environment, this does not mean that the social environment ceases to exist, but it is increasingly mediated by technology and dependent upon it. Thus the replaced and outdated environment remains as a substratum of the new one. And since thinking is slow to move and verbal forms are always a step behind reality, the older environment serves as an ideological reference for those who have been plunged into the new one. Thus when society becomes the dominant environment, nature comes to be regarded as a model, a reference, or a test. Law and morality must conform to nature (natural law, natural morality). I have already shown the inanity of this elsewhere.[2]

It will also be said, however, that we are social animals. This, too, is our nature in some way. But this is hardly an adequate formula. This trait does not characterize us among animals. If what is meant is that we have never lived alone, that is true. If what is meant is that there has always been a human society, this does not correspond to what we can know. I believe that for millennia people lived as though grafted upon the natural environment, and that at that time they were not social animals. The determinative environment was not really their own.

---

2. See Jacques Ellul, *The Theological Foundation of Law*, trans. Marguerite Wieser (New York: Doubleday, 1960; repr. New York: Seabury, 1969); *To Will and To Do: An Ethical Research for Christians*, trans. C. Edward Hopkin (Philadelphia/Boston: Pilgrim Press, 1969). — TRANS.

They are social as they seek to constitute for themselves a different environment, one of their own in which they can be dominant and find fulfillment. But an evolution of this kind is not ontological, nor is it inscribed upon human nature. Yet there will be constant research into what human nature really is. And it will finally be said conclusively that the most constitutive factors of the social environment are really natural. The phenomenon of the state is typical. Once the state is set up and becomes dominant, it is thought without any doubt or embarrassment that a kind of natural law has led to it, that it is in effect a natural reality. The specific historical formation that the state governs is always naturalized, and citizens all believe that the state that they live in is natural.[3] As we now move into the technological environment, we find again that thinking lags behind. It is held that technology depends on politics, that it is not only a specific form of society but also supposedly a natural phenomenon, that it is simply a utilizing of nature. Such statements lead to enormous errors of judgment and ridiculous imbroglios. We do not know how to live in the new environment and so we passionately act as though we were living in those that are outdated and in part destroyed—a fervent concern for nature and a growing faith in politics.

I must now deal with the final objection that this idea of our determination by environment, our dependence upon it, and our transformation as we change it, is simply a revival of Darwin and a purely materialistic reading of history. I do not think so, first because I refer to changes in environment, whereas elsewhere the only environment that has been considered is nature. For me, then, the relation between animals and the natural environment is not the only one. The two other environments are of our own creation. Human beings willed to live in society, organized society, and gave it its form. Human beings want technology and its multiplication. In the venture they miss the point that the society they want and the technology they invent become the determinative environment to which they must adapt. Their own work becomes their global environment. They did not see this, and they did not will it. But

3. See J. Ziegler, *Vive le pouvoir*.

it is still their own work. Work alone is not what singles out human beings. They are marked by their inventiveness, their creativity, but also by the fact that they have to adapt to their own creation. This is not materialistic determinism. There is nothing mechanical here. Human history is always open and always has to be made, yet it is not simply the product of the human will. Human beings have to make history along with what is there and within the framework of what has become theirs by their own works that have now slipped out of their control. I see nothing here that runs contrary to what the biblical revelation can tell me about our creation in the divine image. I find only the expression of what might seem to be a formal contradiction between our freedom (in the freedom of God) and our subjection to contingency and necessity even while preserving autonomy. In our autonomy we constantly achieve a freedom that again and again turns into a necessity and thrusts itself finally upon us, annulling our freedom, and yet this freedom is not dead.

Chapter 9

THE PREHISTORIC PERIOD AND THE NATURAL ENVIRONMENT

I am not a prehistorian or an anthropologist. Yet I have some idea of what went on prior to 3000 B.C., the date to which one may very generally trace the beginning of "history." To talk about prehistory or protohistory is not to imply, of course, that for 500,000 years people had no history. It is just that we know nothing about it and can reconstitute vast tracts of time only by means of habitat, bones, and tools. There is no documented history in the European (and Chinese) sense. Nevertheless, there were certain phenomena that we can understand and comprehend as history. I do not refer merely to the instrumental transition from the Paleolithic to the Neolithic Age. The main phenomenon is the progressive transition from the natural environment to the social environment. This is true history even though it is not marked by events or precise dates. It seems to me that in the Paleolithic Age, and even more so in the ages before that, the population was much more scattered, groups were much less numerous, and individuals were lost in an omnipotent nature over which they had no control. They lived as parasites and predators, and they were exposed to far more dangers than other animals, since they were finally less well adapted to specific environments, though capable of relative adaptation to many different and opposing environments.

We now know there was a succession of hominoid types, *homo erectus* (between 1,000,000 and 100,000 years B.C.), who knew fire, then *homo sapiens* and *homo sapiens-sapiens* (100,000 to 35,000), who used more techniques (stone, tools, perhaps boats, improved hunting, use of skins, ritual burial). As Neirynck has well shown, technology affected human physiology and vice versa. During this long period, human groups did not make war. The bones of young people show no trace of wounds. The low density of the population and the scattered nature of the groups may explain this phenomenon.

Nevertheless, as population increased a major evolution took place with the greater density of groups. Like Chaunu, I believe that the demographic factor is a determinative one in history. In the historical period the centers of civilization are those with a higher level of population. Depopulation expresses itself in the collapse of social organization. Yet we have to make allowance for nuances if we are not to fall victim to a logic of causality, as though demographic movement were the cause of social or economic phenomena. In reality we do not know the cause. Each element here is at the same time both cause and effect. We cannot say what begins things. Did demographic growth come first and technological, economic, and political development follow? Or was demographic growth triggered by an abundance of food, better weapons, or changes of climate? All these things could play a part both ways. In any event, there was a certain coincidence that produced more complex social grouping. What we find in the historical era is sufficiently general and basic to allow us to transfer it to the long prehistoric "night." I think, then, that as population grew larger there was slow evolution in the relationship between the human group and the natural environment. Able to make more efficient tools and weapons, people also belonged to larger groups that could influence the natural environment. This was perhaps between 8000 and 2500 B.C. There thus began the long history in which the race ceased to be defensive in relation to the environment and was able to utilize it, then to master it, and finally to achieve total domination over it.

In the transition to the Neolithic Age, techniques multiplied. Agriculture appeared around 8000 years ago in six different areas. Domestication and breeding came at much the same time (sheep in Iraq ca. 9000 years ago). Then came pottery, glass, and perhaps the first metallurgy around 6000 years ago. But along with the larger population and increased technology appeared the utilization of nature and war, the first indication of political conflict and transition to another environment.

A recent study of this subject is very interesting.[1] The archeologist D. Vialon shows that 95 percent of the depictions that go back to the Paleolithic Age represent animals. There are few human silhouettes, and none with arms. In contrast, in Neolithic paintings human figures gradually become dominant, along with many tools and weapons. The animal increasingly becomes the *hunted* animal under human domination. This development seems to me to be a vital one, for it shows what really counts in the two epochs. The attention of people in the Paleolithic Age was directed to animals. These were the dominant factors and constituted the real environment, providing food but also creating the main dangers. But when people and weapons replace them artistically, this indicates that the human group (for the figures are mostly in groups) has become the main focus of interest, a primary entourage that gradually becomes a new if as yet fragile and threatened environment. It is with the group and its instruments that people now have to do first. The group is the primary entity around them. A turn is beginning to take place. It is only beginning. In spite of the primacy of the group, nature is still dominant and constitutes the true environment. Yet it has begun to be mediated through the group. I am not saying that in the Paleolithic Age there could not be any form of social organization. But we can say nothing about this except that it was neither very complex nor enduring.

In the protohistoric world I believe that functional groups appeared gradually which were determinative for social organization. We must not oversimplify and say that these functional groups meant a division of labor in the strict sense. The three functions brought to light by G. Dumézil, which seem to me to be typical from the time of the Indo-Europeans, will illustrate what I am trying to say. They form an excellent explanatory model, though we must not apply them universally. In other words, the original organization of the group was neither by tribe nor by family but by function. Human divisions, formations of

1. Denis Vialon, "Les images préhistoriques," *La Recherche* (May 1983).

coherent groups in global society, solidarities, along with taboos and cults, came into being through the discharge of various functions in the group. This runs contrary to most accepted theories but seems to me to be in keeping with observable facts. We must not let ourselves become obsessed with the sexual factor or the preeminence of force. I believe that matrimonial relations and family structures were constituted on the basis of the functions a family group was charged with in society. A family is structured less by its sexual status than by the recognized assigning to it of a specific function for which it is responsible.

This is not division of labor in the classical sense, first because the functions do not necessarily correspond to a particular type of work, then because division of labor relates to individuals — one person is a hunter, another a specialist in tools, and another in pictograms—whereas what I have in mind is responsibility for functions discharged by the whole group. Around the function cluster rituals and rites and the possibility or impossibility of having relations. This carries with it a particularizing of techniques and beliefs, but also their complementarity.

We now know fairly clearly that the Neolithic Age was not one of famine during which the main preoccupation and activity would have had to be finding something to eat. Sahlin has shown that abundance reigned except for an occasional crisis.[2] This relative profusion made a partition of functions possible. It is plain that if we picture the people of this period as famished creatures always on the hunt for food, no social organization or division of functions would have been possible. Nevertheless, the assigned function does not take up the whole time, and is not comparable with actual work. At certain times and in certain places the function of a given group becomes dominant and imperative. Everything must yield to its necessity, which is that of the clan as a whole, since the special group fulfills its role in order that the whole may survive. There are also long periods, however, which are free and allow of reintegration into a common symbolism. Hence I would not call the function an explanatory system covering all individuals and

2. Until recently abundance was common in traditional societies, e.g., in Cambodia before Pol Pot, with easy and plentiful rice crops and good fishing.

groups. But it does seem to me to be a structural factor with reference to which the different elements in society are linked to one another. It is certainly not a natural or spontaneous factor. Once again it is human beings themselves that institute it, not by a clear and express decision, but by a long process. And once effectively set in place (though constantly perfected and revised), it tends to become in effect a factor that seems to be self-evident. What all this amounts to, and the majority agrees on this point, is that in the Neolithic Age at least there was no primitive sharing. Everybody did not do everything or anything. There were express assignments, as may be seen at such times as festivals and funerals.

This social organization, then, was not subject to chance or to primary forces that a positivist realism often puts first. We now know that in prehistoric art the drawing is neither realistic (not because the painters were incompetent; on the contrary, they showed extraordinary skill) nor random: the figures are not placed on the wall of a cave, or in relation to one another, in any haphazard way. The figures are, in fact, signs, and one might almost say that we have here abstract images with precise symbolical value. In the same way, it seems to me that the social organization is full of meaning for its members. All social organization carries meaning. Without meaning it would not be legitimate and would fade out, or at most survive only for a short time by violence. Historians of law and positivist jurists generally forget this. An institution is not valid merely because it exists. It must always be referred to something beyond itself of which one might say that it is the sign. For a long time we have wanted to refer law to a value like justice. This is not impossible. In our own time we pretend that justice is the final point of reference. But this is mere hypocrisy. For a period, and for a historical bloc of civilizations, justice has in effect been the meaning attributed to the institution, that which validates it and leads people to accept it. But this situation is neither universal nor permanent. Other meanings can be valid and can be fully accepted. Hence it is not just because an organization is regarded as useful or effective that people are ready to come under it and obey it. It has to carry meaning in their eyes, meaning for life, for death, for total being, for the future, etc. Meaning

assures us of our true identity and guarantees us a certain specificity. When I consider the great variety of possible meanings,
and the fact that in known societies social organization survives
only if it can provide us with valid meaning, I have to believe
that things were the same in prehistoric societies, and therefore
that division by function was accepted only if it also had symbolical force, if it was not just rational organization but carried
an image in which people could recognize themselves (I would
not say individually, but as a group).

This hypothesis seems very likely to me, but it would not
be unilateral or uniform. For the factors of social organization in
different groups are to my knowledge very different and not at
all comparable. In other words, I do not believe that anything is
universal. In history I have never found a universal factor, whether
for individuals or societies. I do not believe that there is a given,
fixed, and permanent human nature, not even general characteristics. If we want to find universal factors in societies, we never get
beyond words. It is our practice to generalize extensively. We say
that people are religious, that there is religion in every traditional
society, that law is religious, or that social organization is religious.
What do such statements mean? To explain them in terms of Latin
etymology (*religare* or *relegere*) is dubious, for the religious facts
do not correspond except in the Christianized Greco-Latin
sphere. What is religion? We would have to be very clever to say
what it is when we look at such different phenomena as the Inca
rites, the myths studied by Lévi-Strauss, Scandinavian beliefs,
Buddhism, Zen, Shamanism, etc. Religion as such does not exist
in the strict sense. I cannot group together all that is traditionally
called religion. The diversity is too great even on essential points:
many gods, one god, or no god, an afterlife or no afterlife, a goal
or no goal, etc. To arrive at a general concept of religion presupposes an abstract gymnastics that in no way corresponds to the
reality here and now of the actual situation. And what applies to
this universal factor applies to nearly all the terms that we now
use as if they were universals.

I must emphasize how smoothly we slip in our Western
terms and institutions. Thus among us the sexual relation between men and women is organized as marriage. We describe
as marriage every such relation in every epoch and society. But

with us marriage is a whole complex, and we measure other institutions by our own. Again, among us the relation between
people and things is organized as one of property. We thus talk
of property among the Etruscans, Kanakas, etc. But this is not
possible.

One example that has always seemed significant to me is
that of slavery. We talk about slaves among the Aztecs, the Egyptians, the Hebrews, etc., and we project a certain model, either
that of Roman slavery in the 2nd century B.C., or slavery in the
Americas in the 17th and 18th centuries. But there is no real
comparison. The Hebrew slave had nothing in common with
the Roman slave except the existence of a master, though under
such different terms that the word itself meant nothing. In much
the same way we misuse the word *family*. We say that there is
a group relation between man, woman, and child, and we give
this relation a name. But we ought not to understand the relation in terms of what we mean by family. We ought to submit
to the reality that is proclaimed from within the society, to accept what the group says about itself, and not to put it in a Western form or to translate it into our own terms. In my view this
is why typologies are so artificial. I do not believe in concepts
like patrilinear, matrilinear, etc. These are things we invent for
the purposes of our own classifying and reasoning, but always
at the expense of the unique features of a given group. As I see
it, these unique features, these special details, these oddities,
these peculiar usages, are what constitute the true character of
an organization or institution. Looking at all the constitutive features of an institution, we tend to pick out those that suit ourselves, and we make of these our criteria of classification, but
in so doing we deform irrevocably the reality that we thus
master. If we want to make some advance in understanding
(rather than rationalized or global knowledge), then we must
analyze the details. No universal form will enable us to trace a
global geography or history of the race. We have referred already to the great diversity contained in a word like *social*. I
might decide to explain human history by the typology of families or of power, but this would be an arbitrary decision. In the
social as in the biological sphere there is a tremendous proliferation of forms and components, and we cannot impose upon

them any hierarchy, but only note the successes and failures. It is impossible to align them in such a way as to be able to trace a history in them.

Nevertheless, even though there can be no coherent knowledge, we can pick out certain features that are general enough to be comprehensive. The first is that by all accounts human beings have been extremely inventive in the creation of social forms in the natural environment into which they were plunged. No single model corresponds to particular features in human nature. There are instead many models that we must not try to reduce to schemas. In all types of natural environment human beings have been able to find the most adequate and effective social structure. The problem was always the same, namely, how to survive in this singular universe in which we are placed. The responses were not stereotyped but appropriate. In other words, there was not just an involuntary adaptation of the biological organism but a voluntary and selected adaptation (I would not say calculated or conscious and considered) of the adopted social form. The remarkable thing about this adaptation is that it was chosen and not left to chance or to arise ex nihilo. Perhaps it came by way of a series of trials and errors, but certainly on the level of the intellect and judgment. We know that prehistoric people could note their mistakes and probably profit by them and try to correct them. There was thus a multiplicity of social forms. It might be objected that we know nothing explicit about these. That is true, yet given the diversity of environments and the different forms of resistance that they demanded, we are forced to assume that people responded differently according to circumstances.

A second feature that seems to me to be fairly general is symbolization. We have alluded to this feature already. Human beings were not content merely to set up a type of family or functional group. They projected it in a form that would explain and justify it. They symbolized it in order to give it permanence, legitimacy, and meaning. At the same time they ritualized it. In association with each social institution rites were created that permitted individual identification and conformity. Rites guarantee social stability, and no institution can evade this fact. An institution does not survive on its own. It can exist only by

way of either violence or the ritualization that guarantees conformity without judgment. Symbolization is neither the expression of a religious feeling nor a movement toward a divine universe. It is obligatory if the social body, however small, is to
survive. As I have said, symbolization offers a guarantee of permanence. It opposes the tendency of all things to grow old and
break up and pass away. It makes possible an orientation to a
system of complex relations with the environment. Rites are a
fixed frame to which to refer for lack of natural stability. Natural stability does not exist, whether in the nature around us or
in the order of shifting human relations. The elementary example of the man-woman relation shows this. A couple is essentially unstable and may break up for any minor cause. The
rite that we call marriage has brought stability, so that the couple
may stay together in spite of every fluctuation.

Nevertheless, in apparent contradiction of what I have just
said, I also maintain that when a human group gives itself a
form that implies the existence of a power or authority, a process
of compensation begins. This is always true in history, and I
have no hesitation in projecting it back into prehistory. In
society no force has ever been at work without giving rise to a
counterforce. There has always been white magic as well as
black.[3] Here again we must avoid two extremes. On the one
hand, this creation is not an organic, spontaneous, or automatic
one, as though society secreted its own antibodies. On the other
hand, it is not the fruit of reflection, of some philosophy or
theory. Humanity stands between the two. There is voluntary
creation, but only as dictated by circumstances. This factor of
compensation seems to me to have played a decisive role. It
prevents the new force from increasing indefinitely. (We have
seen that authoritarian states cannot come into being except
when the factor of compensation disappears.) It has brought
progress by constant criticism of power and institutions. It has
set limits to human action. It has given birth to what would later
be called ethics. I believe that it was present from the appear-

3. We shall see this again in the next chapter; here I may simply refer to
one of the most remarkable institutional examples, that of Rome with its consul
but also the people's tribune as a counterforce limiting consular "omnipotence."

ance of the first social forms. It was so because of the conjoint appearance of material power and symbolizing power.

Finally, two factors seem to me to be always linked and to work together in every social form: a factor of complexification and one of simplification. The former is obviously tied to refinement of adaptation on the one side and on the other to the idea of function that I referred to earlier. The more a group tends to grow, the more new problems arise, for example, securing new food, extending territory, and relating to other groups. There thus develops a trend toward more complexity. Division of functions and work becomes more detailed, and the more developed use of tools poses a demand for several specialists. Power always gives rise to various forms of intervention and therefore to complexity. In fact, as we begin to get more information about the groups called protohistoric, we find ourselves in the presence of extraordinarily complex groups. We are far from the simplistic concept of a communal society. From the beginning of the century anthropology and ethnology have shown how complex primitive groups were and how mistaken it is to equate the primitive with the simple.

Nevertheless, this complexification was accompanied by its opposite, by a simplification of forms and systems. This often went hand in hand with the attempt to give meaning to the social world. Myths might be complex, as Lévi-Strauss has shown, but one aspect of them is that they give order to reality. In this sense they simplify. By taking us to another and representative world, they elucidate. Society expresses and orders itself through the myths that it produces. With symbolization, then, there is in society a tendency toward simplification. It is hard to think of complexification and simplification going together, and yet this is what happens as society gains awareness of itself. In general, evolution is understood as complexification. Primitive society is supposedly simple, and the more it evolves, the more complex it becomes. But primitive society is not simple.[4]

4. I note the same idea among exegetes, who in analyzing ancient documents start with the hypothesis that the simplest document is the oldest. They forget that evolution can go the other way, that the oldest document may be very complex, and that there has been a later work of simplification.

There is also a tendency to purge out forms. That is to say, an awareness develops that certain rites, organizations, or taboos are superfluous, and there is thus a move to suppress them. Starting with a totality that is complex and overdeveloped, people try to find more simple and effective social forms that are better adapted to concrete situations. The purging of social forms is an expression of progress and has played a part in every epoch, though it has never, of course, been permanent. We need to consider each case on its own merits, which I cannot do here.

In closing, I want to emphasize that I am only too well aware of the objections that might be brought against these last pages. I have perhaps illegitimately used the features of historical societies to explain the phenomena of prehistoric societies. Yet to the extent that it seems to me that there is continuity and not discontinuity between them, this does not seem to be out of the question. I must state again that the main difference relates to the fact of our knowledge or ignorance of this history, not to its reality.

Chapter 10

THE HISTORICAL PERIOD AND THE SOCIAL ENVIRONMENT

One might date the beginning of the historical period to around 3000 B.C. The Xia Dynasty in China dates to around 2000 B.C., though an article in *La Recherche* traces Chinese history back to 4000. The first Egyptian dynasty (Menes) dates back to 3000, and the history of Kish, Ur, and Uruk to 2700. In many parts of the world comparable phenomena appeared at roughly the same time without any links among them. Transition is made from the Neolithic Age to human groups of a new type whose features we can better discern. I do not propose to trace their history here but to look at the common aspects and determinative characteristics of these societies from a sociological standpoint. Five features seem to me to apply both to ancient historical societies and to our Western world, marking these societies up to the radical change that has been taking place in the West for the last two hundred years.

(1) The first significant feature is that with historical advance there is an increasing transition to the voluntary and artificial, though naturally not without periods of recoil, for, as we have seen, there is never unbroken "progress." When I use the term *artificial,* I have in mind human intervention in nature. This does not characterize the historical period alone, for once *homo faber* came on the scene, the artificial modification of the natural environment began. But an artificial environment was not created all at once; the natural still permeated it. Historical societies advanced slowly toward an artificial environment. I am not using

the word *artificial* in a pejorative sense. I do not say that nature is good and offers us a model that we must always follow. This would mean the negation of all human history. In historical societies nature is not negated but mediated. Society becomes our chief milieu. It is by society, and thanks to it, that our basic needs are met. But it is also from society that the greatest dangers come (e.g., wars). Certainly the natural environment is still there, and from it society draws its primary resources. Sometimes the natural environment can itself become dangerous, as in the case of volcanoes, tornadoes, etc. But the primary resources have to be exploited by the collective labor of the social body, and typhoons do far less damage than tyrants.

What do I mean when I speak of a transition to the voluntary? The more society evolves, the more it seems to be organized deliberately. First there was a fairly spontaneous grouping, with, as we have seen, norms and taboos and prohibitions and functions and forms, all created by human beings, but with little calculation or pretense at organization. This is shown by the mythical reference to founding deities and the sense of belonging to a sacral universe. From the beginning of the historical period rites and the sacred have existed, of course, but their status declines, and there is a trend toward autonomous organization without any necessary reference to the transcendent. Little by little society in turn comes to be viewed as an object to be fashioned. It ceases to be a mere collection of people. It takes on a being of its own. Standing on its own, it can be contemplated as a thing apart, as a foreign body. People distance themselves from it. They can then impose upon it rules that are increasingly thought out and willed, and less and less inspired and spontaneous. Family and function are no longer rooted in the natural world but are subjected to regulations according to conscious models.

Once it is seen that rules are created voluntarily, it is seen also that they can be changed. For a long time an attempt is made to preserve them, to guarantee them by reference to a religious model, or to affirm that they are natural and sacrosanct, but this is finally impossible in face of the awareness that one can set up new rules for the social game and that one can also change them. Copying yields to reflection. This trend is reinforced by the appearance of writing, which is a tremendous factor in laicizing society and making it artificial. Writing makes possible the universalizing of a decision or insight. It strengthens leadership, since leaders can now make their will known to wider groups. It makes the composing and preserving of records possible. Above all, it makes possible a type of transmission other than what I would call proto-hereditary. It detaches knowledge from that of ancestors and challenges the validity of what is ancient, that is, the idea that things are as they are because oral lore passed down from one generation to another says that this is how they have always been. A different kind of social validity had now to be invented.

Another decisive factor was the invention of law as a means to change society when rules ceased to be the revelation of the deity and became a creation of power. Social organization was now the result of voluntary intervention according to calculation, consent, and authority. Very quickly in Egypt, at Ur, and in China this manipulated society found acceptance. This possibility and concern gave birth to what would become the main preoccupation in the historical period and for the social environment, namely, politics in the larger sense. We have to realize that politics is an activity that is linked to the existence of society as environment. If we change the environment and society ceases to be the chief environment (as is now happening), politics will disappear.

(2) In the transition to the voluntary and artificial there arose another important phenomenon: the possibility not merely of relations but of the influence of one group upon another, of one society upon another, facilitated by writing. In the Prehistoric Age influence of this kind was virtually impossible because groups were so dispersed and because their organization and symbolical representation were so tied to their distinctive entity, being an ontological part of it and therefore incapable of being exported to other groups. Naturally, the change did not come about swiftly, but progressively over the course of history influence and transfers became possible. Institutions and even religions became gradually detachable from a first group and as a result of conquest, travel, or commerce could be imitated by other groups. Thus a multiplicity of possibilities was presented.

There was more than one response to a given situation. Other groups obviously responded in different ways. Discovery of this could lead to hostility as well as imitation. Our inventive resources, however, are infinite. As evolution becomes more precise, society becomes an artificial environment.

This artificiality contains two elements. On the one hand, group organization is more a result of reflection and is not at the mercy of inevitable natural factors, of the constraints and compulsions of the natural environment. A new freedom is thus experienced, though this is at once reduced by the existence of a social environment that becomes increasingly obtrusive and demanding. On the other hand, there is a multiplication of artifacts, of fabricated objects, of tools, of furnishings, of pottery, and of weapons. Naturally the ongoing creation of useful objects fashions a new human background, especially with the construction of houses. All this leads to a genuinely new environment, that of the town. In the town, which emerges around 3000 B.C., everything is in fact artificial. This is the real symbol of the different environment, its features being organization, proximity, and exclusion of the natural. The town is *the* human universe or domain, surrounded by a universe that is not yet mastered even though there is no longer total dependence on it, the countryside close at hand and the forest at a distance. Special rites and taboos exist for entry into this universe. The gods are no longer the same, nor is the human attitude to them.

(3) Fairly soon after this first phenomenon comes social hierarchy. In prehistoric society the group probably had a chief. But the existence of an authority was not enough to create a social hierarchy. In such societies the hunter was not superior to the picker or the sorcerer to the fisher. Hierarchy demands a specification of groups along with a unitary conception of society. There has to be some idea of the kind of organization that is desired for this society. Hierarchy comes by way of many criteria, such as sex, age, role, and especially descent. Often it is an eponymous ancestor who makes possible the establishment of a hierarchy and correlation among groups. I believe that the first major distinction was between families that could claim an eponymous ancestor and those that could not. The former constituted what would later be called the aristocracy or

nobility. What is it that distinguished them? The existence of a history. The eponymous ancestor had an outstanding and memorable history. He was a hero, a demigod. He was endowed with exceptional powers or in some cases was the victim of an equally extraordinary destiny. He could serve as a model of life and conduct for those who claimed him and were supposed to repeat his noble deeds. The history of successive heroes was passed down from generation to generation in these families, often in the form of legends. Families which had a history of this kind were radically different from families that did not, whose recollections went back at most only to two generations. The former families came to constitute a ruling caste, while the latter became the common people, within which there was often a functional hierarchy as one function came to be viewed as more noble than another.

The aristocratic families that preserved the memory of their history also had another essential role. As a frame for the whole people, they carried in effect the history of the whole society. Their history was the history of all. They were truly the memory of the society. The existence of their eponymous ancestors, their network of relations expressed in mythical terms, ended up by constituting a network of correlations between the different social groups. These groups tended to focus on this point in an explicit and orderly way. They received definition and designation as a result. Etymologically, definition means placing between boundaries, having precise limits in relation to others. When one is set in one of such groups, it is impossible in principle to leave it.[1] Definition then takes on a new form, that of law. At the same time, the group acquires a designation. It carries a distinctive sign denoting its place in the city. This designation is often mythical either by way of origin or of characterization, and this process, even though it might seem primitive to us, still goes on today. One has only to think of the mythical stereotyping of certain groups in our own society, for example, Jews, communists, fascists, or Arabs.

(4) In the midst of this creative evolution of a society

1. On all this see Louis Dumont's detailed study, *Homo hierarchicus* (Paris: Gallimard).

whereby it becomes increasingly human and complex, law comes on the scene at the junction of artificial voluntarism and the development of social hierarchy. As I see it, law is neither a reflection of the divine nor an ideological reflection of economic relations. It is not at root natural and ought not to try to express natural relations. It is entirely artificial. It is simply the regulation that people judge to be useful if society is to be able to function and relations between groups are to be stabilized. In talking thus I will no doubt shock lawyers and please those who regard law as unimportant. But I do not intend to disparage law when I describe it in this way. It is enough to recall that if there are no rules one cannot play a game. Without legal regulation one cannot play the game of society.

Law is a specific phenomenon the heart of which is found in different forms in all societies. We have to remember, of course, that for us Westerners law is closely tied to justice. Normally it is fashioned in such a way as to establish or obtain justice. This link may be self-evident to us, but it is in fact a special one. It has a Jewish origin, justice being the basis and law a secondary phenomenon designed to achieve it.[2] But it also has a Greek origin, and here the issue is philosophical rather than theological. The Romans made of law a structure which was complete, effective, and concrete, but in which justice was of little importance; they assimilated the problem of justice by way of Greek thought. For us, then, the link between law and justice is both self-evident and inevitable, but in human history it is simply an accidental and local fact. In other places the law created has a different origin and significance. Individuals and groups were forced to make law in response to a triple challenge: they very soon felt the challenges of space, of time, and of relationships. (a) That of space corresponds to what I have already emphasized regarding groups that settle down, so that society becomes the true environment, though it is always encircled by what is still a powerful natural environment. From the very dawn of history the natural environment has always seemed to be hostile and dangerous. Protection was needed

2. See Jacques Ellul, *The Theological Foundation of Law*, trans. Marguerite Wieser (New York: Doubleday, 1960; repr. New York: Seabury, 1969).

against it, and the rule of law was a means to this end. Thanks to law, limits and boundaries have been drawn between the subdued civilized world, the new environment made by and for people, and the ancient external world. The whole of the human world is covered and controlled by law. Brute force, a relationship of domination, can reign outside. A type of regulated relationship that is quite different obtains inside. The same distinction may be seen in the deities. City deities are civilized, and there may be normalized (i.e., legal) relations with them. Outside deities are savage, unknown, and unpredictable.

The word *unpredictable* brings us to the second original function of law. It is a response to (b) the challenge of time. People soon saw that things change quickly and that they are unpredictable. But it is impossible to live in an uncertain and fluctuating universe. Since time cannot be mastered, the thing to do was to establish in a number of areas a fiction of stability. Law discharges this function of stability. Deciding to act as if things did not change, people formulated laws that would remain in spite of social reversals and changes in government. Law maintains social stability in face of the uncertainties of the future. Between a husband and wife, a lender and borrower, a tenant and landlord, things are always changing. There are changes in feelings, in financial circumstances, in the economic world. Lenders might claim back their money at any time, and those who rent a house might act as if they owned it and refuse to move out. Law regulates relationships of this kind, so that in principle they cannot vary according to circumstances. Once a relationship becomes a legal one, the parties agree to act as if the situation would remain the same even though differences come with time. This is a way of making provision against the uncertainty that the passage of time brings.

Finally, those who live in society face (c) a third challenge, the presence of other people. When a group is small, all the members know each other and there is thus no threat, for any that might arise is known in advance. Only strangers are menacing and a priori hostile. But when the number of people grows, the members of a society (even a microsociety) cannot all know each other. They cannot know one another's reactions. There is inevitably relationship, but this spontaneous relationship may

be dangerous. Law intervenes to regulate things. It mediates between individuals or between families. It offers possibilities of
action other than direct action. It regulates means, so that one
knows what to expect. It assigns to each person a role. And once
social roles are clear, we know a priori what the other can or
should do. When personal relations are good, legal mediation
is unnecessary. It becomes necessary when I do not know the
intentions of the other with whom I have dealings.

To explain the development and usefulness of law I have
used the term *challenge*. In so doing I have had in mind the theory
of Toynbee. I know that it has been criticized and that like all
grand explanatory systems it has now been abandoned and
forgotten. Yet I believe that it is basically true. Every society, like
every individual, faces challenges and will evolve according to
its ability to take them up, to absorb them, or to neutralize them.
There are many kinds of challenges that confront a society. Some
are internal: economic, demographic, moral, or revolutionary.
Some are external: invasions, wars, disasters, epidemics,
droughts, and climatic changes. We can imagine all kinds of challenges which either immediately or over the long haul trigger
one or many reactions. A society faced with a challenge may also
respond in hundreds of ways according to its own genius and
its state of evolution. Sometimes there is a complete ignoring of
the challenge, as in the case of Byzantium when faced by the
Arabs. Either there is trust in one's own power, or there is no
wish to face the threat, and life goes on as if nothing had happened. Thus when Islam had conquered almost all the provinces
of the empire, and all that remained to the emperor was the city
of Constantinople with its outskirts and a couple of islands, he
continued to issue decrees and to sign them as the ruler of the
whole empire. Failing to see the real challenge, people sometimes defend themselves against other things. The great challenge to Ethiopia was the famine, but the government was pre-
occupied with the war in Eritrea. What is in reality a challenge
sometimes receives an enthusiastic welcome as though it were a
gift and blessing. This is the case today in Europe's handling of
Islam, which is the greatest threat to it since the great invasions
of the 7th to the 10th century.

In France I see not only an inability to respond to a challenge but a kind of death wish. It is ready to welcome that which will destroy it. It opens its arms to it, whether it is American culture, the Americanizing of food, games, morals, and the economy, or communism (though this has lost its party), or, more seriously, Islamization, on the pretext that we have to defend immigrant workers. Those whom he wills to destroy, Jupiter makes mad. France is mad with affection for what will cut its throat. To say anything against Islam is, of course, horrible sacrilege. We have to help the poor immigrants who have come to give a lift to the economy of France, and France has a lasting vocation as a welcoming country.[3] In reality, it is the whole of Europe that in face of the many challenges confronting it is showing signs of an unconscious death wish. Though we reject his arguments, we have to say that finally Spengler is proving right. The various attitudes in face of challenges all testify to decline because of the inability of the social group to find a response, or because of its failure to see the danger. But the challenge is there, and it has often been shown that when there is an adequate response and a parrying stroke is found, the group is enriched and develops and becomes more complex. The more challenges it meets, the more vitality it achieves. Challenges in Toynbee's sense, of course, are not the only problems with which the group has to deal.

Furthermore, when we talk about a "response" to the challenge, the term may be misunderstood. We are not thinking on a global scale of the mechanism that has been much used the last thirty years, that is, psychophysiology or stimulus-response. The response I have in view is never a reflex. It is never the unconscious result of physiological adaptability. Decision, choice, and reflection play a big part, at least in a response that is good enough to meet the challenge. This response will be voluntary, calculated, and selected. But lack of response, failure to see the challenge, passivity, and a death wish are all due to the absence of reflection, energy, and social choice. I believe

3. I do not understand this argument, for while aliens who have come to France from countries like Spain or Portugal are welcomed even though they are not refugees, genuine refugees like the Vietnamese or Cambodians are not welcome in France.

that the close connection between a vital reaction and reflection, or intelligent intervention, is a distinctive feature of human history. When we study the historical threats that have menaced societies, we note that the choice of responses is often greater than the challenge. The society under attack does not simply repulse the aggression and return to its prior state. The response entails a modification of the group. The challenge does not simply evoke defense but brings to light hidden resources in the group and results in social or economic improvements. Thus the challenge prevents the society from reproducing itself in its identity.

(5) Another distinctive feature, then, is that an adequate response is much more than a match for the challenge. We cannot know in advance how a social body will react. Each group will find its own defenses and adaptations according to its own nature. Here again we come across the extraordinary inventive capacity of the human race. There is as much diversity in collective responses to challenges throughout history as there are institutional and technical creations. In looking at the reality of human history, then, we cannot draw up a clinical table of human aptitude or ineptitude. The very complexity prevents us from tracing a kind of flat evolution, whether of a given society or even less of humanity as a whole. This is the great temptation that is always present when historians attempt great syntheses or general explanations (including that of Toynbee). The creativity and inventiveness also stop us from drawing lessons from history, let alone from postulating laws of historical evolution. We can analyze an epoch and find similarities between it and our own, for example, the Roman empire in the 4th and 5th centuries. But this does not mean that we can foresee what will happen in the next half-century. History does not teach us how to understand our own time or to choose a solution. It is not without value, but more as a spur to the creation of something new than as a collection of ready-made remedies. Each historical situation is different from all others. If we need to know others, it is in order to see how we have reached the point where we are. History can help in diagnosis, but it offers no cure, and even less does it cause us to bow to ineluctable necessity. If we are convinced that the predictions of Nostradamus

or the scientific laws of history hold in effect the future of society, then this means that we lose our creative abilities, and hence that the society to which we belong will not be able to come up with the new thing that is needed.

Among the means of adaptation and response, I want to draw attention particularly to the mechanisms of compensation. It is these that permit a social body to maintain itself and to achieve equilibrium. We shall see later that in all known societies and every known epoch there is a permanent trend toward unlimited growth. In effect, a developing historical society sees the coexistence of many tendencies, institutions, and more or less competitive factors, which adjust more or less well to one another, and which produce social movements of different kinds. But little by little, in this play of forces, some tend to take the lead over others and to secure power for themselves. Every movement (e.g., toward the voluntary, the artificial, or the hierarchical) contains a totalitarian impulse, seeking to become absolute and to exclude all others. It is perhaps a human trait that there always has to be something more. We shall see, however, that if this impulse has its way, it will bring with it many disorders. But most often mechanisms of compensation come into play, not to fight directly against the dominant tendency, but to make it bearable to those subjected to it.

Thus, on the one hand, in a society in which power tends toward absolutism, or the hierarchy is more static and strict, or law proliferates, extending to all human activities and regulating without end, we find increasing means of evasion. These might be of two types. First we have an increase in holidays and sports. The members of this society find a form of freedom here. It may be sterile and feeble, but it is satisfying in appearance, and appearance is what counts for them. This is why we see a multiplication of sports in societies that achieve strong integration. From this angle we need to reflect on the societies of the free world with their proliferation of sporting events, courses, television, information, etc. These are an indication of the development of an authoritarian, crippling, and omnidominant society. The second form of compensation is religious evasion. Apparent escape from the severity of a totalitarian society is found by looking to heaven and despising the things of the world. This is a very satisfying compensation so long as the religion is free and spiritual, not institutional, since institutional religion is itself authoritarian and hierarchical.

On the other hand, if in a society the dominant tendency is passion for a freedom of incoherence, if this society has plunged into laxity and virtually everything is allowed, if there is no respect for the rule of law, or for social relations, or for moral norms, then we find compensation that again may be of two types. First, an organizing power comes on the scene. Spontaneous social solidarity tends to disappear, but instead there arises an external coherence imposed by an external power, for example, a strong, centralized state. Naturally, this cannot create artificially a true solidarity, but it can prevent disintegration and maintain for a time (for as much time as the society needs to regain its balance) a coherence of compensation. The second type of compensation, as in the first instance, is religious. In this case, however, the religion will be strongly moralistic and institutional, and it will set the social body in a network of constraints desired and sanctioned by belief. The two types of compensatory mechanisms are found in almost all societies and in all historical periods. But I am not trying to explain them, nor am I saying that we find them in every case. They are not the fruit of a conscious decision by one part of society. They are not a product of wisdom and intelligence. They are also not the expression of a kind of natural law of balance which spontaneously produces in a society the counterforce it needs if it is to make good headway. We would have to explain how such a law could arise, where it would come from, and why it would seem to operate in some cases but not in others.

I also believe in the working of what I have called the unbearable factor. There are times and situations in society when things are intolerable, when people can no longer stand them. They then react in a more or less adequate manner—often with mistakes—in an attempt to make a society livable again. They often find a way. In effect this reaction to the unbearable does not simply produce the opposite of that to which they are subjected. It is a strange one. People do not merely do the opposite of what they find painful to them. Often they are not clear how the situation has arisen. They merely want to be able to live in the social body, to make it livable. Thus they often produce something new. (One of the great tragedies of the modern world is that once the absolute revolution was achieved in the USSR in 1917, all protests, all movements of liberation, all struggles against injustice and intolerability were annexed and integrated into the one recognized and admitted revolutionary current, i.e., Soviet communism. We see here the outstanding modern example of the sterilization of the human ability to create something new in society and history.) These material or ideological upsurges have thus far produced a situation which has again become livable and tolerable. Thus it seems to me that the social evolution of humanity is made up of the constant interplay of the organization of power and the rise of an opposing power.

There is a major difference between the two. The first is voluntary, considered, and organized. The second is (or was until communism disturbed things) spontaneous and not thought out, becoming aware of its indispensability only at a second stage. All exclusion of this opposing force, or inability to produce it, incurs the penalty of social totalitarianism or political arrogance. But we must not entertain false ideas of this counterforce. It has to rise up from the depths of the people and not from a small elite that is dedicated to organizing it, with the result that in effect it will instead reproduce power itself. We have a good instance of this in French syndicalism. Between 1880 and 1914, impelled by anarcho-syndicalists, this was a genuine counterforce. It engaged in accurate criticism and initiated actions that gave workers, not so much an amelioration of their condition, but rather a possibility of expressing themselves and of exerting influence in innovative ways. But today syndicalism is no longer a counterforce. It is simply a part of the power game. It works through the usual political forms, playing the same game as other groups. The unions no longer have any important role in making society livable and stopping a plunge into politico-technological hubris. A counterforce has to come from the grass roots. But I do not want to be misunderstood. The grass roots, the people, cannot be said to have any particular virtue, whether intelligence, inventiveness, or foresight. What we have is simply a reaction to what is felt to be oppression. In other words, it is because people are effectively oppressed that they look for a way to reduce the oppression and can thus eventually become a counterforce. It is from the oppressed that there comes the novelty that is needed if a society is to regain its meaning and togetherness. But this creation is possible only if the oppressed are not dragooned in advance, if a place is left for spontaneity, if the movement they can launch is not at once taken over either by the ruling power itself or by an organization identical to it. The existence of various methods of compensation is the only guarantee that a society will have enough vitality to go on.

There is, however, nothing necessary or automatic about this. The development of a social tendency might not run into any counterforce or counterbalance. Then there will be some complex results, and not merely the simple historical event of the disintegration of the society. That will happen only after long periods of trouble and rigidity. It seems to me that one can think of many possibilities. First, there is what I would call the accumulation of social problems. When some activity threatens a certain aspect of life in society, there can be a reaction that tends to reestablish equilibrium. Something is done about the cause of the problem, its origin, in order to reduce or eliminate the problem itself. But sometimes today we find a boomerang effect. The problem triggers action on its real cause, but instead of checking the problem this action aggravates it. Thus problems multiply and no way is seen to deal with them. For it is of the nature of social problems that they resist any efforts to deal with their effects. I will give two simple examples.

The youth problem has many causes: idleness, poor lodgings, the breakup of families, and also the publicity given to the exploits of motorcycle gangs, etc. If we deal with this problem at the level of results, trying to fight against drugs or stealing by repression, or if we merely try to deal with secondary causes, providing proper housing or employment, we find that repression severely aggravates the problem, and that it will now manifest itself in resistance to the pseudo-remedies as young people mess up and degrade their lodgings, refuse to go to work, and contribute to the greater disintegration of their families. Reaction to the causes has the result of making the effects even worse.

We find the same in the case of the traffic problem. At a certain point the increase of traffic and its speed makes life almost impossible in some areas, causing serious inconvenience. Attempts have been made to facilitate the flow by widening streets, providing underground parking, etc. But again these efforts have only made things worse. As Gabriel Dupuy has shown (and others, e.g., Ziv, for American cities), to make the flow of traffic easier is to increase its volume. Open a new freeway and it is immediately full of vehicles. People who have not been using their cars begin to do so when the flow of traffic improves. Roads that are supposed to relieve congestion become new points of congestion. And everything becomes more complicated when the various phenomena intermesh, when there develop in society problems that reciprocally affect each other.

This is not the only feature of social crises. When a certain tendency enjoys unlimited development, two results are possible. The first is a break in the society, a break in communication between its component elements (a short circuit), a break within one of the components, a split into currents so divergent that they cannot meet and combine again. Society then plunges into disorder. But it is a totally unforeseeable and surprising disorder, which does not correspond, therefore, to the necessary disorder, the plunge into the "great age" of Mircea Eliade, into the chaos of origins in which it can find new strength. That disorder is known in advance. It has its place in the march of time. It is for a definite period. It gives new vigor to the whole social body. But the incoherent disorder of unlimited growth has a tendency to be impossible to foresee or arrest. If the absolute monarch no longer has a jester as a counterpart, he ends up by being put to death. This takes place through an uncalculated revolt in which society takes a total risk but which is never a true preservation of social relations nor the source of a new, acceptable society. The whole history of historical societies, whether in Europe, in China, or among the Incas, is punctuated by risks of collapse of this kind (and to talk about revolts against misery is always far too simplistic).

But there is another possibility. Growing social power might finally reach what Illich calls a threshold. At a certain point it might produce the opposite of what it produced in the first period. In a reversal of direction the results are the reverse of what was anticipated. The work of Illich on education and medicine is well known. If we discount some exaggeration, and look in the right places, we might say that he is right in the main. Overmuch education can work against culture. Literacy among Africans and American Indians leads to a radical destruction of local culture and gains nothing. People are taught to read and write, but to what end? They have no access to Western culture, and their own society is deprived of its culture. The same is true to some extent in Europe, where it can be seen that formal education makes some young people less adaptable, and prolonging their studies gives rise to all kinds of behavior problems among adolescents.

Illich's thesis regarding too much medical care has run into heavy criticism. Nevertheless, it is true that too many medications create new illnesses. Many hospital beds are occupied by people who have overdosed themselves. In other words, the effect of medications has been the opposite of that intended. There is a similar threshold in law. In countries like France there is an incredible proliferation of texts, decrees, orders, circulars, and ministerial letters. I have often given the example of legal regulations pertaining to schools and universities — six thousand pages of texts. In other areas there are even more. No one in the world can reasonably act on this deluge of texts, in which there is inevitably at times disorder and contradiction. What is the point then? The aim is to order and control everything minutely, analytically, and rigorously, down to the smallest details, by legal texts which seek to foresee every possible contingency. But no one can really make a synthesis of all these rules, or even know them, so that everyone acts independently of them — I would not say disobeying them, but simply ignoring them and applying some general rules of good sense and insight. An excess of regulation can lead a society into a situation of lawlessness. This is always the sign of a fundamental crisis in society, the prelude to a crisis of authority.

In this sketch of certain crisis factors, I must recall Kondratiev's theory of cycles, even though it is now contested. In the economy there is a system of slow swings, higher prices alternating with lower prices, the latter being a sign of the slow-ing down, the sluggishness, of economic life. These alternations come in cycles of about thirty years (at least in Western society for the last two centuries). They are normal, so that there is no need to worry about them. The correct response of the social body will bring readjustment. Having learned from previous cycles, economists can now deal better with recessions. But if the cycles combine with a long-term general trend (e.g., a continued depression), then a cycle may bring on a true crisis; this occurs when the cycle of upsurge and of economic recovery no longer compensates the trend. This phenomenon manifests itself in a curve in the form of an arch. Accelerated growth slows down when the economy overheats. Then, having passed the top, it begins to decline slowly. But instead of a correction, as in a cycle, the fall speeds up and leads to an economic collapse which is a real crisis. Each such crisis is different from all others, so that traditional remedies do not help. I will not attempt a description or diagnosis of the present crisis. I will simply express my agreement with those who think that it is not just an economic crisis but a social crisis of global proportions. The economic crisis is simply the sign of a crisis that is political, moral, social, and psychosociological, and that has been developing over what many people were stupidly calling a glorious period.

When a society notes the accumulation of the various factors that I have recalled: the absence of a process of compensation, the unlimited growth of a trend, the reversal of trends, the piling up of problems, the existence of a trend toward economic depression, we are in the presence of a serious crisis in which a society may explode, break up, or be absorbed into another society. Such a society is on a razor's edge and its history may be over. It may simply disappear like the Roman empire, the Byzantine empire, the Ottoman empire, or the Aztec empire.[4] The political and economic cards may be redistributed among old and new groups, as in Egypt's New Kingdom, in the Roman empire between the 1st and the 4th centuries, and in China in the 14th century.

---

4. We must not think of a solid and glorious Aztec empire being destroyed by brutal conquerors. It was surprisingly fragile and artificial.

But the crisis that we are approaching today is of yet another order. For it entails the transition, not from one form of society and power to another, but to a new environment. For approximately the last five thousand years we have lived in the environment that I have just described, that of society, in which politics plays the major role. Across the hazards of history human beings have adapted very well to this environment and have made remarkable progress. But everything is now changing. The present crisis is not one that we can overcome by social, political, or economic modifications. It has not arisen in these sectors. It has nothing in common with previous historical crises. This is a total crisis triggered by transition to a new and previously unknown environment, the technological environment. There is only one comparable crisis, but we can draw no lessons from it, for we know nothing about it. I mean the transition of the Protohistorical period: the transition from nomads to agriculturalists, from farmers to townspeople, from natural authorities to political authorities, and the drawing of boundaries, etc. The present change of environment is much more fundamental than anything that the race has experienced for the last five thousand years.

Chapter 11

THE POSTHISTORICAL PERIOD AND THE TECHNOLOGICAL ENVIRONMENT

What we are now experiencing is inaugurating the long crisis of insertion into a new human environment and its organization—the technological environment. For the last two centuries industrialization has been preparing the way for it, but it is only in the last thirty years that technology has begun to impose itself everywhere, to change everything, to take over all social activities and forms, and to become a true environment. Now a true environment has the following features: it enables us to live, it sets us in danger, it is immediate to us, and it mediates all else. Technology fully meets this description.[1] In the first place, we moderns are unable to live without our appliances and technical gadgets. We can survive neither in a natural environment nor in a social environment without our technical instruments. Our gadgets are as necessary to us as food. Even at the elemental levels of food, lodging, and clothing, we consume the products of technology. We could not go back to earlier forms of production and consumption.

At the same time the technological environment creates very great dangers for us. They are so great that they threaten

---

1. I will be very brief in this section because I have already shown how technology has become the human environment in *The Technological System*, trans. Joachim Neugroschel (New York: Continuum, 1980).

to bring about the disappearance of the whole human race, something that has not happened since Paleolithic times. In addition to nuclear risks there are ecological risks in face of which human beings show incredible thoughtlessness. One example will suffice, namely, the worldwide devastation of forests. In Europe we have acid rain, in Africa the clearing of forests, and in Amazonia the stupefying attempt to remove the whole forest block. If we continue along this path, in thirty years there will be no true forests on earth. The elimination of forests will reduce the production of oxygen in the oceans because of the expansion of oily layers. Then there will not be enough oxygen, and at the same time the quantities of carbon in the stratosphere will increase. We will then not have enough air to breathe. Here is a first danger created by the technological environment.

This environment is also immediate. We are surrounded by technical objects just as we were surrounded by natural objects in the first environment. We have only to lift our hands and we come across a technical object, whether in the home, on the street, or in public places. Our relation to them is direct, with no screen, no distance, no reflection, no awareness. This environment is just as evident as were forests and torrents and mountains, then such representatives of power as rites, myths, social imperatives, the family, etc. Conversely, all other relations are mediated by technology. It forms a screen of means around all of us, and we are in touch with nature or the social group by means of communications: television, cinema, telephone, or photography. These instruments make possible much more rapid and numerous relations. They also keep us informed of all that is happening in the world and acquaint us with many pseudonatural milieux that we could not otherwise know.

The creation of the technological environment is achieving two main things. First, it is progressively effacing the two previous environments. Of course, nature and society still exist. But they are without power—they no longer decide our future. There are still earthquakes, volcanic eruptions, and hurricanes. Famines and droughts still cause even greater distress, as in Africa. But humanity is no longer helpless when faced with such disasters. It has the technical means to respond, and it is only due to lack of will, of political decision, and of a global mobilization of means that the scourge spreads. We can act, but we do not, and this is why nature is always menacingly present as an environment that is subordinate and no longer basic.

The same applies to society. It remains as a secondary environment. We still have politicians and police and an administrative organization. But each of these has to have technological gadgets that make it more efficient and active. It has not yet been appreciated that this entry of technology means control over all the persons involved, all the powers, all the decisions and changes, and that technology imposes its own law on the different social organizations, disturbing fundamentally what is thought to be permanent (e.g., the family), and making politics totally futile. Nevertheless, it will be said, politicians make the decisions. But politicians can decide only what is technologically feasible. No decisions can be made that run contrary to technological growth. All decisions are dictated by the necessity of technological development. Nothing else matters. Like every other social organization, politics continues to exist as a kind of theater in which we play out the comedy of freedom. Culture does the same in identical fashion. When politics tries to make decisions that run against technology, it can do so only negatively, that is, by preventing technology from doing certain positive things. We have here the same process as when the social environment replaced the natural environment: an attempt to show that there is alliance and partnership, the earlier values being taken up into the new milieu.

Thus one of the great themes today is technological culture. We are supposedly adding technological knowledge to our humanist legacy. At least this is not an attempt to raise technology to the rank of a true culture, to find in it a source of values, intelligence, a critical spirit, a universalism. A technological culture is in fact impossible, for technology is the negation of culture. We find a similar desire to show that technology becomes social inasmuch as it simplifies and amplifies social actions, or that it creates a new art. This is merely playing with words; there is no substance to it. The art created by painters, sculptors, and musicians imitates what technology alone proposes and permits and has nothing in common with what has been produced as art, and called such up to about 1930, since

Prehistoric times.[2] People are always talking about humanizing technology, but this talk has no effect whatever on its development. All questioning of technology on basic grounds (e.g., by ecology and the ecological movement in its early days) has either been ruthlessly dismissed or integrated into the technological world. This world sometimes seems capable of producing a counterforce, for in the period of transition from one environment to another susceptibilities have to be taken into account. Thus we find the concern for human relations in the 1950s and the movement of technology assessment today. But these simply serve to allay disquiet and thus to make development easier.

The second result of the domination of this environment is that human beings have to adapt to it and accept total change. At issue here is not just a slight modification or adaptation but an essential transformation. A first aspect of this radical adaptation concerns the relation between human beings and machines. If machines have to be perfectly adapted to us, the reverse is unavoidable. We have to be exactly what is useful for machines, their perfect complement. Human life is no longer merely a matter of muscle and reflex. We now have to have our gadgets. We can see the mutation very clearly and decisively in the academic world. The humanities are now disparaged. Traditional culture is valueless relative to machines. At the beginning of the 20th century, and again in 1930, people in the industrial and commercial world began to ask what good such studies as history and Greek are. How can they help us to make money or to forge ahead economically? Today we are putting much the same question, but in a new way: How do they serve the technological world? How do they make us a proper complement for machines? This is why there is such an incredible stress on information in our schools. The important thing is to prepare young people to enter the world of information, able to handle computers, but knowing only the reasoning, the language, the combinations, and the connections between computers. This movement is invading the whole intellectual domain and also that of conscience.

2. Cf. Jacques Ellul, *L'empire du non-sens* (Paris: Presses Universitaires de France, 1980).

But this is not the only feature. Part of the human mutation is the appearance and consecration of the human guinea pig in furtherance of science and technology. Since science and technology are plainly dominant, we have to test their effects and usefulness on people. Experiments are becoming ever more numerous and varied. I was horrified many years ago to learn that in the United States, for scientific reasons (to study the evolution of the embryo), pregnant women were being paid to have an abortion at a given stage, and we have gone much further than that today. Remedies, pharmaceutical products, are being tested on people for pay. There is experimentation in the field of what is everywhere called genetic makeup. We are growing used to the idea that people are simply guinea pigs upon whom it is quite legitimate to conduct scientific experiments. "Humanity is our most precious resource" is a slogan that has been taken up in many forms the last few years. But let us remember that if humanity is only a resource, this implies that we may treat humanity as simply a factor in economic production. Leases are taken out on resources. In the genetic field there seems to be no limit to what can be done (implants, test-tube babies, surrogate mothers, etc.). The imagination has free rein. But genetic manipulation is designed to produce exactly the type of people that we need. Much has been made of the book *1984,* but what is in prospect is really Huxley's *Brave New World.* From birth individuals are to be adapted specially to perform various services in society. They are to be so perfectly adapted physiologically that there will be no maladjustment, no revolt, no looking elsewhere. The combination of genetic makeup and educational specialization will make people adequate to fulfill their technological functions.

Beyond that, American experiments directly on the brain have shown that the implantation of minute electrodes (with the consent of the subject) might induce specific impressions, desires, and pleasures, and effect obedience to orders no matter who gives them and with no need for speech. At an experimental stage this has caused no scandal. But is it not apparent that this new form of intervention in human nature will finally suppress human freedom altogether, will bring about complete obedience without choice, and will result in the perfect adaptation that technology needs? People will no longer be a hindrance to proper conduct. The more perfect technology becomes, the more refined and complex and subtle and swift its processes, the more human conduct has to be perfect. We can no longer dream or forget or have other centers of interest. An instrument panel in an automated factory is no place for the recalling of poetry. The technological environment demands a radical transformation of humanity. Previously human adaptation followed the slow rhythm of evolution from generation to generation. Only over centuries did people become social, political, and urban. No one decided for them that they had to follow this pattern. Today the technological environment is coming upon us very quickly. Technology develops with ever increasing speed. In every sector and in all directions the new environment is being formed explosively. Hence human adaptation to it cannot be extended over many centuries. We have to adjust rapidly.

Examination of the last thirty years will be enough to demonstrate this incredible rapidity. Technology cannot wait, for it soon becomes unusable. Everything has to be done in a single generation. Nor can the adaptation be spontaneous, following our physiological and intellectual rhythm. To move quickly, we have to move by act of will. We cannot wait for progressive and cumulative adaptations. We have to create at once the kind of people that machines demand. Human language has already been modified to become that of the computer. Some numbers and letters have been modified so as to correspond exactly to the form that the computer gives them. This is an almost unrecognizable occurrence, yet it is of major importance.

A problem arises, however. For a long time those who have been genetically manipulated so as to conform to the technological model will be a small minority. Most people will still be at the social stage or even the natural stage. What will be the relations between these groups? They will certainly not understand one another. There will be no more in common between them than in the transition from the first to the second stage there was between nomadic brigands and the first city merchants five thousand years ago. On the one hand there will be a kind of aristocracy marked off by its total and infallible adaptation to technical gadgets and the technological system, and on the other hand there will be a vast number of people who are outdated, who cannot use the technology, who are powerless, who are still at the social stage but who live in a technological environment for which they are totally unadapted.

In this respect I must make a final observation. When I talk about adaptation, readers might think that I mean adjustment to various minor differences in environment. Thus people in hot countries adjust their clothes and habits and customs accordingly. But the changes of environment that I have in mind demand a total and fundamental mutation, so that I am inclined to say that the Prehistoric people of the natural environment had nothing in common with the historical people of the social environment, and that we are now witnessing a mutation of the same order. We have only to think how alien the bushmen or aborigines of Australia were to all that the 19th century regarded as human nature. By a change of environment what is regarded as human nature in one epoch is transformed and a new model of humanity emerges. It might be argued that I am exaggerating and that the environment cannot have this impact on human nature. But that argument is a mere hypothesis based on the conviction that there is such a thing as an inalienable and basically identical human nature. For my part, I am not so sure. Furthermore, no one has ever been able to say clearly what this human nature really is.

Nevertheless, I have still to answer a question of my own. Why have I given this sketch of the development of three environments in a book entitled *What I Believe*? It is true that at a first glance all that I have written here seems to have nothing to do with my fundamental beliefs, with what is fundamentally existential for me. Yet at root what I have presented is not a scientific theory. I cannot prove the impact of the environment or the relation of human beings to it. I do not pretend to be able to give strict answers to the many questions that confront anthropologists, ethnologists, and historians. I have put forward a simple hypothesis. But all hypotheses include a great deal of intuition and belief. Conversely, all beliefs finally express themselves in hypotheses which will be more or less strict and more or less daring, but which we have to take into account if we are to get the complete picture of an epoch. I would say in fact that this relation of human beings to their environment and these changes of environment do form part of what I believe. And if some disappointed readers are tempted to say: "And is this all that Jacques Ellul believes?" I would reply that what is at issue here is evaluating the danger of what might happen to our humanity in the present half-century, and distinguishing between what we want to keep and what we are ready to lose, between what we can welcome as legitimate human development and what we should reject with our last ounce of strength as dehumanization. I cannot think that choices of this kind are unimportant. What I believe with this theory of three environments has to do very definitely with the need to formulate what kind of humanity we want and what kind we repudiate. The relevance of this aspect of what I believe is by no means negligible.

PART III

END WITHOUT END

INTRODUCTION

I believe in the secret presence of God.

I am not now composing a catechism. Nor am I trying to show the compatibility of faith in God with modern rationalist and scientific thought.[1] I am simply suggesting that a secret God exists. Later I will try to say who this God is for me, but for the moment I will simply present the possibility of his secret presence in human life and history, from which we can never break free. But here a first problem arises.

When people do succeed in breaking free from belief in God, they simply create another religious belief to replace it. We always assimilate religion or God to a specific image, to specific rites or groups, to a specific conception, and when we banish these (as the Catholic Church and the Christian God were banished in France), we think that we have achieved freedom of thought. But we then proceed to an apotheosis of reason or science and we have new gods. When we think about God we run up against innumerable questions and obstacles. First there is the great diversity of gods that people have worshiped. If I am a Christian, it is by accident of birth. The diversity suggests that our imagination simply projects our desires on the sky, or that our fears create gods (which consequently have no objective existence), or that we are simply acknowledging in some way that something transcendent exists. In any case, however, the gods are all equally false, though they reflect

---

1. There is an excellent discussion of Christianity and science in *La Recherche*, 169 (September 1985), in a dialogue between P. Thuillier and P. Valadier.

a little something that may be true. One might also try to fuse what is common to all beliefs and thus achieve a syncretism. But either way one cannot say that one god is more true than another. For me to say that my God is true is inadmissibly presumptuous. One way out is to transform all religious records into myths. Another way is to regard all religions as equal without trying to distinguish between what is imagination and what is reality.

　　　The next major obstacle is that of evil. If God were God and good, he would not permit all the evil that takes place on the earth. Some of this evil comes from natural events and disasters (for which God is responsible if he is the Creator). Some of it comes from human actions, but if human beings were made in the image of God, why is there wickedness in them? Why could not God change them and make them good? Then there is death. We can understand that death is a natural reality. When we study cells and consider the laws of organisms, we see that death has its place. But if creation derives from an act of will, how can the Creator tolerate death with its train of sufferings both for those who die and for the bereaved who loved them? Suffering and death are a scandal that cries to heaven and that we cannot evade. We all know the famous dilemma of unbelief formulated by Bakunin: Either God is omnipotent but bad, or good but impotent. To this dilemma there seems to be no solution. Familiar, too, is another of the same kind: Either God is absolutely perfect (in the etymological sense) and he cannot be the Creator, for it is impossible to add anything at all (even a nut, as Anatole France said) to perfection, or God is the Creator and he cannot be perfect, for he was lacking something, and hence he cannot be God. A very old heresy evaded this dilemma by stating that God is not the Creator but that creation is the act of an inferior spirit (Yahweh) that is often regarded as evil.

　　　To this kind of reasoning we must add the findings of science. Historical science unpacks the sacred texts to show that they are not inspired but simply give us at best certain human opinions about God. Physics, biology, and astronomy scrutinize matter and nowhere find even the slightest trace of a beginning denoting the existence of anything other than matter. Insofar as science succeeds in formulating scientific laws of matter and of the functioning of the human brain, there is no place for miracles. Miracle as a transgression of the laws of nature is strictly impossible. Once a law is there it admits of no exceptions. All stories of exceptions are legends or musings. The main point, however, is that God cannot act. If he exists, he is completely paralyzed.

Furthermore, the God of religions is radically incompatible with our reason. Religious people talk about truth, the absolute, eternity, and omnipotence, but what do such words mean? In reality, they mean nothing at all to our intelligence and reason—they have literally no meaning whatsoever. They have no content for reason, for science, or even for the imagination. The proof is that when the sacred texts speak about such things, they have to resort to anthropomorphisms. But what are gods that are angry, that punish, that reward, that are jealous, that make war, or that repent? It is easy to say that this is just a manner of speaking, but since we cannot speak in any other way, is there any point in resorting to such a concept of God? One important theological current, that of negative theology, honestly recognizes that we can know nothing about God. God is hidden, secret. We can speak about him only negatively. We can say what is not God, or what God is not, but we can say nothing more. The Christian religion seems particularly fragile with its supposedly legendary records and its astounding belief that God could incarnate himself in a man. For centuries theologians have tried to comprehend what this incarnation might signify. They have invented various interpretative systems, but none is satisfying. Thus theology has given up and abandoned the problem. The usual surrender by Christians when they cannot answer questions is the statement: "It is a mystery." Strictly speaking, for reasonable people, this is saying nothing.

Another important factor in this whole process is what the gods have made of people. In the name of religion people have waged cruel wars. Convinced of the truth of their religion, they have tried to impose it on others and overcome their errors. Religion has always caused division, hatred, and misunderstanding. People of one religion cannot stand those of another religion. This intolerance is not all in the past. In the name of the communist religion millions of people are reduced to slavery and wars are waged (Afghanistan, Vietnam, and Ethiopia). In the name of the Muslim religion other wars are shedding blood across the world (Iraq and Iran, Lebanon, the Sudan) and an invasion of the whole world is in preparation. Who can deny all this when the Christian religion, the religion of love, has been as bad as the rest with its own wars and conquests, its own suppression of heresy by force, its own intolerance and lack of understanding? There can be no denying all this. And finally there is the terrible impact that Christianity has had on the Western psyche. Westerners have lived under terror of judgment by a terrifying God. They have been made guilty by an idea of sin. They have wandered through a world filled with prohibitions. They have run up against sexual taboos. All this has brought disasters in its train, for they have sought overcompensation in a drive to dominate, to conquer, and to expand.

Confronted by this monstrous process which has been going on since the origins of Christianity, it would be absurd to reply with arguments or to attempt apologetics. I will be content to make two kinds of remarks. First, science, though more modern, is less certain. Second, this type of objection rests on a strange misunderstanding to which, we have to admit, Christians themselves are prone.[2]

Modern science is much less certain of itself because of its very advances, which have opened up immense vistas but also posed increasingly difficult riddles. To be brief, I will simply recall Heisenberg's uncertainty principle, the challenge to Einstein's thesis that God does not play dice, the discovery of complex systems and feedback, the principle of nonseparability, the recognition of open systems, and the abandonment to a large extent of something that was always regarded as fully established, the mechanism of causality. All the sciences are now engaged in new researches and in mounting uncertainty, biology as well as history, chemistry as well as psychology. We have found out that pure science does not exist, that science is never pure, not even mathematics. A great contemporary math-

2. On Christian responsibility in this whole matter see Jacques Ellul, *The Subversion of Christianity*, trans. Geoffrey W. Bromiley (Grand Rapids: Eerdmans, 1986).

ematician even wrote a book on the theme that pure mathematics does not exist. Other scientists are venturing beyond the limits of science. All of them seem to feel a need to state publicly their beliefs, their ethics, their views of life and meaning. They are posing questions which science in its new form seems to be raising again concerning God. Without going so far as the dubious speculations of the gnosis of Princeton, I believe, for example, that the commonly accepted theory of the big bang that started the universe poses a problem. This universe did not always exist. At a single point there was an unimaginable and incalculable concentration of energy which exploded and at a stroke produced the matter of the galaxies. Where did this energy come from? Attempts have been made to explain it by a permanent movement of concentration and deconcentration, a kind of breathing, but this satisfies no one. A very different example is provided by the physicist Bernard d'Espagnat with his theory of veiled reality which we cannot know but without which reality cannot be explained and cannot continue. Thus there is no longer any way forward that can preserve for science its glorious certainties.

The other side of the change that is bringing correction has occurred in the understanding of Christian revelation. Almost all the arguments that I adduced are based on a mistaken understanding, on a metaphysical elaboration that is alien to biblical revelation and that has been superimposed on it. The God who has been thus presented is not the God of the prophets or the God of Jesus Christ but the God of the philosophers. Speculating on the divine nature, on the relation between God and the world, on God as origin, these philosophers finally constructed a totally intellectual image of God that derives from Greek philosophy, and it is this image that the rationalists of the 18th and 19th centuries tore to pieces. Theology also constructed a system which thought it could encompass and explain everything (apart from the mysteries). But when this theological explanation of natural phenomena collided with the scientific explanation, instead of reflecting afresh on the sure data (of the Bible), theologians stuck to their system and opposed reason and scientific experimentation. Some of them thought they could solve the problem by postulating two spheres, the real world for science and the spiritual world for religion. But this was another mistake. For the real can no more be separated from the spiritual than the body can from the soul. The spiritual without body is a vapor without substance.

The main problem with all this kind of thinking was that it ignored dialectic. It was purely logical and linear and rational. During the last three-quarters of a century, however, there has been considerable development. Theology is no longer going with the times but has gone back directly to the sources, and this will be enough to defuse many of the conflicts. We need to see that science and revelation are not two different spheres but have two different ends. The one is designed to give explanation, the other to give meaning. But this meaning is inexhaustible, for it changes as that changes to which meaning must be given, and it becomes more profound as there is better understanding of the Scriptures through new investigation.

This whole detour was necessary to make the point that the biblical God is hidden and yet present. I believe in God's secret presence in the world. God sometimes leaves us in silence, but he always tells us to remember. That is, he recalls us to the word which he has spoken and which is always new if we rebuild the path from the word written to the word lived out and actualized. He is a God incognito who does not manifest himself in great organ music or sublime ceremonies but who hides himself in the surprising face of the poor, in suffering (as in Jesus Christ), in the neighbor I meet, in fragility. We need to lay hold again of the elementary truth that God reveals himself by the fleeting method of the word, and in an appearance of weakness, because everything would be shattered if he revealed himself in his power and glory and absoluteness, for nothing can contain him or tolerate his presence. God cannot be known directly but only through that which is within the realm of human possibilities. This is why imposing ceremonies and ornate basilicas are absurd. Solomon recognized this in his prayer at the dedication of the temple: "Behold, heaven and the highest heaven cannot contain thee; how much less this house which I have built!" (1 Kgs. 8:27). There then follow the intercessions of Solomon for the poor, for aliens, for the hungry, for sinners, and for suppliants. In all these situations of our human weakness God comes to us. But we can be sure that in our situations of wealth and power and domination and expansion and high technology and unlimited growth God is not present. He tells the rich that they have their reward; why then should they have God as well? This is why God is silent in our Western world of opulence and technology. He is certainly present, as in the rest of the universe. But he is present incognito and in secret. He is present as he was when the serpent spoke to Eve and she was enlightened about the tree and took the fruit in order to be as God. He is present incognito and has enough respect to allow the creature to choose its own destiny after issuing a warning. But is not all that I am going to say about this secret God pure imagination on my part?

I find striking confirmation of it in the life of Jesus Christ himself.

Twenty years ago, when there was a debate about nonviolence, I was the first to stress that what characterized the action of Jesus in his life on earth was not nonviolence. Indeed, we all know how his indignation boiled over against the merchants in the temple. From this incident some theologians even inferred that he did not reprove revolutionary violence, so that they were ready to direct the action of the poor against wealthy merchants. We are also all aware of the violent charges Jesus hurled against the scribes and hypocritical Pharisees, against the rich, against Chorazin and Bethsaida, etc. What constantly marked the life of Jesus was not nonviolence but in every situation the choice not to use power. This is infinitely different. Not using power is not weakness. Weakness means inability to do what I would like to do or ought to do. Not using power is a choice. I can, but I will not. It is renunciation. This general and specific decision not to use power does not rule out occasional acts of violence. But this violence is an expression of brutal conflict, whereas the nonuse of power is a permanent orientation in every choice and circumstance. Power is there, but one refuses to use it. This is the example set by Jesus. The consideration that the omnipotent God, in coming among us, decides not to use power, is one of the most revolutionary imaginable. We do not yet see it at the moment of Jesus' birth, for then the child that God has chosen to be the Messiah is weak.

At this moment God strips himself of power and presents himself to us as a little child delivered up to us. That is not a problem for Jesus. The nonuse of power as a way of life may be seen in his messianic career from its beginning to its end. It may be seen when he asks John the Baptist to baptize him, renouncing the possibility of a baptism of fire. It may be seen when he is three times tempted to manifest his divine power and three times refuses. It is not necessary that an obvious intervention of God should show at the level of power that he is the Son of God. The temptation is ongoing.

We know that Jesus sometimes refused to work miracles. These were miracles that people wanted as proof that he was the Messiah. In these circumstances he refused the request. He never performed miracles except as a sign of his love. The clearest example, because in this case Jesus specifically expressed his choice and decision, was that of his arrest. When Peter wanted to defend him with the sword, he stopped him and said: "Do you not think that I could have twelve legions of angels that would come to defend me?" (Matt. 26:53). He was able to mobilize celestial forces, but did not choose to do so. Finally, on the cross, he refused to work the miracle that they asked of him: "If you want us to believe in you, come down from the cross" (Matt. 27:40). He did not come down. The whole time, then, the extraordinary choice was operative not to take the way of power as Messiah and Lord. Note in passing the radical difference from Islam, which can think of relations with unbelievers only in terms of power. The choice of Jesus was in line with many prophetic injunctions to the effect that horses and chariots could not protect Jerusalem, that God alone would defend them, that they should seek only his protection in demonstration of their trust in him, that he was their wall, their shield, and that they should renounce all others (cf. Isa. 31:1; Ezek. 17:15).

But this permanent orientation of Jesus, this express choice not to use power, places us Christians in a very delicate situation. For we ought to make the same choice, but we are set in a society whose only orientation and objective criterion of truth is power. Science is no longer a search for truth but a search for power. Technology is wholly and utterly an instrument of power; there is nothing in technology other than power. Politics is not concerned about well-being or justice or humanity but simply aims at achieving or preserving power. Economics, being dedicated to a frenzied search for national wealth, is also very definitely consecrated to power. Our society is the very spirit of power. The main difference from previous societies is that they also undoubtedly sought power but did not have the means to achieve it. Our society now has the means to achieve unlimited power. Thus we Christians today are placed in the most difficult of all situations. We have to repudiate both the spirit of the age and the means that it employs. If we do not, if we yield even a fraction to these forces, we will betray Jesus Christ just as surely as if we committed some individual and limited sin. For this is a choice for life (nonviolence being part of it), and no other is possible. Pretending that we can express the Christian faith in works of love (aid to the poor and sorrowing, etc.), or in revolutionary acts to achieve justice, is treason if we engage thereby in the use of power. For the last word of love is that never in any circumstances will it express or indicate power in relation to others. Today only a nonuse of power has a chance of saving the world.

Chapter 12

THE SEVENTH DAY

"And God saw everything that he had made, and behold, it was very good. And there was evening and there was morning, a sixth day. Thus the heavens and the earth were finished, and all the host of them. And on the seventh day God finished his work which he had done, and he rested on the seventh day from all his work which he had done. So God blessed the seventh day, and hallowed it, because on it God rested from all his work which he had done in creation" (Gen. 1:31–2:3). We may recall something that is generally known, namely, that the number seven is the number of perfection. The fact that everything is very good means that God's work is complete, and the number seven expresses this completion. After finishing his work, God rests. This divine rest is the crowning of creation. Rest, not the creation of man and woman, is the final stage. God leaves his work and rests. This rest is not divine leisure or recreation. It is infinitely more than that—it is plenitude. Because God is love, he cannot let his love be without object. He wants someone before him to love. Thus he creates. He creates on his own scale, which we are learning day by day as we find more and more galaxies. But love is happy only if the loved object responds to love and loves in return. God's work is done when he sets in this universe the tiny being that is capable of something that is beyond the capacity of the rest of the universe, namely, love. Man and woman are created for love, to show the love of God, to respond to it, to address to God the love and adoration of all creation. With their creation, creation is complete. Since God's love will no longer fall into the void and silence, he ceases to create. Created also to love one another, man and woman are the image of the God who is love. They are the image of God because they are wholly made for love. Thus God set his own image and likeness in creation. He then had no more to do, and so he retired into the rest which is the summit of life, the full achievement of everything. The sabbath, which would later be a lesser symbol of this rest, is a decisive day for us. As we read in the Zohar, the sabbath was not created because of the six days but the six days were created with a view to the sabbath. This rest was not one of idleness but of completeness, when everything was very good. God rests; he ceases to act; he stops creating. But obviously he does not stop being who he is, the Almighty and the Creator. He can always be so afresh. He simply ceases to act.

The fundamental point here is that the the biblical God is not a cause. Though hundreds of theologians have thought so, he is not the supreme cause. In effect a primary and universal cause that functions as such cannot stop. If you think of physical mechanisms in which one thing causes another, the first can never decide to stop. It functions until it wears out or breaks. A cause cannot cease to be a cause without ceasing to be. It must produce its effects to infinity. God is not a cause, then, for we are told that he decides to rest. This divine decision, which takes into account that he had made everything good and that it is all complete, implies his total freedom. This point is not without importance, for if we are in the image of God, then we have been created free. God shows us freedom by deciding to stop. In this way he freely defines the sphere of his activity. But we are thrust into this creation with a function that I would venture to call ontological. We are called upon to love, and in freedom we have the possibility of doing so. But if God decides to stop working, it is also so as not to impede or block the freedom of his creature. This is basic, and it marks the distinction from all other religions. God respects his creature to the point of not acting in order to secure its freedom, including the freedom *not* to love, not to respond to God's love. God retires in order to leave the field free for us. When the break came between God and us, our pure freedom of love changed in nature and became independence or autonomy.

But God still did not suppress this feeble reflection of what had been freedom.

To continue, God enters into rest, leaving it to human beings to manage their patrimony and make their own decisions. But this does not mean that he became absent or indifferent. This was not a retreat into a Nirvana in which the final stage is nothingness, nor was it fusion into some great All. How could that be possible if God is love? God cannot cease to be interested in what becomes of his work. This is why it is so essential that God is not an abstraction or a force but a person. To say that God is a person is not an anthropomorphism but an expression of the fact that God decides and yet at the same time respects the being that is his image. Certainly the statement that God is a person does not tell us clearly who God is in himself. These stories are not trying to tell us who God is in himself but merely to tell us what relation he sets up with us. Their purpose is simply to teach us who God is for us, in relation to us, and with reference to us. All gnosis, all knowledge of God merely for the sake of knowledge of God, is ruled out. The first thing we have to learn is that God for us is a person who gives us freedom and who has entered into his rest.

But this is not the end of the matter. After the seventh day there is certainly nothing more. We see this clearly from the fact that at every stage of creation we are told that there was an evening and a morning. But there is no such statement about the seventh day. There is no eighth day. But this means that the seventh day is not yet over. We thus live on the seventh day. We are set in the rest of God. The whole human adventure that we have tried to sketch, the whole of human history, takes place on the seventh day. I would venture to say that the work of creation continues in this human history. But a tremendous statement is made that might well shake the foundation of many evaluations of human history: "God blessed the seventh day." Let us leave on one side the superficial explanation of exegetes who want to see here no more than a kind of justification of the sabbath — an etiological myth. I believe that there is much more to the story than that. If all human history takes place on the seventh day, if this day is not yet over, if it is ongoing (with the implication that thousands of years of human history, beginning at the end of the sixth day, constitute the seventh day), then all history is set within the blessing of God, for God blessed the seventh day.

This changes our whole outlook. I maintain that neither history nor any event within it makes sense as such, but that this setting of human history within and under God's blessing changes everything. For he blessed this day. He blessed all that takes place on it. We must not forget that blessing means three things. It (1) is a good word, a word of reconciliation, of pardon — good news. But this word also (2) brings salvation and (3) implies an act of kneeling. In Revelation the adoration of the elders and the beasts is accompanied by this same declaration that history is under God's blessing. With all its many disasters and pitiless wars and the collapse of civilizations and the difficulty of launching a new truth or making people listen to words of peace and love, this history is included in the pardon, the act of kneeling, and the salvation that were declared before it began. No matter what might be the beginning or continuation! Hence we have to look at this history in another way.

But this interpretation raises a serious theological difficulty. If all history takes place on the seventh day, and this day is the day when God rests, then God does not make history or himself continue his creation in this history. He does not direct events. His creation is complete. To those who insist that God is behind the events of history, I put the simple question: Where do we place the totality of history? At the end of the sixth day? But this was the day of our creation, of our debut. Between the sixth day and the seventh? No, for the text presents the seventh day as already present, already in being. It is solely in this present, in the reality of the seventh day, that all history takes place. Consequently, if God is at rest, then it is we who have made history, we with our own intentions and possibilities and abilities. History is not a product of God's action. But this seems to challenge what is an almost unanimous idea of theologians: that of providence. In his providence, we are told, God not only knows and foresees all things but combines all things. Every life is directed totally by this providence and every historical movement is in reality an act of God. This idea seems to me to be inaccurate biblically and false theologically. It is a target of anti-

Christian objections: If God does everything, then he does what is evil. Why? If he does everything, he does it badly, for nature and history alike proceed badly.

This idea of providence arises with the logical thinking that tries to establish coherence on the basis of divine omnipotence. It robs human beings of freedom and implicates the freedom of God in the whole venture of creation. I do not believe in providence. If there is such a thing, then God's will is necessarily done in every situation and his rule is incontestable. But what then becomes of the teaching of Jesus that we should pray: "Thy kingdom come, thy will be done"? Why pray for the kingdom to come if it is present already in providence? Why pray that God's will should be done if it is done already in virtue of providence? This prayer shows that God's will is not done, that we seek it, that it is contingent, and that we cannot count on God's intervention in every situation to change it. Praying for God's kingdom and will shows that there is no such thing as providence. The Bible never uses the word or anything equivalent. I know, of course, that some texts suggest it, and we cannot evade them. In Matthew 10:29 we read that not a single sparrow will die without the Father's will. This is the usual translation. But the Greek says simply: "without your Father." It is to make things plain that "will" has been added. But the addition changes the meaning completely. In the one case, God wills the death of the sparrow, in the other death does not take place without God being present. In other words, death comes according to natural laws, but God lets nothing in his creation die without being there, without being the comfort and strength and hope and support of that which dies. At issue is the presence of God, not his will.

Searching further, we come across the saying in Deuteronomy 32:39: "I kill and I make alive." I do not think that this makes every birth and every death a specific act of God. I believe that this statement contains three truths. (1) God is indeed the Lord of life and death because he is the Creator of life and in the face of death he is the power of resurrection. (2) To the degree that all creation plays the game of life and death, he is truly the Lord of all creation. (3) We have here a proclamation of the free omnipotence of God (which the whole passage is teaching), but the reference is to spiritual life and death, not detached from their physical reality, but implying relationship with God. In keeping is the great statement toward the end of Deuteronomy: "I have set before you this day life and good, death and evil. . . . therefore choose life" (30:19). We have here no vision of a providence which causes life or death, but of a free God who does everything that we might live, who points out to us the way, and who exhorts us to live by choosing the good. A final text is found in several places, for example, Ecclesiastes 11:5: "God does all things." But Psalm 115:3 gives us the true meaning: "God does whatever he pleases." This is obviously true. The same applies to the verse at the end of Job (42:2: "I know that thou canst do all things"). The fact that God does all things does not mean that he is the great clockmaker, the mechanic of the universe, nor that his will is a totalitarian will that does not allow a place for any other will. In Ecclesiastes the confession that God does all things is the confession of one who has tried all things in life, who has made all kinds of experiments, who has sought happiness and wisdom in every possible way, and who has come to see that all that we do is vanity of vanity, so that like Job he finally confesses: "As for me, I have not been able to do it. God can do it. I have been able to accomplish nothing, and it is God that does all things." That has nothing to do with providence.

And now the other side of the matter in Scripture: How can we arrive at the idea of providence when we read the story of the Hebrew people in the Old Testament? There is no question here of a set divine plan that God infallibly realizes. On the contrary, we have here a God who intervenes occasionally, raising up a judge or a prophet to accomplish his will. This God modifies his plans and projects according to human wills and decisions. This God repents of the evil that he first meant to do. This God lets himself be deflected by prayer. This God gives constant warnings to the people that this is what will happen if they continue in the evil course that they have adopted, but with the promise that it will all be changed if they change their conduct. In other words, God accompanies us, imposing nothing on us by force, and not doing everything. But we must not fall into the opposite error and think that God is inconsistent, that he does not know what he wants, that he acts haphazardly. In reality the telos, the goal, the end is truly fixed. What we are trying to bring to light is simply God's patience. This patience is not just the fact that he waits for the end of history, letting human beings make their mistakes, tolerating their doing all kinds of things. His patience is an expression of the rest into which he has entered.

God has entered into his rest. Hence he is not to be viewed as providence. Yet he has not abandoned his creation. He does not let things develop and unfold on their own. He is neither absent nor indifferent. Being love, he is passionately linked to this creation which is his and from which he awaits the response. If all had gone well, if human beings had remained wholly in the image of God, if they had given God the assent and love of creation, God's rest would have been complete and things could have gone on by themselves. But with the breach there came about the extraordinary situation that as human beings make their own history, with their folly and pride and their desire to be as God, they trouble God's rest. God is in his rest, but he is constantly disturbed and invoked and drawn in to salvage the venture. God is in his rest, but the human history to which he cannot be indifferent is in no sense a rest. Nothing in creation is rest. All was very good, said God, but at once there began a venture that was not good.

The Bible sets before us God's intervention. He intervenes in this history in two kinds of circumstances. He does so first when human evil reaches a frenzied degree: evil directed against God (idolatry, pride, and self-centeredness), and evil directed against others. When the cup overflows, when humanity passes the limits of tolerable evil, whether tolerable for others or for God, then God acts to set matters straight. The tower of Babel offers the clearest example. God is in his rest, but the building of the city and the tower of Babel is a twofold offense against God, a repetition of the fall of Adam. Thus the text tells us that God "came down to see" (Gen. 11:5). Several exegetes talk about anthropomorphism in this connection, as though God did not know what was happening. But that is not the point. The point is that God is in his rest, and he leaves his rest (comes down) in order to intervene.

He also intervenes, however, when human distress reaches a climax, when misery is so great that the creature that God loves can no longer bear it, and especially when there seems to be no human remedy for the evil, the suffering, the unhappiness, and the distress, when no human means are at hand to deal with it, and there is no hope. This intervention may also occur when, even apart from suffering, people seem to be trapped by a kind of necessity that marches on ineluctably, when they cannot control the power of circumstances, when they are simply being conditioned, for God wants the beings that are still his creatures to have at least enough independence or freedom to be able to turn around and love him. Thus God intervenes, whether to relieve suffering and respond to anguished questions (such as that of Job), or to solve a collective political situation for which there is no human solution. In so doing, God upsets the historical facts in such a way as to replace an implacable situation by a fluid situation in which people can act. God does not reestablish the condition of Eden. He simply enables us to live again. He is constantly waiting for us to recognize him, to recognize him in his love. He thus intervenes occasionally, contingently, and sporadically. Jesus states as much when he says that not all lepers were healed by Elisha (Luke 4:25-27), and not all the blind were cured. He himself certainly did not heal everybody. There is no return to the beginning by a monumental act of God. (This would be to treat us as nonresponsible objects.) Here, then, we have a first essential characteristic of the divine action.

The second is no less important. God rarely acts directly. Events like Babel or the Flood in which he himself intervenes in history are very rare. Most often he sends a human being, one responsible for delivering his word or, at times, displaying his power. This one may be a judge or a prophet or sometimes a king. But it may be a foreign people that manifests his wrath or his justice, or even a foreign king who manifests his kindness and magnanimity, like Cyrus according to the well-known texts which call him God's shepherd and anointed (Isa. 44:28; 45:1). But when God sends a foreign people against Israel, he does not prescribe its acts. This people is not a docile instrument in the hands of a God who organizes everything. God announces that he will raise up the Chaldeans, a violent people that will invade Israel. But he does not approve of this people, saying of them "their own might is their god" (Hab. 1:6-11). We thus find the surprising statement: "Ah, Assyria, the rod of my anger, the staff of my fury . . . against the people of my wrath I command him . . . but it is in his mind to destroy, and to cut off nations not a few" (Isa. 10:5-7). Even nations that God uses to punish Israel are under malediction (Damascus, Edom, and Moab — Amos 1) because they act atrociously, increasing evil and obeying the spirit of power. Hatred and pride have seized hold of them and they have used odious means. Thus, even though they are at first launched by God, God lets them act in their own way, and then turns upon them because they have been guilty of unheard-of wickedness.

God's intervention in human history is complex. Its aim is not that human history should issue in the kingdom of God but that individuals or peoples should recognize that Yahweh alone is God. The same is true on the individual scale. God does not direct our lives. We have no providential guardian angels. We have no direct line to God, and the Holy Spirit does not dictate to us what we must do. But God is always there with us in the silence, and it is a question of faith, knowing that he is present even when we do not experience it, even when we are unhappy; knowing that God is alongside us and for us, that we are not alone even though there is no miracle in reply to deliver us; knowing at every moment that he can indeed intervene when some disaster crushes us or when we are on the point of doing something dreadfully wicked. God is not dumb, or blind, or deaf to the cry of his creatures, though he is also not an automatic dispenser of the graces and privileges and miracles that we demand. The teleology is the same. When Jesus meets a man blind from birth, and his disciples ask him why this man is handicapped in this way, and whether he or his parents sinned that he should be so afflicted, Jesus answers: "It was not that this man sinned, or his parents [the infirmity is not a punishment, it is a result of natural circumstances], but that the work of God might be made manifest in him" (John 9:3). In other words, God's work was not to make him blind but to give him back his sight.

This interpretation, which explains why we might feel abandoned, or experience God's silence, or suffer his inaction, or not see why he seems to be governing the world so badly, is confirmed in both Genesis and the Gospel of John. In Genesis 2:1-3 we have what seems to be an astonishing contradiction. The heavens and the earth were finished, "and on the seventh day God finished his work which he had done, and he rested on the seventh day from all his work." Everything is complete by the seventh day, but it seems that there was still something to do, for we are told that God finished his work on the seventh day. If everything was finished, what need was there to say this? There is indeed duality here, for on the seventh day, the same formula being used in each case, we read that he both finished his work and rested from it. Everything is complete, yet God still did something. God enters into his rest, but he still has something to do. We can understand the contradiction if we accept the contingent action of God whereby he lovingly continues his work (not a work of creation, for creation is not continuous) even though he has entered into his rest. The two facts revealed here are both true. God is no longer the Creator doing new works of creation, but he is always attentive to the doings of the exceptional creature that is called human and that he is able to sanctify. It is precisely because he is resting that he may seem distant (he is present only in Jesus Christ) and silent and perhaps even absent. It looks as if he has abandoned the world, as if there is dereliction.

The relation between this rest of God and his occasional interventions enables us to understand some sayings of Jesus. Thus he says: "The Father who dwells in me does the works" (John 14:10). God's presence on earth is actualized in the person of Jesus Christ. The Father does the works of Jesus that are a witness ("believe at least because of the works that I do"), but a localized and specific witness to God's presence, to his intervention in the world. We also recall the enigmatic saying with which Jesus answered the Jews when he had healed a paralytic and was accused of breaking the sabbath: "My Father is working still, and I am working. . . . The Son can do nothing of his own accord, but only what he sees the Father doing; for whatever he does, that the Son does likewise. . . . As the Father raises the dead and gives them life, so the Son gives life to whom he will" (John 5:17-21). Here we see clearly that God is not the One who does everything, that there is no question of continuous creation, that he acts only in some cases and at specific points. So, too, does the Son, for this action of Jesus was a specific action, and yet he says that all that he sees the Father do, he himself does. Undoubtedly when he says that "my Father is working still" with regard to a single healing, he is not saying tha⸱ ⸱⸱s Father is the supreme cause. He is saying that God works in human hearts and seeks reconciliation, which is achieved in Jesus Christ.

Precisely in saying "reconciliation" (between God and us) we are saying that human beings and their acts and history cease to disturb the rest of God. We are saying that they rediscover their true being in God's image as those who respond to God's love, and God can fully enjoy the rest to which the text refers, when there is on the one side the healing of a sickness and on the other side the reestablishment of the sabbath in its truth. Jesus Christ has suppressed the two things that disturb God's rest. Human history troubles God because it causes terrible human suffering to which God cannot remain indifferent, and also because it engenders a terrible misunderstanding of the being and will of God, which are love. Here are two impossibilities which God cannot tolerate, and this is why he is still working up to the time of Jesus. Why not beyond that time? Because everything was to be restored in Jesus Christ and all misunderstanding was to come to an end in him, since he is the Truth. After Jesus Christ God was again to find untroubled rest. But the Truth has not enlightened all people, and history has pursued its bloody and aberrant course. It is not that what Jesus Christ accomplished has met with a setback. The point is that human beings have found new ways to fight against God. What Jesus Christ accomplished is forever: salvation, pardon, assurance of the love of God, resurrection, and reconciliation. God finds his rest after himself bearing all the demonization of societies, but the work has still to go on with the action of Jesus Christ through those who take up this action and carry it forward ("I am with you always, to the close of the age," Matt. 28:20), and with the action of the Holy Spirit, who constantly begins again what we tear down. We are already in the seventh day, but if everything has already been accomplished, everything has not yet been consummated.

The rest of God—a rest which will not again be challenged or modified—has already been achieved with the reconciliation that has been effected. But oddly this reconciliation is unilateral. God is reconciled to all people, but all people are not reconciled to him. In Christ reconciliation has been made, but people still continue both to accuse God and not to accept that his will is both perfect and benevolent. No matter what our denials may be, our future is that of entering ourselves into this rest. We need to consult a passage in Hebrews: "For we who have believed enter that rest, as he has said: 'As I swore in my wrath, they shall never enter my rest' [referring to Ps. 95:11, which has in view the revolt of the Hebrews after the Exodus from Egypt], although his works were finished from the foundation of the world . . . for whoever enters God's rest ceases from his labors as God did from his. Let us therefore strive to enter that rest, that no one fall by the same sort of disobedience" (4:3-11). This rest, which is acceptance of reconciliation with God and salvation by faith, is promised to everyone, to all creation, and to all humanity. History will reach its goal in this rest by a way that we are completely unable to imagine.

But again we must not reverse things. This rest is not the rest of death. There is much misunderstanding of the requiem that Roman Catholic priests pronounce at funerals. At issue is not the rest of death that the deceased find. Prayer is made that God will enable them to enter into his rest, which is that of accomplishment. For God enters into his rest when he finishes all his works and sees that they are very good. This rest is not a sleep, not an inactivity. It is not passive—it is the fulfillment of love in virtue of this accomplishment. It is not static—it is participation in perfection. What is more, the promised rest is a transvaluation. God has worked, he has created, he has produced a universe. Even if he did it by his word alone, he acted (there being no difference in Hebrew between word and act). His work being finished, the fulness of rest brings to light the primacy of being. God is totally himself when he has created. Creation being finished, he exists in the perfect unity of being.

The promise made to us and our work and history is that of the same transition from doing to being. In the course of our human venture, individual, collective, and total, we have done a great deal. We pass our time in doing. Entering into the rest of God is entering into the fulness of being. Rest is not boredom or satiety. It is the discovery of love finally achieved and realized. It is the amplitude of fulfilled being. This is the point of the placing of all human history on the seventh day.

We do not yet have this rest even in faith, in spite of Hebrews. The fact that faith has to show itself in works is the proof. Furthermore, faith is not constant; it is not the permanent truth of my life. We are thrust into the turmoil of all that there is to do. In order to give us respite from this turmoil, God instituted a day that would enable us to know his own rest. It is a prophetic day, the seventh, the sabbath. The sabbath is very important, and we should not be surprised that the Jews gave it so important a place in their faith and rites. The promised rest of God is actualized here at a point in my life. But we have to receive this gift that is given us. As for God, so for us the sabbath is not a vacation, a day of leisure, or a day of indifference. One of the horrors of our society is to have made Saturday and Sunday into a weekend for all kinds of purposes, and therefore into a time of absence. At this time modern people are simply nonexistent, though they have the impression of existing when they leave work. But true existence comes only with entry into the rest of God. Any other use of the sabbath is in fact the boomerang of a curse. When Saturday and Sunday are used to get away, they become a repeated sign of the curse on Adam when he was chased out of Eden, out of the rest of God.

On the other hand, we must not make of the sabbath a day of legal restraint, of redoubled observance of the divine commandment. I have in mind not merely the minute rules that were progressively created by later Judaism but also the Calvinist understanding which makes Sunday a day of tedium and constraints. I also have in mind the Roman Catholic rule that has made it obligatory, under severe threats, to attend Mass on Sunday. The sabbath is a gift of God to remind us that we are not constantly under the burden of the toil that results from our break with God, and to remind us also of the hope that we shall enter into his rest. It can be received and lived out only in faith. It cannot be authentic otherwise. Either we believe in the truth that God is with us and that he gives us the sign or firstfruits of the great reconciliation, so that we can live out the sabbath in different ways but always in worship and without constraint, or we evade or regulate, and then the sabbath is no more than an inverse sign of what God has promised.

We have to live out the sabbath in all the richness of its meaning. For I do not believe that the sabbath has been annulled by the resurrection. The sabbath and the Lord's day belong together as the end of work and the beginning of life. But to hold fast to the sabbath we need to keep it by finding our own way of life, yet always having in ourselves its threefold symbolical meaning. It tells us first that the condemnation represented by the constraint of work is lifted for a day as it will be at last in eternity. We are no longer under condemnation. Second, it is the promise that we shall enter into the rest of God when history comes to an end with the end of time as God decides. At the heart of our history this sign is set. The rest is for us, and it awaits us. Third, it is the sign of the reconciliation promised and effected in Jesus Christ. One is thus tempted to replace the sabbath by the day of his resurrection. For what was promised has now become reality in this resurrection. But if the fulfillment is real before God, history still goes on and there is an ongoing need to recall the promise as such. Furthermore, if God is reconciled with all of us, a vast majority still does not know it. Thus we need to show them a visible sign of what is promised. The celebration of the sabbath and the Lord's day is a sign to unbelievers, inducing them to receive the promise for themselves. We recognize that the two days have become solemn days for internal use by Jews and Christians and that they do nothing to awaken the desire of unbelievers.

The sabbath in virtue of its three meanings, and the Lord's day in virtue of the resurrection, ought to be marked by two attitudes: freedom and joy. This is a day of great freedom. We are free for a day, and we should act as free people, always in a spirit of adoration and also of joy. It is alarming to see how gloomy Christians look when they worship. Joy ought to be a sign held out to all people that on this day the burden of the world, the constraints of society, and boredom and anguish are all lifted. This is a joy that leads, not to distractions, but to adoration. Are we full of joy that we may worship the Savior in truth? This is our personal question. If so, we can appreciate Jesus' teaching about the sabbath in the Gospels. It is often said that he broke the sabbath laws. I do not believe that he meant to break them. He wanted to make this day a day of joy and freedom, a day of reconciliation and of the presence of God's love. Is not this precisely what he showed us when he healed on the sabbath? Is it not the sovereign freedom of fellowship with the Father that he showed us when he let his disciples eat the ears of grain? "You shall enter into my rest"—let us take this promise with full seriousness, living out the sabbath in the joy of the rest which comes with resurrection and life.

Chapter 13

GOD FOR ME

What can I say? All has been said already, and we know better than other generations that we cannot really talk *about* God, though believers can talk *to* him. All that we say is inadequate, and what point is there in endlessly trying to achieve an equation between the One who is and what I can say about him. The very nature of such an undertaking seems to me to be mistaken. I cannot attempt a philosophical discourse because I am not a philosopher and have no philosophical instrument by means of which to engage in a profound exploration. Nor is there any point in apologetics. Why try to prove that God exists? Even if we managed to do so, who would be led thereby to a knowledge of the living God? Why and for whom should we engage in apologetics? What is the point? To prove that God exists as some kind of object is simply to cause people to think of him merely as an object. But surely we see that this is precisely what God is not, at least the God to whom the Bible bears witness. I do not see how I can present a defensive apologetics or become an advocate for God, justifying what he does. I know that it is God who justifies me and us. He has no need of an advocate. He can defend himself very well. Nor can I focus on my own experiences of God. I dislike talking about my relations with the God in whom I believe. I find testimonies quite intolerable, since it is finally the self that emerges as the hero of the exceptional experience. I contrast firmly such outward displays with the reserve of Paul, who merely alludes to his spiritual experiences and says little about his intimate relation with the Savior, letting others do it for him. To make a parade of these experiences is ultimately to talk about oneself and not to bear witness to God. Even St. Augustine did not avoid this.

I must say first that it is infinitely easier to say what God is not for me. He is certainly not the being decked out with qualities the reverse of my own nature: impassible, immutable, eternal, omnipotent, etc. All that is simply a mirror image. Nor is he the being decked out with human qualities that I value, but carried to the absolute. For one thing, I have no conception of what "absolute" means. Absolutely righteous, holy, free, authentic—I do not know at all what these things might mean. I am too much tied to history to have any idea of the absolute, and what I know about justice or freedom prevents me from tacking on to them the adverb "absolutely." It is not anthropomorphism that restrains me here but the simple inability to understand what I would be saying. Perhaps I am too much influenced by Feuerbach, but a human image absolutized or invested with all that the human cannot contain seems suspect to me. Above all, it does not interest me, whether from a spiritual, an intellectual, or a human standpoint. It makes no difference to me if God is impassible or absolutely righteous. The traditional approach that finds in God a supreme cause or creative force also leaves me in the same state of coldness and indifference. I am not concerned about anything that has to do with the God of the philosophers. To my great shame I admit that I have never been able to read Spinoza. He does not interest me.

At the other extreme, God is not what mystical or sentimental exuberance describes as love, life, spirit, etc. I certainly do not want to say that God is not love for me, or that he is not the force behind life, or that he is not spirit, but I distrust any reversal of such statements. If we say that love is God, we can hardly evade Cupid. During the past twenty years we have seen among young people how incredibly dangerous such a formula can be. Similarly, to say that life is God is to introduce a banal pantheism. Neither the love that we know, nor life and its various forces, nor spirit as we can lay hold of it in some form, can be equated with God. The God in whom I believe assumes these things in fullness and totality but is not assimilated to them. The love that I know in the world gives me a fleeting reflection of him whom I call God, a parable, but only on the condition that

I do not go on to make an identification. The same applies to the joy of a birth or the wonder of a spiritual activity.

Finally, God is not the celebrated God of the gaps. On this view, when we cannot explain certain phenomena, to satisfy ourselves we refer to God, making him the explanation or cause or reason that we cannot find elsewhere. God is thus an easy temporary replacement until we find the real explanation, which will, of course, be scientific. This kind of procedure is stupid. I see nothing of it in the Bible, absolutely nothing along these lines. It is also presumptuous to think that science answers the questions that people are asking when they talk about God. This is the attitude of an ignorant and arrogant scientism, certainly not that of real scientists. An interesting point to note is that at the very time when science is recognizing its own limits, some theologians, a half-century behind as usual, are going the way of scientific triumphalism, explaining that God's domain has been terribly reduced as a result of the glorious progress of science. The tendency here is to make of God no more than a vague spiritual essence, or in any case something different from what science might eventually come across. In other words, God is totally detached from the reality of the world and reduced to an insubstantial vapor. To save him they repress him. For me God is certainly not the God of the gaps.

In conclusion, I want to say that this whole undertaking is impossible as I see it. For me God cannot be described or displayed or demonstrated. Thus what can I say? Yet I have promised to attempt the impossible, and I will present some reflections along two lines.

I

My first reflections revolve around the central conviction that I cannot have a single coherent image of God. I cannot say at a given moment that God is simply this or that for me. He is, but he is also other things at the same time which may finally be the opposite. I cannot attempt a synthesis or reconciliation between the different elements in what I believe I can understand about God. I thus renounce here any attempt at intellectual coherence.

In my thinking there are three different levels. The first is that of what I have learned intellectually about God, the result of the work of theologians and the evolving consensus of the church. Jesus is the incarnation of God, true God and true man. God is the Creator. God is Three and One. He reveals himself progressively. He intervenes in history. He creates new heavens and a new earth. There is nothing original here, but it corresponds to a great truth. I am aware of the linguistic problems that arise, but they do not trouble me. Most of the questions that are put on the matter are false questions. As for the rest, we are wrong to think them new. The problem of the adequacy of language has harassed theologians from the very first, as we see from the debate between Eunomius and Gregory of Nyssa or the dispute about universals. We have made few innovations, and the formulation of the thinking of the church has gone on in spite of all the difficulties. We cannot presume to set aside the knowledge of God handed down by the church. Nor can we have the feeling that it is of no direct concern to us today. Arguments that suggest as much, for example, the anthropomorphism of its definitions, their strictly cultural character (inasmuch as they express the beliefs of a given culture that another culture cannot assimilate), or their dependence on this or that philosophy, seem to me to be weak and superficial. Without going into detail, I would simply say that after serious and profound study of all these critical systems, I have concluded that none of them is convincing or can sway my own convictions. To want to change a name or representation is of little interest. To say that we must not think of God up there because he is down here is simply to ask for a change of signpost. To talk of the ultimate or the unconditioned (which seems to me to be exactly the same thing as the classical ingenerate) is no doubt not incorrect, but it is also no more true than to talk of the eternal or the absolute. I thus accept with little difficulty the teaching of church fathers and theologians, at least those who have produced the traditional teaching of the church.

But can I stop there and receive this deposit of the faith (in spite of the scandal this formula represents today) as adequate and well packaged? For two reasons I have to say, not that everyone was wrong up to the present day, nor that this

way of thinking about God is historically outdated, nor that it
is idealistic and hence does not concern us, but that I cannot
stop there and merely accept it. My first reason is simple: if God
is God, he obviously cannot be totally known or circumscribed
or put into a human formula. There is always something more
to know and understand and receive. All theologies and all
knowledge of God will always fall short. It is a commonplace
of theology that the finite cannot contain the infinite. My second reason is different: if God is the God of Jesus Christ, he
demands of me a personal decision because he has set up a personal relation. This personal decision presupposes action on my
part, including intellectual action. I cannot spare myself the
trouble of facing up to this revelation of God, of trying to express in my own way what this personal relation to God entails. Not being wholly satisfied with what the church's tradition teaches about God, I have to go my own way and try to
think out the question for myself.

Concerning the second level of reflection upon God, I am
at once inhibited by something that many theologians have come
up against, and this is perhaps because I belong to my age and
setting. The point is that if God is God, I cannot know anything
about him on my own, and even less can I say anything about
him. God is the Wholly Other. If he were not, he would not be
God. If he is, I cannot even conceive of what is at issue. Since
my process of acquiring knowledge is tied to what is familiar, he
is truly unknowable. I have neither the right nor the ability to
manipulate him in such a way as to be able to know him. What
I might say on the subject does not concern God.

We are back to the problem of name. In his own revelation God reveals himself as the One whom we cannot name.
To be able to pronounce the sacred tetragrammaton I vocalize
it. This enables me to pronounce the word, but the word is not
really the name of God. It is just another thing of which I am
capable. A way which seems to me to be completely invalid is
the analogical way. Based on the declaration that we are made
in God's image, a whole theological trend has thought that we
can infer God's own reality from what may be said about us.
This view is reinforced by the statement that Jesus is the full,
perfect, and sufficient image of God. Now we should at least

distinguish between these two statements. In the first, we run
into a twofold difficulty. On the one hand, there has after all
been a break between God and us. Does the image of God still
remain after this break, or has the break been so total that nothing remains intact and unscathed, so that we cannot stride across
the gulf and act as though there is analogy between God and
us? On the other hand, can we believe that everything in us is
in God's image, and if not, can we say what is? The insoluble
nature of these two questions invalidates all research based on
an analogical method. But this approach, common in the Middle
Ages, has now been replaced by the affirmation that Jesus is
true God, that all that we can know about God is in Jesus (he
and the Father are one), and that we have only to look at Jesus
to know who God is.

From these true propositions the transition is smooth to the
further proposition that it is useless to talk about God or to pose
the question of God. God is not in the sky. He is nowhere except in Jesus. Jesus alone is before us. At the same time, Jesus is
reduced to an exemplary man. Now if the statement that Jesus is
God is basic for me, I can neither accept the reduction to exemplary humanity nor be content with agnosticism concerning the
One whom Jesus calls his Father. For there again the difficulty is
insoluble. Jesus undoubtedly says that those who have seen him
have seen the Father, but in that very place and with those very
words he presupposes, not the suppression of the Father, but his
distance from us. He is not saying that there is no Father nor telling his disciples not to bother about him but to remain peacefully
agnostic on the subject. The Father is he who fully reveals himself in Jesus, but it is a matter of his revelation and not his replacement. The Father himself encounters us in Jesus. The same
Father has designated Jesus as the Messiah.

The difficulty that we cannot avoid is this: What does
Jesus reveal of God? Those for whom Jesus is simply a good
man, a complete man, a politician, a liberator of the people and
the poor, simply suppress this difficulty. But in so doing they
suppress Christianity itself, for why should people passionately
attach themselves to this interesting historical personage called
Jesus? He was just one of the many religious heroes and no
more. In the Middle Ages scholars debated the difficulty in the

form of the problem of the two natures. What is finally of God in Jesus? This is just as unanswerable a question as the question: Who or what is God? But Jesus teaches us at all events that God is the Father. Thus I believe that we hold two links of the chain, even though it plunges down into the darkness. On the one side God is indeed unknowable. He is beyond anything that we can understand or be. He is completely hidden. He is truly the Wholly Other about whom I can say nothing. But on the other side he is the Father, and I can play here a Barthian game (which after all I find very satisfying) and say that as the Wholly Other he is the Father and as the Father he is the Wholly Other.

Nevertheless, a Christian who is accustomed to consulting the Bible cannot stop there. For if the route of an intellectual return to God is closed, we are nourished by the idea that this God who is hidden from our efforts, to whom we have no access, still reveals himself to us. He discloses something about himself when he intervenes. Certainly he is never known face-to-face. He is never known except by his free decision to unveil himself here and now. We never know his being or its depths. What we can grasp of this revelation is never constant. God reveals himself here and now as the need arises in a given human situation. There is thus no metaphysical unveiling (we never grasp the being of God), nor can we add up the fragments which God has revealed, now to one and now to another, and which we can receive only as parts of a puzzle. We often try to put these pieces together, but to do so shows that we have not understood the revelation at all, for it means that we are again trying to grasp the being of God when all that he has given us to see is simply his intervention. Moses did not see God in the burning bush. He saw the burning bush and knew that it was a sign that God was speaking to him. In revelation, then, we recognize the signs that God is speaking to us, the works that he has done. There is nothing more illuminating than this continually repeated situation. When God is there, when he acts in our lives, our society, or our group, we do not know or feel anything special. It is only afterward, when God's work is done, that looking back we can say: "But it was God who was at work, it was he who changed the situation, it was he who passed by," just as we read that Moses and Elijah saw God's back (cf. Exod. 33:23; 1 Kgs. 19:11) when he had passed by.

Thus God in his revelation does not satisfy our intellectual curiosity. He cannot be put together again in human knowledge on the basis of his intervention. He is this or that to this or that person according to the historical circumstances. Nothing can guarantee what he is in himself. This is why we see him reveal himself in what seem to be contradictory ways. Thus he is the God of thunder who makes the mountains tremble when he comes down to the earth. But he is also an indescribably light breath which passes by for Elijah after all the catastrophic events. He is the Almighty who yet chooses the way of total weakness, the being that elects to die. God does not reveal himself like an object that one might unveil. He does so as the One who intervenes at the heart of our lives and history. We cannot infer his being from this intervention.

Nevertheless, one has to move to another level. I have in mind the God of Pascal whom we know in the heart. Incontestably, apart from the way of intellectual knowledge, there is the God that I sense to be present in my life, acting and revealing himself on another level than that of the intellect. Is this mystical? I know nothing about that. What I know for certain is that this God is not to be confused with a phantom, an imagination, an illusion, a psychoanalytical projection. We feel God in the heart, but this God is known in my concrete life and not in ecstasy. In my experience, then, it is not a matter of *ek-stasis* but of the very opposite. This God does not make me take leave of myself. He comes for a moment into the life that is mine and modifies and reorients it. He produces what I certainly am not, but what I may become in virtue of this intervention. Naturally God cannot be reduced to my experience of God, and he certainly cannot be proved by my experience. The formula of Frossard: "God exists, I have met him," is stupid. I do not question Frossard's experience. But the meeting is strictly ineffable and there is nothing else to back it up—no proof or demonstration. We can testify only to what Scripture presents to us, not to our own experience. It is possible to have an existential relation that is strictly incommunicable. Yet we know also—this is the problem—that this God speaks and that we are gripped by a word of God. If there is word, there is communication, and there is thus the possibility of communicating the same word to others. Unfortunately, then, we have to reject that simple proof.

The revelation is not for me a matter of mystical contemplation. It is more like what many of us are familiar with; a word suddenly becomes so true to us that we can no longer doubt it. We know well how astonishing this experience can be. I read in the Bible texts that I have read a hundred times, that I know by heart, that are part of my objective knowledge of the biblical God, and suddenly the word that I know so well intellectually takes on an unexpected significance, a blinding force that constrains me from now on to accept it as truth, as a truth at once comprehensible, irrational, and rigorously certain. At this moment I can do nothing to challenge or reject it. It is suddenly placed at the core of my life. But I cannot transmit this experience as such. I cannot tell how the biblical text has become truth for me. I cannot offer any proof or guarantee. I do not know whether it is God's plan that the same word should become truth for someone else. I can bear witness only to what has happened. If I cannot communicate, what is the significance of this word that God speaks and of the fact that God himself is Word?

God is said to speak because in Hebrew the word is not distinct from the deed, because it evokes and provokes and literally creates something new. Thus the Word means more than it does for us today. It cannot be reduced to mere discourse. It is not absorbed into oral language, though it also adopts this language. This fact guarantees its absolute freedom, protecting it against linguistic analysis and also ruling out any facile idea of a translation of this Word into our words, any idea that we can hear it according to the laws of discourse and thus put it into the same form. The God in whom I believe is not the God who — to simplify — whispers words in the ears of a prophet that the prophet then has to repeat aloud. He is indeed the Word, the creative Word, always creating new situations, but he is a Word that is not the prisoner of linguistics and has nothing in common with our words. Human language can encircle this revelation on all sides but it cannot exhaust it or give a strict account of it. The Word is the designation of him who is unnamed.

Here at once is contradiction. He who remains hidden speaks to my heart. He convinces me and sets me in his new creation. Interpreting, I understand the words of this new birth, but they are not my words. I can tell only what God has done for me, not who or what he is. I can look back on the way in which he has directed my life, but I cannot deduce from this either his being or his future interventions. I see very well that he structures what I know and that he himself does not enter into any structure. His presence forces me out of my own categories. Undoubtedly, I cannot remain silent, but if it is possible to witness directly to what God does in this history and to what he enables me to discern in order to get beyond it, I have to talk in an indirect way. I use myth or parable or poetry. I have to adopt the dialectical method to be able to give an account of this contradictory totality that reveals itself to me as God. My approach in language can never be fixed. I can never stop at any moment and say: "God is there," or: "God is this." The God whom I feel in my heart can never be indicated except in parable or myth. He cannot be denoted in a descriptive or intellectual way. Conversely, if I offer a parable, of what or of whom is it a parable? Of the God who reveals himself to me in the totality of my life, the God of Jesus Christ who is the same, the God whom Jesus Christ shows to me in fulfillment of the Law and the Prophets, the God whom he shows to be in some sort the relation that exists between being, love, life, and word, and all that this symbolizes of freedom, ineffability, proximity, power, communication, and authenticity.

These three levels of apprehension that I have tried to sketch, the God taught in the church's tradition, the God whom I try to understand and whose revelation I try to hear, and the God whom I feel in my heart, are not identical, and yet there is a certain relation among them, for it is the same God who offers himself to me for adoration and who gives himself to my incredulity as he puts to me the question of my life.

There is at this moment in France a big movement to bring together, to set in dialogue, to assimilate, and finally to merge all monotheistic believers, that is, Jews, Christians, and Muslims. It is stated emphatically that what characterizes these three religions is that they are all in some sense locked into one another in opposition to all the world's other religions, for they all refer to one single, universal, and all-powerful God, the same God. The widespread view is that they believe in the same God under different names, Adonai Elohim for Jews, Theos-Christos for Christians, and Allah (which is close to Elohim) for Muslims. God is finally the same, and therefore they should unite.

This analysis is wrong on every count. First, in regard to the exclusiveness of monotheism, these three religions do not have a monopoly of it. It has often been noted that in what are called polytheistic religions, though the gods take specific forms, there finally reigns an indefinite, unnamed, and mysterious spirit. Among the Greeks, the powers above the gods are Chronos, Ouranos, and then Fate (sometimes Ananke). Even more secret is the power above the gods in Egyptian religion, the Unnamed with whom no relations are possible but who seems to dominate all things. In many religions of the North American Indians an indefinable spirit rules on whom all things also depend. One cannot say that these religions are monotheistic, but we should perhaps moderate our pride in this matter. I do not even mention Akhenaton's attempt at monotheism.

My second and even more serious point is this: Can we really say that monotheism is the essential and central feature of the Christian revelation? It is the great merit of Moltmann to have reminded us in this time of theological confusion that Christianity is trinitarian before it is monotheistic.[1] The Trinity is really the distinctive characteristic of Christianity. One God indeed, but the great objection of Jews and Muslims to Christianity is that it is not strictly monotheistic, since in their view Christians worship three Gods. From the days of the church fathers theologians have debated endlessly in an attempt to reconcile the oneness of God with the threeness of the Trinity (one God in three Persons). But if we lay primary stress on monotheism, we forget that the revelation in Christ is primarily trinitarian. The stakes are serious, for to stress monotheism is to make Jesus Christ secondary. But if we maintain that Jesus Christ alone reveals who God is, that he alone teaches us the

---

1. See Jürgen Moltmann, *The Trinity and the Kingdom*, trans. Margaret Kohl (New York: Harper & Row, 1981).

love of God, that he alone is the image of God, that he alone
makes a covenant between God and us, that he alone is our salvation through his death, that he alone is our hope through his
resurrection, that he alone is the truth, then other monotheists
regard us as polytheists. If we want to engage in a pleasant dialogue, if we want to appear to be people of goodwill, if we are
ready for agreement on a common basis, we shall have to set
Jesus Christ aside. We shall just have to stop being Christians.
The Trinity is not a matter of theological accommodation to difficult problems. It is not a human invention. It belongs to the
very essence of the biblical revelation. Creation by the Father,
the incarnation of the Son, and transfiguration by the Spirit are
the architecture of revelation. Moltmann was right when he
even went so far as to say that monotheism engenders authori-
tarianism and totalitarianism both ecclesiastically and politically.
Trinitarian thinking ensures at the same time both divine and
human liberty.

These harsh statements do not necessarily involve a break
with the Jews, even though they naturally cannot recognize
Jesus as the Messiah and the Son of the Father. Although Jewish
thought centers on the one God ("Hear, O Israel, Yahweh is
one God, the only One"—Deut. 6:4), we also find the Word of
God. This God is Word. We find, too, the Wisdom of God and
the Spirit of God. In the relevant texts each seems to have its
own specificity. I am not saying that each is God, but each is in
some sense hypostatized. The Spirit of God breathes into the
dead bodies in Ezekiel's vision (Ezek. 37). The Word of God
was scarce at certain times. Both Word and Spirit are "of God,"
yet each has its own role and individuality, and the two cannot
be simply equated. Similarly, the Son is inseparable from the
Father ("I and the Father are one"—John 10:30), and the Spirit
proceeds from the Father and the Son, and yet they are one
God. I am not saying that everything is identical here. Indeed,
some elements in the Old Testament revelation might be cited
in opposition. Nevertheless, there is at least a possibility of understanding and cooperation between Jews and Christians, for
they believe in the same God.

The same thing is not possible with Islam. It is ridiculous
to say that Islam recognizes Jesus because it admits that he is

the last of the great prophets. The real question is whether he is the Son of the Father, God of God, God incarnate in love. Muslims are self-consistent. Such ideas are all unthinkable for them. There is no ground on which there might be agreement and understanding. An even more important point is that the God of Islam has nothing in common with the God of Jesus Christ. Theologians no longer make this identification in their desire to accept Islam and find points in common. Muslims have pushed to an extreme the idea of exclusive monotheism: Allah is a radically and absolutely self-sufficient God. He is everything; he needs nothing; one can add nothing to him. Creation is neither useful nor necessary. Allah is imperturbable and immutable. He does his will with no consideration for anyone or anything. Thus the only possible attitude in face of him is total submission. We should never forget that Islam means submission —blind and unlimited obedience. When something happens, the only human response is: "It is written." Certainly, Allah is merciful, but we should not forget how much abstract distance and sovereignty there is here. A dictator can be merciful when he pardons those under condemnation.[2] Allah is the direct opposite of the God of Abraham and Jesus Christ, who is love above all things, and to whom creation is indispensable because he is not content merely to love himself. Undoubtedly this God is transcendent, but he is also present in all human history to be with us. Because he is love, he hears our prayers and joins with us in the adventure that I have sketched. Because he is love, he suffers from our sin. We need to read the fine passages in Moltmann on the passion of God, on the divine anxiety, on the tragedy of God, to see to what extent God is devoted to us, is unable to think of being without us, does not want to be able to be thought of as being without us. He has nothing in common with the gods to whom he has often been assimilated, the gods of total arbitrariness, supreme indifference, and cruelty. We cannot bridge the gulf between the God of the Koran and the God of the Bible.

2. It is strange that Christians who hate the term *charity* because it denotes the distance and superiority of those who exercise it are the very ones who want at all costs to reach an agreement with Muslims without seeing that the merciful Allah is exercising "charity."

My opposition to Islam does not relate to some peripheral matter. It relates to the very cornerstone of the building. To want to make Jesus Christ the greatest of the prophets is not to have understood the gospel at all. Jesus cannot have been the prophet of Allah. In our monotheistic fraternization we are making exactly the same blunder as we do when we translate Elohim by Theos, which carries with it the whole of Greek mythology. At this point we have to cry an absolute halt. We can engage in dialogue, but we can make no concessions either on the deity of Jesus Christ or on the nature of God as love.

II

I must now look at another aspect of my understanding or convictions. My approach will be quite different from that which precedes. I will not be talking about attempts at knowledge or about experience. I will be starting with the situation, not my own but that of the world in which I live, of our technological society and collective venture. How is the God of promise, the God of the successive promises fulfilled and at the same time renewed in Jesus Christ, how is this God present in this history? The question is neither theological nor abstract, but existential. It is not a political problem (God present through the poor or revolutionaries, for example). That seems to me to be superficial and mechanistic, in spite of appearances. At issue is a hypothesis on the basis of knowledge of our technological society, that is, from the standpoint of the situation into which we have come.

If we realize what the technological system is, then we have to think of it as encompassing everything. On the one side it is a totality. On the other side it grasps, modifies, and qualifies all aspects of human life, social, political, and intellectual, all human relations including artistic research, and it transforms them into something else. It finally absorbs, subsumes, and assimilates all that arises outside it. All opposing acts and ideas finish up being put in the service of the technological system and finding their place in it. The technological system encompasses all things totally, ineluctably, and invincibly.

Now if spiritually, in "religion," we are ready to be brought solely into a horizontal relation (along the lines of Feuerbach), this has some important implications. First, we have no point of reference by which to pass judgment on the system. We cannot refer to Jesus of Nazareth, for he was a model only for a traditional society and not for a technological society and has nothing in common with what we know. He cannot be a model or a point of reference, nor can he be an inspiration to us. In its global character, the technological system excludes what is prior to it, making it completely unimportant and obsolete. In our day it absorbs everything outside it, making it part of the system. This is what is happening to Third World countries. This is their new form of slavery. No external reference can exist, least of all the life and conduct of Christians.

Second, if we cling to the hypothesis of atheistic Christianity, there can be no possibility of criticism. If no external point of reference is imaginable, there can be no view of the system except from within. Hence one cannot criticize it according to different criteria. All studies take place within the system from the very outset. There is no possibility of criticism either in the sense of questioning or in that of distancing oneself. To be able to criticize one has to be outside what one criticizes. Self-criticism means obviously that outward thinking affects one and forces one to put questions. There is needed something to rest on, a scale of values, an instrument of external analysis, to make criticism possible. A surgeon in diagnosing and treating a tumor has to be outside the patient. But the technological system rules out any other scale of values. Being global, it will not allow any other point of view. It renders all such inoperable. It takes over the instruments of analysis and criticism and advances the classical dilemma: Either you want them to be effective, and if so they will have to be technological, being part of the system and strengthening it even as they criticize, or they will be nontechnological and for that very reason ineffective and useless.

The third consequence, if we continue to accept the theory of the death of God, is that there is no exit or outcome for this world, whether in its actuality or in its historicity. The only possibility is to take the technological path. No other life is possible. The hippie experience is a recurrent phenomenon with no other meaning. One cannot open up this world from within to something else. Technology has subjugated everything and closes itself off progressively. It becomes quite literally the equivalent of fate, of Ananke, of destiny: on the one hand it allows no variation; on the other hand it seeks totality indefinitely even in its contradictions (and there are, of course, thousands of contradictions within it, but they all promote its progress). No future hope is possible. Everything is determined by the play of the technological system. I am not saying that this system functions well but that it alone functions. It may lead to disaster, but nothing can stop it functioning. One can envision only two eventualities. On the one side it functions badly, chaos ensues, and everything is destroyed in practice because of the very globality of the system. On the other side it functions well, and one can imagine the equivalent of the best of all possible worlds, but with an equally disastrous result, for what it produces will not be a kind of artificial paradise, stabilized and normalized, but real entropy, which in turn leads to a second degree of chaos. Both these consequences are tightly linked to the global character of the technological system. There can be no other hope for the future. Here, then, are the three implications of horizontal theology.

If hope is still possible, if there is a possibility of humanity continuing, if there is any meaning in life, if there is an outcome other than suicide, if there is a love that is not integrated into technique, if there is a truth that is not useful to the system, if there is at least a taste, a passion, a desire for freedom, and a hypothesis of freedom, then we have to realize that these can have their basis only in the transcendent, and specifically in the transcendent as it is disclosed in Christianity, that is, in the Transcendent who reveals himself in such a way that human beings can comprehend and receive him, the Transcendent who speaks in the Word but who is nonetheless transcendent for so doing. A pure transcendent that cannot be known, that is the object of negative theology, is nonexistent for us. Even if such a transcendent intervenes it is only as a deus ex machina. But what Jesus Christ reveals to us is not just the example of Jesus of Nazareth, or his permanent presence among the poor, but the Transcendent who has drawn near to us. Classical and commonplace theology? Certainly, but there is no other. All other theological discourse is reduced to zero by technique. The Transcendent, however, is outside and cannot be assimilated. Thus, no matter how far the technological system extends, he alone can furnish us with a point of reference, a viewpoint, a different critical apparatus. He alone can enable us to mount a critical operation in relation to the system. He alone can prevent us from being entangled in the dilemmas of technique on the one side and its moral evaluations on the other. All this is not guaranteed, of course, nor is it given in advance. It is not easy. At this level of analysis we cannot expect the Transcendent to intervene as such. It is we that have to act. But there is at least the possibility that our intervention may take place—the intervention without which human action cannot be rescued from global encirclement. At this level, then, the Transcendent does not act but is a condition of our action to arrest global encirclement. He is the presupposition without which there can be no concept of anything external to modern technique.

In effect we have to recall here what we said very summarily about dialectic. Dialectic expresses the movement of life itself and is indispensable for history. But if technique becomes fully global and there is no transcendent, no dialectic is possible. But if there is no dialectic, there is no history, and thus human life will be no more than a meaningless passing of time, and we shall finally be back in a cyclical system. We shall see later why this is impossible in Christian thinking. Those who from a philosophical or theological standpoint hold the contrary view, or rather do not in fact ask this question or see its important implications, simply show that they have no conception of what the reality of the technological environment is today.

It might be objected, however, that the God who is necessarily transcendent in this situation is not very different from the gods of nature when nature was our human environment. At that time, too, people needed a transcendent deity that would enable them to combat nature, to have a point of reference regarding it, and to achieve the certainty that they could survive in this hostile world and master it. Two preliminary observations must be made regarding this objection. First, the technological environment is an artificial one. It is abstract by design.

Hence the transcendent God has to be consciously heard and clearly recognized as such. He has also to be universal and not specific. Second, the technological system, precisely as a human creation, comes from within humanity; thus it demands heart allegiance and works out means of taking inner possession, manipulating people from within as they were never manipulated before in the whole course of history. Being part of the natural world was spontaneous and direct, but today being part of the technological world is produced by techniques of transformation, so that an equivalent of the ancient gods of nature would not be adequate. What is needed is a transcendent that is genuinely transcendent and is not just believed to be so by us, a transcendent that is not the product of the human brain or heart; otherwise, he would be no more than a reflection of the technological system itself. The gods of nature, which were viewed as transcendent, were themselves a reflection of the natural world. The God of Israel was not. He was truly different from all the rest. This same God, being transcendent, is not in the least coincident with the technological environment either, because he is not the product (even a product necessary and indispensable to human survival) of the human heart or human thought. He alone can act to save us at this time.

But there is a second line of reflection. We have said that the Transcendent has also to be he who reveals himself, who gives himself to be known. Thus we do not have here a transcendent hypothesis that we ourselves set up in order to have an external point of reference from which criticism is possible. It is not the case that, seeing criticism to be necessary, we have given ourselves the means to achieve it in the same way as the geometrician sets a point outside a figure in order to have a point of reference (though it may be forgotten in such a comparison that the geometrician is not actually in the figure). On such a view, the transcendent would be no more than a human hypothesis. But at the end of the preceding discussion we noted that the transcendent, to play such a role, cannot be a mere fiction or hypothesis that will fade from view once the conclusion is known. Necessarily in the movement of revelation we are in the presence of a transcendent that acts and yet that is also self-existent. Because he reveals himself, this world can never be a closed reality. It cannot find fulfillment in itself or shut itself up in a total system.

The technological system comes under the historical law of Babel. This was a city meant to enclose the whole race and its gods. It was a universal city. It had no place for the transcendent. The walls of Babel were meant to shut out God, or to leave him only a gate. But just because God is the God who reveals himself, he says: "Let us go down and see," and Babel collapses. God opens it up from outside. In the same way, as without choice we have to continue in a movement toward the perfecting and developing and improving of the technological system, and as we therefore have to continue closing up the system that holds us captive, finding no opening, no break from within, behold, we receive the assurance from him who cannot be swallowed up or assimilated that he will come down and see. If we hear this word, and if we believe in the God of Jesus Christ, the transcendent Father who has already come, we can find a hope and live out a hope no matter what may be the situation of the world in which we are. An opening is always possible. Thus meaning can be received, discovered, and given. A different history is possible from that of technicizing, of our immersion in the technological world. This will be a history that is no longer automatic and necessary. It is one that we can invent, and it will not issue in disaster of any kind. Because a transcendent can effectively reverse the data, it is possible for us to make our own history without being radically defined or circumscribed, without being carried headlong by fate. This is the only guarantee and the only possibility.

But is not this a deus ex machina that intervenes from outside to resolve things? Is it not the God of the gaps that we set in this transcendent sphere because we cannot solve our own problems, making it his job to solve them for us? The equation is tempting but impossible. All theologies that refer God back to this world are in reality ideologies conforming to this world's sociology. Why is it that they find no place for the Father God, the unheard-of Transcendent, the Creator, him who can intervene with miracles and mighty works, and his vertical purpose? Exclusively (i.e., to the exclusion of any other reason or ground) because the technological system convinces us that there is nothing outside itself. This subject would involve us in another line of research: What is the status, role, and function of theology in a technological society? I have touched on this incidentally in some of my books,[3] but a systematic study is needed. It would show that this modern theology is an exact reflection of technique, an ideological product which is designed to help it fulfill itself, close itself off, perfect itself. To affirm a transcendent over against technique is the way of nonconformity today, of not being conformed to the present age. This is what is required of us.

A final point is that this Transcendent is not a deus ex machina or a God of the gaps because, as we well know, he reveals himself, he manifests himself in sovereignty, by a free and in our view contingent action and not one that is obligatory or under the constraint of any necessity. In other words, even if we fully believe in this Transcendent, we have no guarantee of his existence. No liberation intervenes automatically. He *can* intervene. Moreover, all that we know of him in Jesus Christ is that he loves his creation, his creatures, and that he comes to liberate and to save. We believe that he will intervene, and if we live in this hope we ourselves are moved to act in this love. Our own action is undoubtedly at issue; it is not enough to have the purely subjective conviction about a transcendent. The subjectivity of faith will not suffice. It cannot replace the objectivity of the Transcendent. I will not enter into the debate between Barth and Bultmann. This debate can go on forever at the philosophical level, but we are not doing philosophy here.

I would like to take up the objection that Marx had against the young Hegelians. He said that when they think that revolution by idea is revolution, and attack private property on the philosophical level, they end up with an idea of revolution and destroy an idea of property, but the economic and legal reality of private property is untouched and the condition of those who are exploited is not changed at all. In the same way, we do not have here a phenomenon that is purely subjective. The technological system is terribly objective and real and external to us.

3. See, e.g., Jacques Ellul, *The New Demons*, trans. C. Edward Hopkin (New York: Seabury, 1975).

This and not our idea of it is what we have to master or combat in a given case. The idea of a transcendent reduced to my faith, of a risen Lord who lives only in the heart of his disciples (and in ours), may give us a desire to act but not the possibility of doing so. I will have an impression of being liberated but no more. What is at issue here is a Transcendent who intervenes objectively, effectively, and in person. But only the possibility is at issue. He is not bound to intervene.

When we read the biblical account of the early stages of the liberation of the people of Israel from Egypt, we see in fact that God was silent for many centuries between Joseph and Moses, and many generations of his chosen people had to weep and cry and pray and suffer, not understanding why God did not come, but then one day God remembered, one day he turned to Israel, one day—we do not know why. There is no historical certainty and nothing mechanical about this decision. We are faced with our own problems and struggles. But faith believes that God will finally make his sovereign decision. It rests on knowledge of the fulfillment of his promises. It rests on the reality of his presence in Jesus Christ (the presence of the Transcendent in Jesus Christ, without which he would be no more than an interesting example of a certain ideal of humanity). This kind of faith enables us to live because the game is not yet over, and the game is not yet over because the Transcendent himself may intervene. Into this openness, this "play" between the pieces of the puzzle, I can insert myself as a living person. Thus the Transcendent is the Creator of something new within the technological system itself, and this new thing is the effective hope that he generates. But this is in truth an external creative act. It is not a spontaneous natural production of my belief and ideology. Those who do not accept the Transcendent as the final reality beyond our knowledge and experience have to admit that there is no future apart from technique's end, in every sense of the term, and this includes the end of humanity, in the sole sense of its termination.

Chapter 14

UNIVERSAL SALVATION

I am taking up here a basic theme that I have dealt with elsewhere but which is so essential that I have no hesitation in repeating myself. It is the recognition that all people from the beginning of time are saved by God in Jesus Christ, that they have all been recipients of his grace no matter what they have done. This is a scandalous proposition. It shocks our spontaneous sense of justice. The guilty ought to be punished. How can Hitler and Stalin be among the saved? The just ought to be recognized as such and the wicked condemned. But in my view this is purely human logic which simply shows that there is no understanding of salvation by grace or of the meaning of the death of Jesus Christ.

The proposition also runs counter to the almost unanimous view of theology. Some early theologians proclaimed universal salvation but almost all the rest finally rejected it. Great debates have taken place about foreknowledge and predestination, but in all of them it has been taken for granted that reprobation is normal.

A third and the most serious objection to the thesis is posed by the biblical texts themselves. Many of these talk about condemnation, hell, banishment into outer darkness, and the punishment of robbers, fornicators, idolaters, etc. As we proceed we must overcome these obstacles and examine the theological reasons which lead me to believe in universal salvation, the texts that seem to be against it, and a possible solution. But I want to stress that I am speaking about *belief* in universal salvation. This is for me a matter of faith. I am not making a dogma or a principle of it. I can say only what I believe, not pretending to teach it doctrinally as the truth.

I. God Is Love

My first simple thesis is that if God is God, the Almighty, the Creator of all things, the Omnipresent, then we can think of no place or being whatever outside him. If there were a place outside him, God would not be all in all, the Creator of all things. How can we think of him creating a place or being where he is not present? What, then, about hell? Either it is in God, in which case he is not universally good, or it is outside him, hell having often been defined as the place where God is not. But the latter is completely unthinkable.

One might simply say that hell is merely nothingness. The damned are those who are annihilated. But there is a difficulty here too. Nothingness does not exist in the Bible. It is a philosophical and mathematical concept. We can represent it only by a mathematical sign. God did not create ex nihilo, out of nothing. Genesis 1:2 speaks of *tohu wabohu* ("desert and wasteland"; RSV "formless and void") or of *tehom* ("the deep"). This is not nothing. Furthermore, the closest thing to nothingness seems to be death. But the Bible speaks about enemies, that is, the great serpent, death, and the abyss, which are aggressors against God's creation and are seeking to destroy it. These are enemies against which God protects his creation. He cannot allow that which he has created and called good to be destroyed, disorganized, swallowed up, and slain. This creation of God cannot revert to nothing. Death cannot issue in nothingness. This would be a negation of God himself, and this is why the first aspect seems to me to be decisive. Creation is under constant threat and is constantly upheld. How could God himself surrender to nothingness and to the enemy that which he upholds in face and in spite of everything? How could he allow a power of destruction and annihilation in his creation? If he cannot withstand the force of nothingness, then we have to resort to dualism (a good God and a bad God in conflict and equal), to Zoroastrianism. Many are tempted to dualism today. But if God is unique, if he alone has life in himself, he cannot permit this threat to the object of his love.

But it is necessary that "the times be accomplished," the times when we are driven into a corner and have to serve either the impotence of the God of love or the power of the forces of destruction and annihilation. We have to wait until humanity has completed its history and creation, and every possibility has been explored. This does not merely imply, however, that at the end of time the powers of destruction, death, the great serpent, Satan, the devil, will be annihilated, but much more. How can we talk about nothingness when we receive the revelation of this God who will be all in all? "When all things are subjected to him, then the Son himself also will be subjected to him who put all things under him, that God may be all in all" (1 Cor. 15:28). If God is, he is all in all. There is no more place for nothingness. The word is an empty one. For Christians it is just as empty as what it is supposed to denote. Philosophers speak in vain about something that they can only imagine or use as a building block, but which has no reality of any kind.[1]

The second and equally essential factor is that after Jesus Christ we know that God is love. This is the central revelation. How can we conceive of him who is love ceasing to love one of his creatures? How can we think that God can cease to love the creation that he has made in his own image? This would be a contradiction in terms. God cannot cease to be love. If we combine the two theses we see at once that nothing can exist outside God's love, for God is all in all. It is unthinkable that there should exist a place of suffering, of torment, of the domination of evil, of beings that merely hate since their only function is to torture. It is astounding that Christian theology should not have seen at a glance how impossible this idea is. Being love, God cannot send to hell the creation which he so loved that he gave his only Son for it. He cannot reject it because it is his creation. This would be to cut off himself.

A whole theological trend advances the convenient solution that God is love but also justice. He saves the elect to

---

1. This is why books like Sartre's *Being and Nothingness* and H. Carré's *Point d'appui pris sur le néant* are so feeble.

manifest his love and condemns the reprobate to manifest his justice. My immediate fear is that this solution does not even correspond to our idea of justice and that we are merely satisfying our desire that people we regard as terrible should be punished in the next world. This view is part of the mistaken theology which declares that the good are unhappy on earth but will be happy in heaven, whereas the wicked are successful on earth but will be punished in the next world. Unbelievers have every reason to denounce this explanation as a subterfuge designed to make people accept what happens on earth. The kingdom of God is not compensation for this world.

Another difficulty is that we are asked to see God with two faces as though he were a kind of Janus facing two ways. Such a God could not be the God of Jesus Christ, who has only one face. Crucial texts strongly condemn two-faced people who go two different ways. These are the ones that Jesus Christ calls hypocrites. If God is double-minded, there is duplicity in him. He is a hypocrite. We have to choose: He is either love or he is justice. He is not both. If he is the just judge, the pitiless justiciar, he is not the God that Jesus Christ has taught us to love.

Furthermore, this conception is a pure and simple denial of Jesus Christ. For the doctrine is firm that Jesus Christ, the Son of God, died and was willing to die for human sin to redeem us all: "I, when I am lifted up from the earth, will draw all men to myself" (John 12:32), satisfying divine justice. All the evil done on earth from Adam's break with God undoubtedly has to be judged and punished. But all our teaching about Jesus is there to remind us that the wrath of God fell entirely on him, on God in the person of the Son. God directs his justice upon himself; he has taken upon himself the condemnation of our wickedness. What would be the point, then, of a second condemnation of individuals? Was the judgment passed on Jesus insufficient? Was the price that was paid — the punishment of the Son of God — too low to meet the demands of God's justice? This justice is satisfied in God and by God for us. From this point on, then, we know only the face of the love of God.

This love is not sentimental acquiescence. "It is a fearful thing to fall into the hands of the living God" (Heb. 10:31). God's love is demanding, "jealous," total, and indivisible. Love has a stern face, not a soft one. Nevertheless, it is love. And in any case this love excludes double predestination, some to salvation and others to perdition. It is inconceivable that the God of Jesus Christ, who gives himself in his Son to save us, should have created some people ordained to evil and damnation. There is indeed a predestination, but it can be only the one predestination to salvation. In and through Jesus Christ all people are predestined to be saved. Our free choice is ruled out in this regard. We have often said that God wants free people. He undoubtedly does, except in relation to this last and definitive decision. We are not free to decide and choose to be damned. To say that God presents us with the good news of the gospel and then leaves the final issue to our free choice either to accept it and be saved or to reject it and be lost is foolish. To take this point of view is to make us arbiters of the situation. In this case it is we who finally decide our own salvation. This view reverses a well-known thesis and would have it that God proposes and man disposes.

Without question we all know of innumerable cases in which people reject revelation. Swarms are doing so today. But have they any real knowledge of revelation? If I look at countless presentations of the Word of God by the churches, I can say that the churches have presented many ideas and commandments that have nothing whatever to do with God's revelation. Rejecting these things, human commandments, is not the same as rejecting the truth. And even if the declaration or proclamation of the gospel is faithful, it does not itself force a choice upon us. If people are to recognize the truth, they must also have the inner witness of the Holy Spirit. These two things are indispensable, the faithful declaration of the gospel, the good news, by a human being and the inner witness in the hearer of the Holy Spirit, who conveys the assurance that it is the truth of God. The one does not suffice without the other. Thus when those who hear refuse our message, we can never say that they have chosen to disobey God. The human and divine acts are one and the same only in the Word of Jesus. When he told his hearers not to be unbelieving but to believe, if they refused then they were rejected. In our case, however, we cannot say that there is an act of the Holy Spirit simultaneously with our proclamation. This may well be the point of the well-known text about the one sin that cannot be pardoned, the sin against the Holy Spirit (cf. Matt. 12:31-32). But we can never know whether anyone has committed it.

However that may be, it is certain that being saved or lost does not depend on our own free decision. I believe that all people are included in the grace of God. I believe that all the theologies that have made a large place for damnation and hell are unfaithful to a theology of grace. For if there is predestination to perdition, there is no salvation by grace. Salvation by grace is granted precisely to those who without grace would have been lost. Jesus did not come to seek the righteous and the saints, but sinners. He came to seek those who in strict justice ought to have been condemned. A theology of grace implies universal salvation. What could grace mean if it were granted only to some sinners and not to others according to an arbitrary decree that is totally contrary to the nature of our God? If grace is granted according to the greater or lesser number of sins, it is no longer grace—it is just the opposite because of this accountancy. Paul is the very one who reminds us that the enormity of the sin is no obstacle to grace: "Where sin increased, grace abounded all the more" (Rom. 5:20). This is the key statement. The greater the sin, the more God's love reveals itself to be far beyond any judgment or evaluation of ours. This grace covers all things. It is thus effectively universal. I do not think that in regard to this grace we can make the Scholastic distinctions between prevenient grace, expectant grace, conditional grace, etc. Such adjectives weaken the thrust of the free grace of the absolute sovereign, and they result only from our great difficulty in believing that God has done everything. But this means that nothing in his creation is excluded or lost.

II. Biblical Texts

Yet we have to take into account the fact that many biblical texts refer to hell, to eternal fire, to judgment, to the closing of the gates, to rejection, etc. So far as I know, however, if many texts speak about condemnation, none of them in either the Old

Testament or the New speaks about damnation or the damned. I do not pretend that I am engaging here in an exhaustive study of all the passages that deal with condemnation. I will simply pick out a few that seem to me significant.

I must begin with two preliminary observations. First, we must not do what many do and confuse judgment and condemnation, as if every passage that refers to judgment had condemnation in view. Judgment can end with declaration of the innocence of those being tried. I can say without hesitation that we will all come into judgment. But we cannot conclude anything from that. We have to ask what the judgment consists of. My second observation concerns the Old Testament passages. We have to remember that the idea of survival after death or of a resurrection develops only slowly in Hebrew theological thinking, so that this does not include the idea of eternal punishment. Thus many texts that refer to condemnation (often spoken against Israel) do not have damnation in view at all but condemnation on earth and in time. These are temporal and historical condemnations that often take concrete forms (famine, drought, invasion by enemies, deportation, etc.). We have thus no right to read them from another angle and to make them texts about eternal judgment. Concerning the proclamation of rejection in Gehenna, we must not forget that the Valley of Hinnom served as a refuse dump for Jerusalem, so that this proclamation meant: you are being put out with the garbage as an object that was finished or broken or unusable. In this case the object became unserviceable for God.

The worst fear or worst condemnation for Israelites was that God would turn aside or hide his face from them. This expression relates to the condition on earth, not to eternal judgment. We read constantly that God does not reject forever. He "will not keep his anger forever" (Ps. 103:9; Jer. 3:5, 12; Mic. 7:18). On the other hand, his mercy endures forever (Ps. 106:1; 118:1; 136:1; etc.). These two great theological proclamations rule out the idea of a God who damns, for that would mean that he keeps his anger forever. Remembering these restrictions, we may now look at some of the texts that speak about hell and damnation.

We must look first at many parables of Jesus in which he

announces the threat of hell, of the fire that is not quenched, of rejection from the marriage feast, of weeping and gnashing of teeth. But here, too, we must make two preliminary observations. First, it has been recognized for a long time that parables are designed to teach one particular point. We cannot make dogmas out of all the details. In other words, the warnings about hell do not mean that it actually exists. Even if we take a parable in which hell plays a big part, that of Dives and Lazarus, this is not meant to teach us what hell is like (Luke 16:19-31). Its aim is first of all to get us to question riches and the relation between the rich and the poor, and then to send us back to know the truth in Moses and the prophets.

To my knowledge there is only one parable in which hell and eternal punishment are central, and that is the account of the judgment of the nations in Matthew 25:31-46. The first lesson here has to do with the work that even non-Christians can do in accordance with God's will, while the second relates to the reality of eternal punishment. From this standpoint it is embarrassing, and since I will have to say this again about some passages in the Epistles, I will not try to avoid saying it. We have also to observe, however, that these parables are meant to be heard and received as a warning rather than a threat, as the means that Jesus employs to make us face up to a decision that we must make. The parables are not simple fables or pious discourses or a kind of catechism. Each contains both a revelation of the will of God and a strict summons issued to each of us with a view to decision. Evoking the punishment of hell, then, is one of the means used in parables to show that we must choose. The mistake is thinking that the choice has to be made under constraint. Jesus never tries to gain followers by arousing fear, for he asks only for love. He does not try to make people afraid but offers a parable, a representation of what the world would be like without love. Such a world would be hell. And we already experience this hell on earth.

We must now face up to the repeated statements in the Epistles. Here it is incontestable that many passages speak as though God's consignment of some people to eternal condemnation and hell were revealed teaching. Once again we must make two preliminary observations. The first is that there are many contradictory statements in the Epistles. We find teaching about eternal rejection. We also find references to universal salvation. The same Paul in the same letter (e.g., Romans) seems to state contradictory truths. We will try to understand what this seeming contradiction means. Second, the Epistles are addressed to Christians. The punishment announced (the same is true in Revelation) relates to those who have heard God's Word, who have received the revelation, who are part of the church, and who in spite of that continue to live in an unworthy or scandalous fashion. In the Epistles hell and condemnation do not concern others. It is true that Paul specifically affirms the universality of sin in Romans: All are under the dominion of sin, for they could have known God in his works but did not do so. But when Paul tells believers not to associate with immoral and greedy people or idolaters, he adds that he does not mean this in an absolute sense, for that would mean going out of the world (which is made up of people of this kind); they are not to associate with immoral and greedy and idolatrous people who are in the church and who have heard God's truth (1 Cor. 5:9-10). Hence the admonition is given to Christians. They must not spend time trying to find out whether others outside the faith ought to be damned. That is God's affair. They simply know that the salvation in Jesus Christ is for all.

In other words, what Christians learn about the possibility of hell and perdition is that given the love of God and the sacrifice of Jesus Christ there is no condemnation, but all sins (save one) are pardoned. Nevertheless, they also need to know that there is what I would call, adapting a phrase from Karl Barth, a possible impossibility. God being who he is, hell is impossible. It is an impossibility. Nevertheless, you Christians must realize that nothing is impossible for God. Hence the possibility remains that he might decide for this punishment and penalty. You must retain, though not as a dominating factor, a fear that God will make possible that which according to his revelation is impossible.

Having made these introductory remarks, I must now listen to the texts. In sum, they tell us that sinners will not inherit the kingdom of God. "Do not be deceived; neither the immoral, nor idolaters, nor adulterers, nor homosexuals, nor thieves, nor the greedy, nor drunkards, nor revilers, nor robbers will inherit the kingdom of God" (1 Cor. 6:9-10). Paul encompasses every form of sin under the term "immoral" (5:9). We find much the same list in Galatians (5:19-21), in Ephesians (5:5), and in Hebrews (cf. 12:16-17). There is no possibility that such sinners should inherit God's kingdom. Does this mean hell and eternal fire? Nothing is less clear. Naturally, God's kingdom cannot include evil, injustice, and hatred. All evil is diametrically opposed to it. All that is stated is that people who are guilty of such things cannot participate in God's kingdom. We must not too hastily cause confusion by reading in other things.

A first point ought to give us our bearings. Paul says that sin dwells in him (Rom. 7:14-24). This passage is very important: "But I am carnal, sold under sin. . . . I do not do what I want, but I do the very thing that I hate. . . . It is no longer I that do it, but sin which dwells within me. For I know that nothing good dwells within me, that is, in my flesh. . . . I do not do the good I want, but the evil I do not want is what I do. Now if I do what I do not want, it is no longer I that do it, but sin which dwells within me. . . ." Is Paul also excluded, then, from God's kingdom, or is the intention to do good sufficient for him to be saved? The passage concludes with a shout of victory: "Who will deliver me from the body of this death? Thanks be to God through Jesus Christ our Lord." In other words, Paul states that he is a sinner, that he is tied to evil, that he is corrupt within, that his acts are wicked, but that he can thank Jesus Christ for delivering him.

We must link this passage to the statement in 1 Corinthians 15:50: "Flesh and blood cannot inherit the kingdom of God." Now we have to remember that the flesh is not the body or the total being. It is a general term for human weakness and finitude, for the human tendency to do wrong, for human solidarity with sin. It is not evil as such but the possibility of the evil that people do and that cannot inherit God's kingdom. All the specific sins listed in the more detailed passages are in reality an expression of the flesh. But they are not the self. As one can say that committing a robbery does not in itself make a person a robber, so the sins committed by the flesh do not define the whole person. I realize that I am contradicting here the passages that speak about immoral persons, adulterers, etc. as though the acts contaminated the whole being. For the moment let us simply note the contradiction but not forget the distinction between the flesh and the person.

Now certain texts tell us that we shall be judged by our works. Revelation 20:12 reads: "And the dead were judged by what was written in the books, by what they had done," and Romans 2:5-6 reads: "But by your hard and impenitent heart you are storing up wrath for yourself on the day of wrath when God's righteous judgment will be revealed. For he will render to every man according to his works." (The passage does not say, however, that those who are under God's wrath are damned and rejected—simply that they are subject to God's wrath.) The term *works* is a complex one, for it denotes acts but also relations, achievements, and attitudes. All the same, *ergon* ("works") is unquestionably not identical with *psyche* ("soul, person"). The person finds expression in works but is more than works.

Other passages tell us that words are decisive, expressing as they do relations: "On the day of judgment men will render account for every careless word they utter; for by your words you will be justified, and by your words you will be condemned" (Matt. 12:36-37; cf. Jas. 3:2-12). Yet it is not those who say "Lord, Lord" that will be saved, but those who do the will of God (Matt. 7:21). Thus various expressions of the person ("for out of the abundance of the heart the mouth speaks" — Matt. 12:34), whether acts, words, or relations, will be a decisive test at the judgment, but does this test imply a condemnation of the actual person, an eternal condemnation, a definitive rejection and exclusion from grace?

We must come back unceasingly to grace. Receiving grace is not a matter of good works or of being justified by one's words. Once again we recall that Jesus did not come to seek the righteous but sinners. We have to take this statement in all seriousness. When the president of a modern state exercises his right of reprieve, this means that a person has been found guilty and condemned but after the pronouncement of condemnation there is a declaration of pardon. Grace is not exercised upon someone who is not previously condemned. In other words, we must not confuse grace, justification, and sanctification. Those who are justified by faith in Jesus Christ go on to live sanctified lives and do works of righteousness that are worthy of salvation. They do not have to be restored by grace. Strictly speaking, grace is not the act of God which through the Holy Spirit reveals to people during their lifetime the salvation that is in Christ Jesus. It is the act of God that will grant pardon to those condemned at the judgment. We recall the parable of the lost sheep. Jesus does not seek the good sheep that walks where it should, but the sheep that is truly lost, the lostness being that, not of temporary straying during the present life, but of eternal perdition. This is the one that the risen Jesus goes to recover. We must not cut down the reach of God's grace or limit the dimension of it to this life—it will last into eternity. Thus God's grace has an unparalleled dimension and is universal as the concrete expression of his love.

We now come to the well-known passage of Paul which is often used as a basis for the doctrine of double predestination. Paul is interpreting Exodus 33:19, where God says to Moses: "I will have mercy on whom I have mercy, and I will have compassion on whom I have compassion." This saying expresses the pure freedom of God, which we are not contesting. Note that it does not say: "I will damn whom I damn." God has this message for Pharaoh: "I have raised you up for the very purpose of showing my power in you, so that my name may be proclaimed in all the earth. So then he has mercy on whomever he wills, and he hardens the heart of whomever he wills. You will say to me then, 'Why does he still find fault? For who can resist his will?' But who are you, a man, to answer back to God? Will what is molded say to its molder, 'Why have you made me thus?' Has the potter no right over the clay, to make of the same lump one vessel for beauty and another for menial use? What if God, desiring to show his wrath and to make known his power, has endured with much patience the vessels of wrath made for destruction, in order to make known the riches of his glory for the vessels of mercy, which he has prepared beforehand for glory?" (Rom. 9:15-23).

At a first reading this passage seems to be very clear and very simple. But it raises several questions. First, the fact that God hardened the heart of Pharaoh so that he would not let the Hebrew people go does not mean that his eternal salvation was at stake. He was in fact defeated on the human level, he and his army being drowned. This is how Jewish thinking views the matter. The judgment pronounced on Egypt was meant to make known, we are told, the wrath of God. This intention is perfectly understandable, since Pharaoh did not recognize in the words of Moses and Aaron the Word of the sovereign God. God's wrath found expression in what happened at the Red Sea. Also to be made known was the power of God, which came to expression in the miracle of the crossing and the extermination of the Egyptians. The power of God was indeed very evident in this event. But the justice of God was not at issue, nor was this a matter of eternal judgment. Paul then explains that God can make some vessels for beauty and some for menial use. But again it is a matter of use, of what these vessels are made for during their earthly existence. Some people are called to bear witness to the truth of God, while others undoubtedly remain in humble circumstances and live unimportant lives. It is evident that the latter might accuse God of having made them for menial use and not given them a share in a life full of meaning and greater joy. But here again salvation is not the issue.

The only troubling word that evokes the grave problem of reprobation is the word *destruction* ("vessels of wrath made for destruction"). But we maintain once more that this is not a matter of God's justice. As Maillot has noted, both types of vessels are useful.[2] This is why he prefers the term *destruction* to *perdition,* which is sometimes the rendering. If we are going to find here an exposition of the justice of God, then we must not forget that the Savior God of justification includes the God of predestination, who is in effect "subject" to him, God's wrath being only for a moment, while his mercy endures forever. The justifying God is necessarily the predestinating God. Maillot shows very clearly that the passage does not include double predestination and is not intending to say that God has made vessels of wrath in order to damn them.

Above all we ought to read the magnificent passage in

2. See André Maillot, *L'Épître aux Romains* (Geneva: Labor et Fides, 1984).

which Karl Barth forcefully shows that by manifesting God's power Pharaoh renders God no less a service than does Moses:

> The man that is *hardened* is the visible man, . . . who neither knows nor practices repentance. . . . The man to whom God shows mercy is the invisible man, . . . the new-born man whose repentance is God's work. . . . God must be apprehended as the God of Jacob and of Esau. . . . When He manifests Himself to the men of this world as God, He must do so as the angry God who is bound to make His power known. . . . And conversely, when men receive His revelation, they cannot do so otherwise than as vessels of wrath. . . . Inasmuch as it is God who does reveal Himself to men, He confronts creatureliness with the 'And Yet' of the Creator, the immensity of human sin with the 'And Yet' . . . of His covering forgiveness. . . . But what if the process of the revelation of this one God moves always from time to eternity, from rejection to election, from Esau to Jacob, and from Pharaoh to Moses? What if the existence of—*vessels of wrath*—which we all are in time!—should declare the divine endurance and forbearance (iii.26), should be the veil of the long-suffering of God (ii.4), behind which the *vessels of mercy*—which we all are in Eternity!—are not lost, but merely hidden?[3]

But now we run into another passage that seems to be just as restrictive. In John's Gospel we find the celebrated text: "For God so loved the world that he gave his only Son, that whoever believes in him should not perish but have everlasting life" (3:16). God so loved the *world*. The world, like the flesh, is more than the body, the sociological or institutional reality of human groups. It is the totality of the forces that indwell it and that are responsible for the unhappiness, the hatred, the covetousness, and the violence within it, namely, for all that makes it hateful and not lovable. It never achieves good but always evil. This evil means suffering for us that also causes suffering for God. It means unhappiness for us, an inability to achieve happiness except at the cost of greater unhappiness, perhaps for others too. God so loved this unlovable world in order to show the unlimited greatness of his love. He loved it so much and in such a way as to give himself in his Son in order to prevent it from

3. See Karl Barth, *Epistle to the Romans*, trans. E. C. Hoskyns, 6th ed. (London: Oxford University, 1933), pp. 351ff.

rushing headlong to the fate of death which is the outcome of evil.

But the text then goes on to say: "That whoever *believes* in him should not perish but have everlasting life." Simple logic seems to force us to say that those who do not believe in Jesus Christ will perish and will not have everlasting life, and thus "be damned." But how, then, can we explain the obvious contradiction? On the one hand, God loved the world, the whole world without restriction, and made the total, incomparable, and absolute sacrifice. On the other hand, there is the restriction that only those who believe in Jesus Christ will not perish but "have everlasting life." This restriction would leave out all those who lived before Jesus Christ and all those who do not come within the sound of the preaching of the gospel. Thus only a small fraction of humanity would profit by this tremendous act. Yet all the rest belong to "the world" as well; the world is made up of them. The same ambiguity seems to obtain in the verses that follow: "For God sent the Son into the world, not to condemn the world, but that the world might be saved through him. He who believes in him is not condemned; he who does not believe is condemned already. . . . And this is the judgment, that the light has come into the world, and men loved darkness rather than light, because their deeds were evil." People at large prefer darkness. And it is the world at large that Jesus saved. The two groups are identical.

I believe that we can solve the problem as follows. Jesus came to save the world, and he could not fail to do his work, for he is the Son of God and he did all that had to be done. But people prefer darkness to light because they know that their deeds are evil. Thus they remain in darkness, not knowing that they now belong to a world that is saved. Remaining in darkness is their judgment. (Verse 19 is very clear: the judgment is that they prefer the night to the light.) They do not want to repent, to bring their works to the light. Those who believe act according to the truth. This does not mean that their prior works were good but that they let the truth of their life and works be brought to light, and in so doing they act in accordance with God. They then learn that they are not condemned and that they have received everlasting life. As for the rest, their judgment does not mean their damnation. It means that for the whole of their lives they are delivered up to the darkness that they have chosen. They will truly experience all the tragedies and horrors of the world as judgment in hopeless situations in which evil works will multiply and there will be no meaning in what happens because they have rejected both meaning and hope. They have no knowledge of everlasting life and each day are in a situation of death.

Those who believe live in hope. They have already the firstfruits of eternal life. They have within them that which will not perish, the Word of God. They live a double life on earth; in this world which is saved in the eyes of some and is terrifying in the eyes of the rest; on the earth on which some have assurance of the resurrection and the rest only the certainty of death; on the earth on which some see meaning in the human venture because they have the light, and the rest wander in folly and "perdition" because they cannot see the way. But this is a temporary situation of human life. All are encompassed in "God so loved the world and Jesus came to save the world." In the course of human history there are those who know happiness and have the light, and those who are lost on a way with no exit. But the latter are not lost to the heart of God, nor are they outside the love of God. As has often been said, what we suffer here on earth is punishment enough. Hell is on earth, as the Bible itself tells us.

If we take a further step, we find confirmation in the great event of reconciliation. God reconciled the world to himself in Jesus Christ: "God was in Christ reconciling the world to himself, not counting their trespasses against them, and entrusting to us the message of reconciliation" (2 Cor. 5:19; cf. Rom. 5:11). Paul insists on the fact that it is by Jesus Christ that we have received reconciliation. The doctrine of reconciliation is basic, and Paul does not discriminate. We were all wicked sinners, and God showed his love by giving Christ his Son, who died for us. The "us" sets no limit. It does not refer only to converts. All without exception were wicked sinners: "If while we were enemies we were reconciled to God by the death of his Son, much more, now that we are reconciled, shall we be saved by his life" (Rom. 5:10). This is a unilateral act of the God who in an extreme expression of his love decides to reconcile the world as a whole even in all its rebellious, hostile, and autonomous power, saving sinners without discrimination, for there are no greater or lesser sinners in the presence of the holiness, perfection, and absolute justice of God. All are sinners, and all as such have been assumed and reconciled to God by Jesus Christ.

This divine decision that changes human destiny is of supreme importance. In effect, whether individuals will be reconciled or not, whether they will make their peace with God or not, whether they will be penitent or not, does not in any way affect God's decision to reconcile the world to himself. It might change the lives of those concerned but not their ordination to salvation. From the very outset this reconciliation is for all (Muslims, Buddhists, Nazis, Communists, etc.), and it will apply to them whether they know it or not, whether they will it or not. God is reconciled to them even if they are not reconciled to God. Jesus bore insults, unbelief, betrayal, abandonment, misunderstanding, and temptation ("prove that you are the Son of God" — cf. Matt. 27:40), but never for a single moment did he condemn or reject or curse those who were guilty of such things. Instead, he wept over them. He was in fact reconciled to all no matter what they did.

This attitude of Jesus provides us with a model of the Father's reconciliation with the world. People may deny his existence, betray his revelation, and proclaim his death, but God remains the Reconciler. All that we hear is this anguished plea of the Father: "My people, what have I done?" For from the very beginning the whole race is his people. The reconciliation effected in Jesus Christ recalls and fulfills God's dealings with Noah after the Flood when God set a rainbow in the sky and said: "Whenever I want to punish the race again, I will look upon this bow and it will be for me the sign of an everlasting covenant" (cf. Gen. 9:12ff.). That reconciliation was still fragile, and a long history began under the sign of that covenant, but from the very beginning God was reconciled to all of us in virtue of the new covenant which cannot be broken, which encompasses humanity as a whole, and which sets it in God's love rather than imposing a law upon it. The reconciliation of God with the world, with all humanity, rules out the possibility of damnation. I stress again that our human will or disposition can do nothing to change what has been accomplished.

Yet we still find hell and the second death proclaimed in the book of Revelation. Let us begin with hell. Some people are excluded from the heavenly Jerusalem: "Outside are the dogs and the sorcerers and fornicators and murderers and every one who loves and practices falsehood" (Rev. 22:15). This description confirms what we find in some of the parables, and it comes to fulfillment in the well-known account of Gog and Magog in 20:7-10. Satan seduces the nations and gathers them for battle against God and Jesus Christ. But fire descends from heaven and consumes them, and the devil who seduced them, who separated them from God, will be thrown into the lake of fire and brimstone where the beast and the false prophet are. We read that it is the devil, the beast (power), and the false prophet (falsehood) that are thrown into the lake of fire, not beings, let alone human beings, but the forces that from creation have turned people aside from God and introduced absolute evil. It is these rebellious spiritual forces that are in hell. They seduced the "nations." This term is a collective one *(ethne)*, and as I see it again concerns not people but powers, for a nation is much more than the people who compose it. Thus France is an entity that has a kind of reality of its own. We know to what extent nations can be seduced and can regard themselves as gods. Here again the idea is that the nation that sets itself up as a deity in opposition to God is what is thrown outside.

We now come to the second death, and what we find is a parallel statement: "Then death and Hades were thrown into the lake of fire. This is the second death, the lake of fire" (Rev. 20:14). In other words, it is death itself which is put to death (the death of death, according to d'Aubigné). And this accords well with the proclamation of Paul: "The last enemy to be destroyed is death" (1 Cor. 15:26). Paul speaks about the absolute triumph of Jesus Christ, to whom God gives his entire kingdom and power, putting all enemies under his feet (Jesus does not consider human beings his enemies), the last enemy to be overcome being death. The only outcome for death is that it must disappear in the death that slays death.

Yet there is ambiguity in this passage in Revelation, for it also tells us that at the judgment the dead were judged according to their works as these were written in the books that will be open to God at the time of the resurrection. Another book was also opened, the book of life, "and if anyone's name was not found written in the book of life, he was thrown into the lake of fire" (Rev. 20:15). On the basis of this idea of books in which human works are written, Christian thinking gradually worked out the concept of a great accounting system. Each of us has a column of credits and a column of debits, and these will be balanced, good works being added and bad works subtracted. Such an idea runs contrary to the whole gospel and to the thinking of Paul, for whom salvation is never attained by the works of the law. Furthermore, the idea seems to falsify radically the picture of God that the whole Bible presents. The biblical God is not an accountant. "No one is righteous, no, not one" (Rom. 3:10). No one can bring before God works that are worthy of him. In other words, if we were confined to an accounting balance, the result would always be a deficit, the world would be condemned, and no one would be written in the book of life.

My own view is that there is a distinction between "the books," which have to do with our human life on earth, and "the book of life." There is only one book of life (as distinct from the multitude of other books) because this is the book of grace, and there is no accountancy here but simply the proclamation that all are saved by grace in Christ. The books are those of trial and judgment. But after the judgment comes the simple, universal verdict. All are written in the book of life. Yet the verse that follows (Rev. 20:15) then gives us the solemn warning which is addressed to Christians to make them take seriously the possible impossibility of which we spoke earlier. God always reserves to himself the possibility of rejecting people, and this is the secret of his freedom. If he is not an accountant, he is also not tied ineluctably to a kind of global decision which makes the trial and judgment derisory and fictitious. Clearly the book of life is the book of Jesus Christ, who is incompatible with death and all that death is.[4]

---

4. See further Jacques Ellul, *Apocalypse: The Book of Revelation*, trans. George W. Schreiner (New York: Seabury, 1977). — TRANS.

Although I proclaim the truth of universal salvation, I cannot proclaim it as an absolute truth. I cannot penetrate the secret of God. I cannot presume upon a simple decision of the eternal Father. Hence I cannot proclaim this truth as a dogmatic proposition which is scientifically demonstrated. In proclaiming it, I am saying what I believe, what meditation on the biblical texts leads me to believe. I do not teach universal salvation; I announce it.

I still have to reply to two elementary questions. First, if everyone is saved, what is the difference between Christians and non-Christians? And what good is it for Christians to lead lives that are godly, worthy, honest, moral, etc.? Concerning the second point, we must be very firm. Living such a life achieves nothing and in no way assures us of salvation. To lead a virtuous life in order to be saved is completely mistaken from a biblical standpoint. The evangelical view is that I lead a virtuous life *because* I know that I am saved. It is *because* grace has been granted to me that I *can* live an honest life before God. Salvation is not the result of virtue but its origin and source.

Let us return, however, to the first part of the question. What is the difference between Christians and non-Christians? For a long time the emphasis has been on individual salvation. We have to convert people, to lead them to faith, if they are to be saved. This is the goal of many evangelistic campaigns and of much missionary work. But if we accept the certainty of universal salvation, salvation cannot be the point of communicating the gospel. What, then, is its value or significance? It rests on three solid foundations. First, it is a matter of communicating knowledge. All are saved, but only those who believe the gospel know it. This is no small matter, for people are full of anguish and anxiety and fear, fear of the future and of war and of death. They are delivered up to the pain of a cruel disruption. They are desperate because they have lost their loved ones, or think they have lived in vain, or see the world degraded and nature violated and slowly plundered. They are doubly crushed because they do not know that they are loved and accompanied and saved and reunited and promised a future of truth, righteousness, and light. Not to know this is the great tragedy of people today. Communicating the gospel is passing on the astonishing news that no matter what happens nothing is lost and we are loved. "Good news is preached to the poor" (Luke 4:18). It is a matter of the poor (all of us!) and of *this* good news.[5]

But passing on the gospel has a second meaning too, for those who hear and receive this gospel henceforth become the servants of God. They are given a mission, a vocation. This gospel is to be proclaimed on earth. Believers become the servants of this proclamation. I will repeat what I have often said before, namely, that being a Christian is neither a privilege nor an advantage but a charge and a mission. Those who learn the good news of salvation are under obligation to live a different life, to become "saints" because they are now sanctified, and to make it their task to pass on what they have been given. But they have also to become again the image that God has made of himself, his counterpart.

We have said that there are three vital points. The third is our response to the tragic and anguished question that Jesus poses: "When the Son of man comes, will he find faith on earth?" (Luke 18:8). There is no guarantee of the permanence or perpetuity of the gospel among us. Jesus gives us the promise that he will be with us to the end of the age (Matt. 28:20), but there may not be anyone with him. There may not be a single Christian, a single bearer of the good news. This is a possibility that the question of Jesus opens up for us, and we cannot treat it lightly. Again, if we are charged to communicate this gospel, it is also *for* Jesus, so that he may not have the further sorrow of having done everything but finding no one who believes it or knows it. Thus service out of love for Jesus (the only service that we can render him) ought to constrain us to evangelize all peoples and all classes.

A final objection to universal salvation is that of the frivolous or worldly person who says: "It is all very easy then.

5. We find an abominable travesty of this good news in some liberation theologians who reduce the poor merely to the economically poor and exploited, and the good news to news of the revolution, namely, that with Jesus Christ the poor can rebel and liberate themselves from their masters. Face-to-face with Jesus Christ, this is a pure and simple lie. See further Jacques Ellul, *Jesus and Marx: From Gospel to Ideology*, trans. Joyce Main Hanks (Grand Rapids: Eerdmans, 1988).

I do not need to bother about it. I can live as I like. I am not under any religious restraints. There is no need for works, as the Protestants have shown. There is not even any need for faith, since even atheists and pagans are saved." This kind of talk is the only kind that might bring people into danger of damnation. For it is the talk of those to whom the good news has been fully proclaimed, and they despise it. There is the rub. If people refuse to believe in God and in Jesus Christ during a hard and serious struggle, if they wrestle with God as Job did, then the God of Abraham and Isaac and Jacob and Jesus knows and understands ("for he knows whereof we are made"—cf. Ps. 103:14), and he finally grants his revelation. But what is not tolerable, what cannot be pardoned, is that when the love of God is known, when the full extent of his grace is understood, this grace should be mocked. The unacceptable thing is not to be moved by this love when it is known and recognized, not to respond to it, or rather to respond with raillery: "It is all very convenient, we can simply profit from it." This is the kind of hypocritical talk that makes a game of the truth. It involves a corruption of the very being against which there rings out the terrible warning: "God is not mocked" (Gal. 6:6).

Chapter 15

JUDGMENT

In spite of all the explanations that have been given, I realize that there remains a contradiction between the universal love of God and the passages which describe sins that bring condemnation. Such passages speak about the saved and the damned. I ask myself whether they have in view living persons, the very beings that God has created and that participate in his being as the living God even if only by the fact that they have life. I will advance a hypothesis, though with some trepidation, because I am aware how fragile it is. It came to me when I was reading a passage in Paul: "According to the grace of God given to me, like a skilled master builder I laid a foundation, and another man is building upon it. Let each man take care how he builds upon it. For no other foundation can any one lay than that which is laid, which is Jesus Christ. Now if any one builds on this foundation with gold, silver, precious stones, wood, hay, stubble — each man's work will become manifest. . . . If the work which any man has built . . . survives, he will receive a reward. If any man's work is burned up, he will suffer loss, though he himself will be saved, but only as through fire" (1 Cor. 3:10-15).

I realize that this passage has to do with the upbuilding of the church. It follows a passage that tells us that one sows and another waters, but God gives the increase. We are God's workers in the construction of the church. Paul has laid the foundation, which is none other than Jesus Christ. But the church might then be built in different ways. And the work of building that each of us does will be judged. We shall talk about the reward in the next chapter. Plainly it is not salvation. But we should also note that the text refers to another way of living, another type of relationship with God. There are two possible developments, and the second is on a far grander scale than the first ("All things are yours . . . the world or life or death or the present or the future, all are yours; and you are Christ's; and Christ is God's" (vv. 22-23).

I asked myself, however, whether this passage of Paul might not be given an application beyond the sphere of the up-building of the church. Might it not have in view the upbuilding of a life, which is finally a person's work? Christians build up their lives on the only foundation, which is Jesus Christ. But others build up their lives either on a relation to the Christ whom they do not know but who is implicitly present in their lives (Matt. 25), or on a knowledge of God (though there can be no question of constructing a natural theology): "For what can be known about God is plain to them, because God has made it known to them. . . . His invisible nature, namely, his eternal power and deity, is clearly perceived in the creation of the world when they see him in his works" (Rom. 1:19ff.). On this basis, they can build up their lives, whether with hay and stubble, or with stone and wood. But "they have gone astray in their thoughts and their senseless hearts were darkened. . . . Therefore God gave them up to their passions. . . . They worshiped and served the creature rather than the Creator." Thus it is a matter of how people construct their lives as work, of how they lead their lives, on the basis of a certain knowledge of God. In the course of life, in acts and works and involvements and words, some build a full and solid life with gold or stone, but others build an empty and, for God, an insignificant life with hay and stubble. Judgment consists of passing the work of this life through fire. In the one case something remains, preserved by God, and we shall see later what becomes of it. In the other case, the work goes up in smoke and nothing is left. These people have lived in vain.

But Paul then has a statement which caused me a good deal of reflection: "He himself will be saved, but only as through fire" (1 Cor. 3:15). In other words, what this person did in life vanishes, but the work is not the whole person. Even when we make a full tally of a person's passions, intelligence, relations, involvements, occupations, and individual psyche, something is still left, a surplus that is not exhausted, the self. I hesitate to use the word *soul,* for it is too heavily freighted both philosophically and religiously; I refer to the being, the self, from which passions and actions spring. It is this self that is finally saved. The living self returns to the living God who created it. The spirit returns to the God who gave it (Eccl. 12:7). I thus make a clear-cut distinction between the being and what occupied it.

A first stage of judgment, we might say, is the vision that this being has of what becomes of its life's work. Punishment consists, for example, of the fact that nothing remains. God will not preserve anything of this whole life. It is the bitter realization that one has lived totally in vain. Yet we must be more precise, for no life's work is ever wholly evil. The most advanced saints are forced to recognize the evil works they do, as we see from a rereading of Augustine's *Confessions,* and the worst criminal can have in his life a work of love. Thus God does not either accept or reject the whole of life.

I have in mind here the text in Hebrews (4:12): "For the word of God is living and active, sharper than any two-edged sword, piercing to the division of soul and spirit, of joints and marrow, and discerning the thoughts and intentions of the heart. And before him no creature is hidden, but all are open and laid bare to the eyes of him with whom we have to do." The issue here is undoubtedly judgment, but what is meant by this sword that divides soul and spirit? Judgment carries with it separation. The presence of this sword is confirmed in Revelation in the description of the risen and glorified Lord: "From his mouth issues a sharp sword," which represents God's Word (19:15). But why a sword? Immediately after this passage there really begins the judgment of the seven churches. If it were a matter of separating good people from bad, there would be no need of a sword. But the judgment of the seven churches describes in each case a separation of what can be retained as righteous before God from what has to be eliminated. Is not this exactly the judgment that each of us undergoes? It is not a kind of accounting in which good works are balanced against bad works with a view to the condemnation of the whole being, but of separation, of separation within this being between that which is pleasing to God and which he preserves, and that which is to be destroyed and annihilated because it belongs to the devil and to Satan. Human beings to whom God has given life and whom he loves do not go into nothingness or hell, but their wicked and diabolical works do, sharing the same fate as their father the devil. We are thus given a fuller picture of judgment. We do not merely see the works of our lives burn up. We first have to undergo this separation between our being and our evil works. The reward will be to learn that some of our works are pleasing to God. This is my hypothesis regarding the relation between universal salvation and those works of people's lives that are condemned by God and destroyed. What is destroyed is not God's creation but a construction of our own.

Chapter 16

RECAPITULATION

The doctrine called recapitulation *(anakephalaiosis)* was studied closely by the church fathers. Irenaeus of Lyons especially laid emphasis on this part of Christian teaching. God became man because we could not arrive at immortality and incorruptibility unless he who *is* essentially immortality and incorruptibility joined himself to our nature and to the whole of humanity of which we are a part, and recapitulated it in himself. In the 3rd century Hippolytus insisted on the fact that all humanity (the millions of people that compose it) is resumed, comprehended, and recapitulated in Jesus Christ. The doctrine gradually became weaker and lost its importance, but it has a basis in some passages in Paul. In Christ God accomplished "his plan for the fulness of time, to unite all things in him, things in heaven and things on earth" (Eph. 1:10). We have in this verse the Greek equivalent of the word *recapitulate.* Paul is saying that Christ became man, not just to regather all humanity in himself, but to recapitulate all things, all creation, whether things in heaven or things on earth, for human beings do not constitute the whole universe, and it is in this sense that we have to join hands with orthodox theology in calling Christ *pantocrator.* Christ came not merely to bring human beings to immortality but to bring back the original harmony and unity of things, heeding at last the groaning of a crushed creation. Human beings are saved by Christ, but all that was thrust into disorder and rupture and incoherence is also saved.

This concept of recapitulation corresponds exactly to that of the reconciliation that God effects with creation. "He is before all things, and in him all things hold together. He is the head of the body, the church; he is the beginning, the first-born from the dead, that in everything he might be preeminent. For God willed all fulness [the *pleroma* that corresponds to the totality of creation] to dwell in him, and through him [he willed] to reconcile to himself all things, whether on earth or in heaven, making peace by the blood of his cross" (Col. 1:17-20). We note the great difference between this cosmic view of reconciliation and that of Irenaeus, which entails only the recapitulation of humanity. Paul says much more. All things subsist in Christ and all things are reconciled in him, both in heaven and on earth. This does not mean that Christ has become as large as creation but that he has become the head of all things, of this great body which is not just the church or humanity, but the whole universe, both material and spiritual. He is the head who directs and impels it, the one from whom thoughts and volitions and decisions emanate. Reconciliation issues in this recapitulation because for once, for the first time, the whole will of God has been fully done with neither break nor hesitation and yet with complete freedom. Jesus was never a serf or a robot. He was never a being that was conditioned to do the will of a God who was a deus ex machina. He did all things with full freedom of decision, choice, love, and truth. He even interpreted freely the commandments that God had given to the Jewish people, and it was thus that he was fully obedient. He was the perfect image of God. For the first time since the fall of Adam God found his image again, his counterpart, his free and creative partner in prayer and decision. In this shattered universe it was enough that for once the will of God was fully done. Order was then restored, reconciliation was made, and recapitulation could take place.

Naturally, the reader will think (like myself) that these are all dreams. Evil still reigns, disorder is at a peak, humanity is more than ever the victim of war and famine, and there is no trace of this great work in actual life. This is basically true. Yet there are two dimensions. What has been done and can never be erased is reconciliation. This has been effected; Jesus has become the head of this creation. What has always been in effect is that the universe is in God. What is not yet in effect is that the members of this body are in accord with the

head, that people follow the example of Jesus, that human freedom is coincident with the will of God. This helps us to understand how Irenaeus came to think as he did: the invisible
virtues of immortality and incorruptibility were gained for us
in recapitulation; nothing else was changed.

I have a different interpretation. We have talked already
about reconciliation. A single whole has to be gathered under
the authority of the head. I will leave on one side the questions
of things celestial and terrestrial and concentrate on humanity,
from which, as we have seen, God awaits a free response to his
love. In my view what seems to have been missing in the doctrine of recapitulation is a concrete view of humanity. We again
come up against the problem of metaphysics. For Irenaeus what
is recapitulated is humanity in the abstract, the essence of
humanity, the permanent, immutable, unchanging nature of
humanity. There are theoretically fallen beings and theoretically
reconciled beings. There is a humanity composed of millions of
abstract beings gathered into a whole. But completely forgotten
are both the living, changing reality of mankind and the fact
that one cannot speak of humanity in a global sense.

For my part, I clash with both idealism and realism. In idealism, we have only an idea of humanity, but an idea of humanity is not what is saved. People who really exist are saved. They
alone are sinners, and they alone can repent and pray and receive grace and be converted. The whole Bible is anti-idealist.
Recapitulation is the gathering of all living people into a totality
that has never previously existed.

At the same time, the position of theologians like Irenaeus
has to be regarded as one of realism, not in the modern sense,
but in that of the debate between nominalism and realism. On
this view, humanity is a reality, a real entity and not an intellectual abstraction. On the one side there are individual people and
on the other a coherent whole which has its own existence, which
is different from the sum of individuals, which has its own qualities and specificity, which is a "rational being" and "moral person," and it is this entity, already unified and real, that is assumed
in recapitulation. At different times I myself have already declared in favor of nominalism. One can talk about humanity, but
in itself it is merely a word, which is useful for the purpose of

denoting the totality of people, and which serves well in reflection and communication, but which is never anything more. The millions of individuals do not constitute one real humanity. Nor is there one human nature that is always identical and immutable and that one can find in each individual. Nor is there any rational being that is the same through space and time. For me, such things are mere names and no more.

The dimension that is obviously lacking is that of history. This humanity has had a history. In recapitulation, does God take account of the thousands of years of human history with its differences and mutations? In the course of this history many works have been produced: artistic, cultural, and technical, also literary, political, and legal. The same is true in the lives of individuals. In the course of life we all produce many works. Our lives are made up of works, not only great works, but daily activities, relations with family and associates, words that we speak, decisions that we make in politics or love. In recapitulation, does God take these works into consideration? What is our life in abstraction from these works? We hinted at this point earlier when we recalled that we are judged by our works and words, and when we said that we might be saved in our being even though our works were all destroyed by fire. Yet in every case some works survive. Why not, then, those of the race as a whole from its origin, during the long march of its history?

In my view this seems to be shown by the following conviction. God loves us. He loves us fully. And when I say that, I am saying that he does not love a kind of phantom, an evanescent and abstract being with a common nature. Loving us, he loves us in the concreteness of our lives, with all that makes up our lives, our jobs, our hobbies, our hopes, our fears, the things we have created, the beings we have loved. God loves us in the totality of our lives. Thus he does not save an abstract and interchangeable phantom. He loves us in our individuality, that is, in our history *with* its works. Saved people are not judged to be of value apart from their works. The judgment would be terrible if God did not think that any of our works deserved to be saved, conserved. A whole life lived in vain! The result of so many hours and so much energy reduced to nothing! There are no criteria by which to know what God will keep. We may think we have clear data regarding moral and spiritual works, which are good, which conform to God's will, but we cannot evaluate our political and technological works, and we will no doubt be surprised by what God keeps and what he destroys.

But is there any biblical basis for what I have been suggesting? In effect, I am convinced that it is biblical study that has led me to it.[1] When planning to write a biblical history of the city, I suddenly found dazzling evidence of its vast significance along the following lines. In the beginning (Gen. 2) God created a garden (Eden) in which he placed Adam and Eve, a perfect place of riches and delight. Adam and Eve had everything there, trees that produced fruit in abundance and four rivers flowing out of it. God planned this garden as the ideal place for them. But a strange thing happened. There was a break with God, and they could not stay in this place of fellowship and intercourse with God. They were chased out of the garden and began the long adventure of human history. But at the end of this immense journey of "humanity," when both this world, whose elements are to be dissolved (2 Pet. 3:10-12), and the development or the creations of the race will come to an end, there will be a new creation by God, a new place for us where God will be all in all. But this new place is not the same as that at the beginning. This is odd, for in all the myths that talk about a happy beginning for humanity, a golden age, a primal paradise, the end is always a return to the beginning. Humanity finds again the happy place that it lost. This corresponds to a cyclical view of time. At the end of history, the circle is complete and we come back to the beginning.

We know, however, that in Hebrew thinking, in spite of some recent disagreement (e.g., Thibon's *Le voile et le masque*), time is rectilinear and not circular. At the end of the course we do not come back to the beginning. Naturally, there might have been identity between them. That is to say, God might have created a new Eden, a garden, for that was his original idea of what is best for us. He might have kept immutably to his judgment and put us back in a garden. But this is precisely what the

---

1. For more on what follows see Jacques Ellul, *The Meaning of the City*, trans. Dennis Pardee (Grand Rapids: Eerdmans, 1970).

biblical texts do not say. In Revelation, what appears at the end of the age is a city, the new Jerusalem that comes down from heaven, the holy city (Rev. 21:10-27). Thus what is finally given us by God is a city. Nor is this an isolated invention of the Revelation of John or of the apocalyptic movement. In Isaiah the promise of the restoration of Jerusalem might seem to have in view only the historical restoration of the earthly Jerusalem, but the end of chapter 60 shows very clearly that we are now in the age of the creation of a new world: "Violence shall no more be heard . . . you shall call your walls Salvation and your gates Praise. The sun shall no more be your light by day, nor for brightness shall the moon give light to you by night; but the Lord will be your everlasting light. . . . Your sun shall no more go down. . . . Your people shall all be righteous" (Isa. 60:18ff.). These are undoubtedly eschatological promises. Even clearer is Ezekiel's vision (ch. 40) of the new Jerusalem that comes down from heaven. Obviously one might take the view that these prophetic texts relate only to the historical Jerusalem and the renewal of the Hebrew people. But I believe that if we read them plainly we are forced to agree that we have here eschatological promises.

In other words, at the end of time God will place us not in a garden but in a city. God has changed his plan. Why? Because in this new creation of his he takes human history and human works into account. One might say with some truth that the city is the chief human work. It was with the appearance of the city that the true history of human development began. The city is the focus of all invention and interchange and art; the city is the birthplace of culture. I am not saying that there is no rural culture, but it arises in symbiosis with urban culture. The city is indeed our primary human creation. It is a uniquely human world. It is the symbol that we have chosen, the place that we have invented and that we prefer.

But we must proceed with the biblical story. The city in the Bible (apart from Jerusalem) was an invention of Cain. Condemned to wander across the earth, Cain settled down, building a city. He had received from God a protective mark, but he did not really trust it. He preferred to protect himself and to do so he built city walls. From this first act which qualifies it, the city throughout its long history has always been the place that human beings have chosen in opposition to God. It is the place from which they have excluded God, as Babel did, or the place in which they have invented many gods that God rejects, as Babylon did. The city is the place of violence and war (Nineveh). It is the place of money and commerce, the place of corruption (Sodom). The city always has a negative connotation in the Bible. But we cannot change the fact that all human history has taken place in the city. And now we find it beautifully revealed that as the new, ideal, and perfect place that God will give us at the end of the age, God chooses the city, the place of the revolt against him. In the new creation he changes the negative sign into a positive one. Since the human race wants the city, God wants it too. He listens to the prolonged request of humanity. He responds to human expectations. But what he gives is a perfect city from every standpoint, unlike the imperfect and intolerable cities with which humanity has marked its history. What does this change mean if not that God takes account of what humanity wants?

Thus the recapitulation to which Scripture refers is not the synthesis of an abstract humanity but the recapitulation of all human history. This is the first implication of God's choice of the city as his new creation. Human history is not in the least annulled by the gift of the new creation. It would be horrible to think that at the end of thousands of years of effort, courage, hope, work, hatred, tragedy, exaltation, creation, and aspiration, God in fulfillment of his own will would wipe it all out as though it had never been, and with no interest in what humanity has been doing through its long history, paying no attention to it, blindly place us back in an abstract place. No, God assumes all human history, as in his incarnation Jesus assumes the legal injustice of Rome, the sacerdotal betrayal of Israel, and the hope of the people. The heavenly Jerusalem is a kind of condensation of all that human beings have created and wanted and instituted throughout the history of the race. All of it is inscribed on the memory of God. I think that this might well be the meaning of the "books" that Revelation mentions in which all human works are written. Why should we think of these as merely individual works? Why should not the great movements of history be conserved? Are not the great movements themselves always the product of individual actions and decisions? This history, then, is now part of God. But if nothing of ours is lost, if it must all come into judgment, the works done in the course of history must also be taken up by God.

This is in effect the second point. In two verses Revelation tells us (21:24, 26) that into this heavenly Jerusalem the kings will bring their glory and the nations their glory and honor, the kings being the leaders and the nations consisting of people of every type. What they bring is their *doxa*, their expectations, their hopes, their opinions, their beliefs, and also their renown and glory. It is not a matter of their works in the strict sense. But when we talk about beliefs and expectations, we are talking about a reality that incarnates itself in acts and products. Furthermore, what is glory? We obviously need to go back to the Hebrew, and there the word for glory *(kabod)* carries first the idea of weight, of heaviness. In one sense it is synonymous with the goods or wealth or fame or greatness of a being. It is that which manifests a being. The glory of Yahweh is finally equivalent to his revelation. Yahweh makes himself known in his works, in his creation, in his judgments, and these things all express his glory. His glory is not just his majesty but his revelation in his deeds and works. In other words, glory is the expression of that which reveals being.

I know that I am now extrapolating—and some might regard this as illegitimate—but I think that the word has the same sense when it refers to us: the glory of a person is that which his works make visible. Our works are the revelation of our being. Hence when this passage in Revelation talks about the human glory that comes into the new Jerusalem, this is not the glory of a parade or procession or trumpets, etc. What enters in is that which brings to light what the kings and the nations really are in God's truth throughout the course of history. The kings and the nations bring in the works which in God's eyes are true glory in history. If these works enter the new Jerusalem, they are not to be put in a museum. These works are an integral part of the new Jerusalem. That is to say, God takes these works of the nations throughout history and uses them to build up (in part) this actual city.

And now I make a second extrapolation which some might find no less scandalous than the first but which I will make just the same. The nations are composed of individuals. They have no other existence, except it be that which they give themselves in their pretensions to divinity. We are now dealing, however, with nations whose *exousia* ("power, authority") has been destroyed. They have been despoiled of their self-divinization. They can no longer make a pretense of directing history. They have been vanquished with Gog and Magog.

Their only reality is that of the people that constitute them. The realistic Jewish thinking never conceives of a nation as such but only of a nation as an assembly of people. Hence the glory is not that of an abstraction (e.g., France or Greece) but that of individuals. *Nation* is a generic term to denote the people in a specific group. Thus the works that come into the new Jerusalem and form part of it are not just collective works (great military triumphs or imposing monuments). They are the works that reveal the individuals that constitute these nations. They include individual actions. For me, then, the twofold statement of Revelation contains the idea that God allows to be brought into his own work all the things in the lives of all people which he judges to be worthy to be part of it. Our glory is that a fragment of the work that we have done in life, of love, labor, church, character, and relations, is found by God to be worthy. This is the true meaning of the judgment of which we spoke. We have said that into each of us comes the sword of the Word to separate the bad, which will vanish, from the good, which God will finally conserve. What is thus conserved, however, does not float off into the void but is used by God to build his city.

This is also the meaning of the reward, about which people sometimes ask. The reward is not salvation; that is a gift of grace. Nor is the reward the granting of a place of honor in heaven. What would be the point of that? Are not all equally close to God, who is all in all? When the disciples ask for places of honor in his kingdom, the one on his right hand and the other on his left, Jesus firmly rebuffs them. No, the reward is to see that something we have done in life (perhaps only a single word) is conserved by God for use in his holy city. We have brought something new to God that he judges worthy of conservation.

This is a stupendous thought, but not in the least incongruous. God has granted us independence to lead our own lives, to undertake our own works, to build up our own histories. This is a false independence in view of the many determinations imposed by the orders to which we are subject, yet God still grants it, and the more so if we turn to him, for then we receive not merely independence but freedom. In this case we do works that are our own, that God neither expects nor dictates, but that he does not necessarily judge to be bad because they are independent. As speaking beings we have been called upon to cooperate with God from the very beginning of creation (for this is the point of Adam's naming of the animals in Genesis). Even after the fall we have still been called upon to cooperate with God (we are God's co-workers, says Paul — 1 Cor. 3:9). God issues directives, gives signs, makes appeals, and sometimes intervenes, for he always expects us to do *his* work. We finally cooperate with God in erecting this perfect Jerusalem, for if it is exclusively God's work, he builds it with the materials that we bring, materials of all kinds which, when approved by God, reveal a certain human greatness which is our glory.

This is what I firmly believe, and to the utmost of my power it has been the meaning and motivation of all that I do.